A SHEARWATER BOOK

In the Dust of
Kilimanjaro

To my mother and father,
Shirley, Carissa, and Guy,
and the wildlife and Maasai of Amboseli

In the Dust of Kilimanjaro

David Western

ISLAND PRESS / Shearwater Books
Washington, D.C. / Covelo, California

A Shearwater book
published by Island Press

Copyright © 1997 by David Western

All rights reserved under International and Pan-American Copyright Conventions. No part of this book may be reproduced in any form or by any means without permission in writing from the publisher: Island Press, 1718 Connecticut Avenue, N.W., Suite 300, Washington, DC 20009.

ISLAND PRESS is a trademark of The Center for Resource Economics.

Jacket photography and image design by ROBERT VAVRA.
Image production by Patrick Sagouspe, through the courtesy of Victor Díaz and The International Institute of Photographic Authors, La Jolla, California.
Jacket typography and text design by JOYCE C. WESTON.

Library of Congress Cataloging-in-Publication Data

Western, David.
    In the dust of Kilimanjaro / David Western.
        p.   cm.
    ISBN 1-55963-533-9 (cloth)
        1. Wildlife conservation—Kenya. 2. Wildlife management—Kenya.
    3. Western, David. 4. Wildlife conservationists—Kenya—Biography.
    5. Kenya—Description and travel.   I. Title.
    QL84.6.K4W47   1997
    333.95´4´096762—dc21   97-14845
                                                             CIP

Printed on recycled, acid-free paper ⊛

Manufactured in the United States of America

10 9 8 7 6 5 4 3 2 1

Contents

Acknowledgments

I owe my childhood immersion in wildlife and conservation to my mother and father. Because of them, I was lucky enough to grow up in southern Tanganyika (now Tanzania) at a time when people and wildlife coexisted and the tensions at the root of the modern conservation crisis had barely begun. Their love of animals and concern for their future inspired me to take up conservation. My father conveyed a deep concern for people victimized by wildlife as well as for the animals suffering human depredations. In losing his life trying to resolve the conflict between people and wildlife springing up in developing Africa, he inspired my own lifelong quest for a solution.

I owe an enormous debt to those who taught me about the African bush, the conflict between people and animals, and the need to find a just solution. Mohamed Mbwana, tracker and guide on my first hunts, was such a mentor. Then there were our gunbearers and safari companions Dismus Pius, Mwanyuheri, and others whose names have faded over the years. George Rushby, Bill Dick, and other officers of the Tanganyika Game Department inspired me with their enormous dedication to saving Africa's wildlife.

When I began my own research and conservation efforts in Amboseli, Bristol Foster, my supervisor, gave me every encouragement to work on a highly charged topic. So, too, did the University of Nairobi and the Office of the President. Above all, I must thank Daniel Sindiyo, warden of Amboseli at the time. Without his support, friendship, and wholehearted collaboration, my efforts in Amboseli would have been futile. I also wish to thank the Leverhulme Trust and Ford Foundation for taking the risk of funding work on the human side of conservation matters in Africa—at the time, tantamount to selling out to the enemy.

Above all, I wish to acknowledge and thank the Maasai in Amboseli, who have been my greatest inspiration for thirty years. No people on earth have so ably coexisted with wildlife and have lost out quite so tragically as a result. Parashino Ole Purdul, more than anyone else, taught me about the Maasai tradition of coexistence and how it turned sour on them. I thank him for showing me Amboseli through the eyes of a cow and for our long and sometimes contentious dialogue in search of coexistence in to-day's world. That we should come from radically different backgrounds yet forge common ground is a testament to our long and close friendship. Many other Maasai collectively contributed to the ideas and conservation programs outlined in the book. They include Kerenkol Ole Musa, Chief Ole Somoire, Shuhe Ole Mweyendet, Daniel Ole Somoire, John Marinka, Jonathan Leboo, the many group ranch representatives over the years, and the Honorable Stanley Oloitiptip—despite our rocky beginning.

Several wardens in Amboseli have played important roles over the years. They include Joe Kioko, Bob Oguya, and Francis Mkungi. Rangers such as Corporal Kibori and Sergeant Francis, along with others too nu-merous to mention, have played a seminal if unacknowledged role in the conservation of Amboseli. To the directors of Kenya National Parks, the Wildlife Conservation and Management Department, and, more recently, the Kenya Wildlife Service, especially Perez Olindo, Daniel Sindiyo, and Richard Leakey, I wish to pay tribute to their perseverance and fortitude in managing Kenya's wildlife through its most turbulent years. I also wish to thank John Koitie and Yuda Komora among other permanent secretaries in the Ministry of Tourism and Wildlife for championing the changes out-lined in this book, often in the face of great skepticism.

There are many colleagues to thank for their insights and collabora-tion over the years, among them Frank Mitchell, the staff of the Insti-tute for Development Studies at the University of Nairobi, Phil Thresher, Sandy Price, Mike and Judy Rainy, Tom Dunne, Charlie van Praet, Har-vey Croze, Cynthia Moss, Chris Gakahu, Moses Kumpumula, Solo-mon Ole Saibul, Nick Georgiadis, David Andere, Chris Hillman, Steve Cobb, Patrick Hamilton, Virginia Finch, Iain Douglas-Hamilton, Peter Matthiessen, Richard Barnes, Tom Pilgram, David Cummings, and Ian Parker. Foremost among these is David Maitumo, my research assistant and companion for twenty years.

In the last few years it has been my great joy and privilege to work with a cadre of young conservationists at the African Conservation Center in Nairobi, established with the support of the New York Zoological Soci-ety. They include Helen Gichohi, Chris Gakahu, Fred Waweru, John

Waithaka, Evans Mwangi, Andrew Muchiru, Lucy Chege, and Josiah Musau. I wish to thank them all for their inspiring and enjoyable collaboration on research and conservation programs.

Since 1973 my work has been supported solely by the New York Zoological Society, recently renamed the Wildlife Conservation Society. No one has given more support and provided as much input as its president, Bill Conway. His vision and drive created the Society's international conservation program and allowed a handful of biologists and conservationists, including George Schaller, Roger Payne, Tom Strushsaker, and myself, to "follow our noses" and devote ourselves fully to research and conservation. I also wish to acknowledge with very special thanks and deep respect the backing, financial and otherwise, given by Charlie Nichols, longtime chairman of the Wildlife Conservation Society Conservation Committee, and Royal Little. Working with the Society has been a special pleasure, and I am deeply indebted to the support of all its staff.

I also wish to thank Liz Claiborne and Art Ortenberg, who, through their foundation, not only supported the Amboseli project and the Ivory Trade Review Group but have along the way become close friends and persuasive advocates for balancing human and wildlife needs.

Special thanks go to Laurie Burnham, my editor at Shearwater, for all her help in improving the book. Laurie persuaded me to continue rewriting long after I thought the job was done. As a scientist in her own right, she is uniquely qualified to offer advice on what to include and what to cut in striving for a balance between information and communication. I am also grateful to David Quammen for his advice on an early draft of the book and to Robert Vavra for his jacket image.

Finally, I wish to thank my wife and closest and dearest in all things, Shirley Strum. This book would not have been possible without her support and encouragement at every stage—or without those long evening walks across the savanna to put it all into perspective. Our children, Carissa and Guy, have been a source of joy and an inspiration. By joining us in the field they have made it possible to spend time on Shirley's baboon study in northern Kenya and my own projects in southern Kenya without disrupting our precious family life.

Preface

Every day conservationists wage battles around the world in defense of endangered species and threatened habitats. Some of the evocative images include Chico Mendez' courageous defense of the Amazon forest against loggers, Dian Fossey's lonely vigil to save the mountain gorilla in the mist-covered Virunga Mountains of Rwanda, and Greenpeace's open dinghies scudding over pounding seas to stop Norwegian whalers. Less known if no less dedicated are people like Michael Werihke, a young Kenyan who left his job at an assembly plant in Mombasa to raise a million dollars to save the black rhino by walking through Africa, Europe, and the United States.

No two conservationists share identical motives or methods. Some work in virtual isolation, quietly amassing data on the state of the planet; others are radical activists. Some work in government, others in non-governmental organizations. Some are scientists, others hunters, farmers, ranchers, tourists, or school kids baking cookies to raise funds for the endangered tiger. Ask any of them why they are conservationists and you will hear answers ranging from those based on sentiment and compassion to those based on economics, science, pleasure, aesthetics, or the fundamental right to existence. The motives for conservation are as varied as the five and a half billion people in the world.

Yet there is something deeper to conservation than a passion for saving the Amazon, the gorilla, and the whale. For most conservationists, what began as a preoccupation with saving a favorite species or patch of wilderness grew into a concern for all forms of life. Ultimately, conservation boils down to a disquiet over the threats human beings pose to other species and the health of the entire planet on which our species, too, depends.

The specter of standing room only may be receding as birth rates dip steadily around the world, but the runaway consumption of the rich nations and the catch-up ambitions of the poor ones allow no grounds for complacency. The environmental impact of agro-industrialization is universal. No society or ecosystem is beyond its reach. The first signs appeared in the blackened skies of Europe, then spread and fell as acid rain, which killed forests and lakes throughout the industrialized world. Today the impact of more people and greater per-capita consumption of natural resources shows up in greenhouse warming and expanding ozone holes. The global imprint of industrialization affects the Kung! hunter-gatherer of the Kalahari no less than the surfer off Malibu Beach.

Human activity will soon outstrip natural agencies in shaping the composition and behavior of the air, water, and soils of our planet, if it hasn't already done so. This is what the battle to save the Amazon, the mountain gorilla, and the whale is really all about. No one cared a hoot about the spotted owl until it became a flagship for saving the old-growth forests of the Pacific Northwest. Then, like the whale, the spotted owl became an early warning sign of environmental destruction and a rallying point for a greener world.

There is one place left on earth where the Pleistocene herds of large mammals which once roamed every continent still linger. That place is East Africa. Both Nairobi National Park, with its thousands of migratory wildebeest and zebra, and Nakuru National Park, with its million flamingos, abut large cities in Kenya. East Africa offers us our last chance to secure such space for wildlife alongside people.

I was fortunate enough to grow up in the Old Africa, where wildlife was abundant, people few, and both coexisted. I saw this world on the trail of big game and loved every moment of the hunt. It was with growing concern that I watched this world vanish, largely as a result of colonial preservation policies and rising human numbers. But it was not cold rationality or the fact of being witness to the origins of Africa's wildlife crisis that awoke my devotion to conservation. On the contrary, my concern arose from a magical encounter with a sable antelope when I was eight years old. The encounter was so deeply emotional that it brought out latent sensibilities which widened irresistibly like a ripple in a pond until they touched all aspects of my life. My feelings for the sable—and in due course all wildlife and the African herders and farmers who lost their lives and livelihood in the name of conservation—derive from that single moving encounter. The sable antelope was my motivation in taking up the cause of conservation; it remains my emotional touchstone.

As the threats to wildlife grew and I traveled beyond my favorite patch of bush in search of solutions, it became obvious that the problems facing Africa's savannas are everywhere the same—in the high Andes, the deserts of Oman, and rain forests of Sulawezi. Every conservationist has a touchstone. Whatever the touchstone, all conservation inevitably involves tackling the global threats to all species and habitats. And so, like other conservationists, all too often I found myself abandoning my favorite haunts to become a national and even global activist.

Like other conservationists, I, too, have my own reasons to conserve and my own philosophy for how to go about it, based on cultural diversity. Growing up in Africa, seeing things from an African perspective, it is hard to accept anything less. The Maasai see nature differently from the Montana rancher, from the New York stock broker, from the Indian rice farmer, from the Shinto priest. One culture may see the divine in nature, another economic sustenance, another beauty, and yet another the simple fact of coexistence among all creatures.

Pragmatism seems a better approach to saving the diversity and integrity of life than does a pursuit of a single universal ethic based in a sense of moral superiority or virtue. If we take the narrow—mostly western— view that nature is harmonious unless disturbed by humanity and that protected areas are necessary to ensure the survival of wildlife, there can be no hope for wildlife outside parks. Today, on the basis of biological insights, we know that protected areas themselves are far too small and scattered to avert mass extinction. Take the broader view of nature in continual flux and humans as part of it, and there is far more space for wildlife, if we can rediscover the art of coexistence. In short, if we concede there are many views of nature and many ethical and cultural reasons to conserve biological diversity, the prospects for conservation are limitless.

My own brand of conservation aims at winning space for wildlife beyond the boundaries of national parks as well as within them. This comes down to making wildlife something of value first and foremost to the Africans whose lands it occupies, rather than something they fear and despise. Colonial game laws were undeniably elitist and racist and created deep antipathy toward wildlife in rural Africa. Winning a lasting place for wildlife involves reversing a century of alienation—making those who suffer from the depredations of wildlife its primary guardians and principal custodians. Indeed, the continued survival of wildlife in its abundant natural state is rooted in Africa's traditional art of coexistence rather than in prevailing western conservation policies based on segregation. The present enemies of wildlife must be converted into friends.

To explain how a boyhood infatuation with a sable antelope led to the radical realization that its best chance of survival lies in the hands of its enemies, let me take you back to the trailhead where it all began, a few miles from the Indian Ocean in Tanganyika Territory in the 1940s.

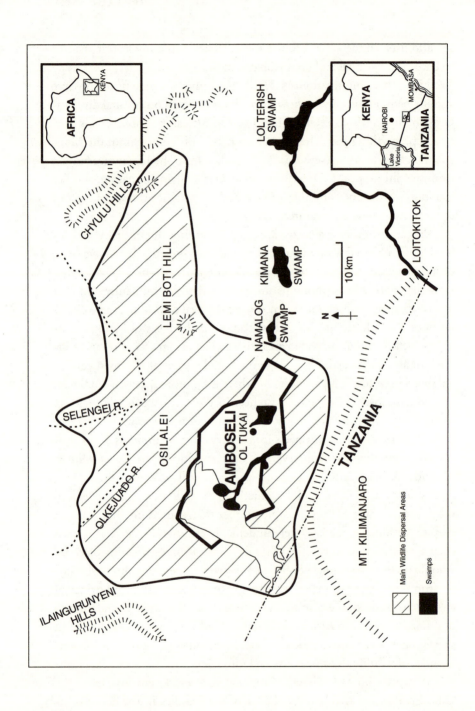

AFRICA

KENYA

CHYULU HILLS

LOLTERISH SWAMP

KENYA

NAIROBI

Lake Victoria

MOMBASA

TANZANIA

LOITOKITOK

LEMI BOTI HILL

KIMANA SWAMP

NAMALOG SWAMP

10 km

N

SELENGEI R.

OSILALEI

AMBOSELI

OL TUKAI

OLKEJUADO R.

TANZANIA

MT. KILIMANJARO

ILAINGURUNYENI HILLS

Main Wildlife Dispersal Areas

Swamps

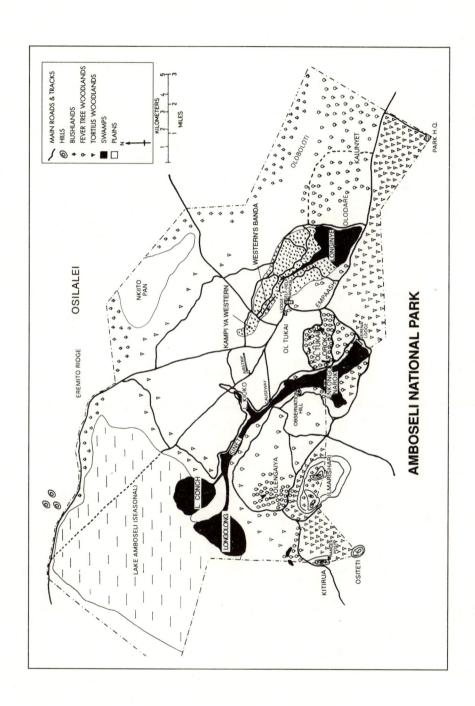

AMBOSELI NATIONAL PARK

OSILALEI

MAIN ROADS & TRACKS
HILLS
BUSHLANDS
FEVER TREE WOODLANDS
TORTILIS WOODLANDS
SWAMPS
PLAINS

KILOMETERS
5 4 3 2 1
MILES
3 2 1
N

EREMITO RIDGE

NKIITO
PAN

LAKE AMBOSELI (SEASONAL)

L. CONCH

LONGOLONG

SINET

L. KIOKO

AIRSTRIP

CAUSEWAY

LENGAIYA

ILMARISHARI

KITIRUA

OSITETI

OBSERVATION
HILL

ENKONGO
NAROK

OL TUKAI
OROK

OL TUKAI
LODGE

SERENA
LODGE

KAMPI YA WESTERN

WESTERN'S BANDA

LODGE
SELF-HELP
BANDAS

EMPAASH

LONGINYE

OLODARE

KALUNYET

OLOBOLOTI

PARK H.Q.

◄ Part One ►

Vanishing Worlds

« 1 »

Dreams of a Hunter

THE SHOTGUN SNAGGED IN the grass and chafed my skin raw under the shoulder strap. My legs ached and buckled as I tried to keep up with the others striding effortlessly ahead, hour after hour in the scorching sun. I remember little of those first hunts except the pain, sweat, and misery. All the hardships seemed worthwhile so long as I carried my precious shotgun. In my eight-year-old eyes a gun made me a hunter, even if I hadn't shot anything bigger than a pigeon with a slingshot.

Seen through adult eyes, Mbwamaji, my father's hunting ground, was a patchwork of tall grass and woodland thicket, but to a kid four feet tall the bush was a confusion of sounds, smells, and discomforts. From my height there was nothing to see except the back of an adult towering ahead of me, a wall of grass on either side and the tops of nearby trees. Whenever the adults froze at the sight of an animal, I tried to guess from their reaction what they had spotted—a buffalo, eland, impala, or whatever—and I got pretty good at it. Trapped as I was in a tunnel of grass, the steady drumbeat of bare feet on the compacted trail seemed loud enough to scare off the animals. The drumming seemed to go unnoticed by the adults; when I told my father about it, he laughed and said I was imagining things. Rivulets of sweat poured down my temples; hordes of flies crawled into my eyes and cloaked my sweat-soaked back like an itchy coat of mail. The adults, catching the freshening breeze above the grass jungle, shrugged at my complaints. "You'll grow out of it, Bwana Mdogo," said our gun-bearer Dismus. An employee at my father's workshop in town, he used *bwana mdogo,* small mister, as a term of respect and affection, but to me it was an irksome reminder of how far I had to go to become a real hunter.

Mohamed Mbwana, our local tracker, was as alert as a pointer, stopping, checking, listening, and scurrying to catch up, indefatigable even though he was well over sixty at the time. His lean, muscular body defied his dour, grizzled face. Oblivious to flies, he seldom wore more than a grubby turban and a black loincloth tied at the waist by a palm thong. On hearing his short sharp warning hiss, my brother, Martin, and I sank to the ground like gundogs, just as we had been instructed. "What do you think?" Martin whispered from under his trilby, delirious with excitement. My father slunk off into the grass, Mohamed crouching low and tense behind like a drawn bow. "Big," I answered, noting my father's concentration. "Too big for a warthog. A buck of some sort."

For a while we followed the rustle of clothes and the crunch of grass until my father's movements faded to nothing. The background sounds grew intense during the long, anxious wait. Off in the distance, waves crashed against the coral cliffs of Tanganyika's coastline; close by, cicadas struck up an ear-splitting screech. Suddenly I whirled in panic at what sounded like a buffalo charging at us through the thicket, only to realize it was a dead frond brushing against the trunk of a borassus palm. Our porter, Wonk Eye, nicknamed for his grotesque bulging eye blinded years earlier by a thorn, turned to us. "I think it's an impala," he whispered with a greedy grin of anticipation.

A loud bang exploded ahead, followed at once by the deafening buzz of cicadas. "Amempiga, amempiga," Wonk Eye yelled at the "thwop" of the bullet. He bounded off in the direction of the shot, his instructions to stick with us forgotten in the excitement. I struggled after him, the shotgun bouncing wildly on my shoulder and a water bottle hammering at my ribs. Mohamed was closing cautiously on a waterbuck lying on its side, gurgling from a lung shot. "Grab the horns from behind," he yelled at Wonk Eye.

The old man unsheathed his knife, pulled back the waterbuck's head and cut its throat in a few swift strokes, muttering "Alhamdulillahi," praise be to Allah, the Muslim's cleansing ritual. The animal's pupils dilated in fear, then fixed vacantly. Bright red blood pumped from the severed jugular, then drained slowly into sandy soil, where it congealed and darkened. Flies drawn by the sickly sweet smell swarmed over the sticky mass.

My frenzy during the kill turned to fascination, then to pity as I watched the waterbuck's life ebb away. My father sat cross-legged under a tree, leaning against the trunk, contentedly gulping sweetened lime juice from an aluminum bottle. I turned away to hide my overwhelming sense of guilt at what we had done to this innocent animal, knowing real hunters were supposed to be strong and unemotional about death.

"Shika mguu," grab a leg, Mohamed told me. I pulled. Martin stood by ashen-faced, watching. He never did like skinning animals. With expert hands, Mohamed sliced through the bulging gut wall from ribs to crotch, releasing a rush of gas. The warm smell of blood, intermingled with the pungent stench of fermented grass, hit my nose. He gave a tug and the animal's stomach tumbled out like a white inner tube, dragging with it a slithering profusion of pleated intestines. My gut heaved involuntarily.

Gripping the heavy hide, Mohamed sliced evenly through the skin and subcutaneous fat, thrusting his hand forward through the soft tissue. A thigh muscle quivered. "Is it alive?" I gasped, forgetting myself.

"No, Bwana Mdogo," Mohamed scowled. "That's his soul crying out for his wife."

I turned to Dismus for reassurance. "Yes," he nodded. "It is dead. Don't worry."

The skinning and dismembering done, Mohamed and Wonk Eye wrapped the meat in the fan-shaped leaves of a borassus palm and strung the bundles on a pole hacked from a thicket.

There was no need for silence now, so we staggered back to the village under our loads, loudly acting out the hunt as African hunters do. Wonk Eye's lurid mime of the death scene made us all laugh, drawing out my guilt like a hot poultice.

A boisterous gang of villagers ran out to join us and escorted us the last half mile back to camp. Their shouts of joy and clucks of admiration drove out any lingering doubts I had about the kill, and in that triumphal moment I knew what it was to be a hunter.

My father, Arthur Cyril Western, saw to it that Martin and I learned to hunt at an early age. Strong-headed and adventurous, he left England for India in his teens, drawn by stories of tiger hunting, pig-sticking, and the wilds of the Himalayas. He joined the Indian army as a passport to adventure and served an eight-year stint in the Third Hussars, a cavalry regiment famous for its Gurkha. Stationed in the northern state of Lucknow, he explored the Himalayan foothills, where his fluency in Hindustani made for easy relations with the hill people and set him apart from the imperious officers of the British raj. He returned to England before the Second World War, married the vivacious nineteen-year-old Beatrice Slack, who lived down the street, and started a family, unsure of where his love of adventure and the wilds would take him next.

"I arrived in Africa by chance," he loved to tell us, "because some dozy war bloke couldn't tell the difference between Hindustani and Kiswahili and sent me to Kenya by mistake." Posted to Kenya and garrisoned at Gilgil, in the Rift Valley, he soon became fluent in Swahili and trained African troops for the Somali campaign. "Left me plenty of time to explore," he added smugly. "Jesus, the Loita Hills! The most beautiful place I ever saw. So wild. So full of game. And the Maasai. Now there's a proud tribe, unspoiled and brave. Sometimes we met them out hunting lions with spears and shields. Most of them had never seen a European before."

By the end of the war, Africa had claimed my father's heart. Six months after returning to England in 1946, he headed back, this time to settle in Tanganyika Territory, where he established an apprenticeship school for African carpenters and joiners in Dar es Salaam. My mother and their four young children—Sheila, Martin, and I and, four years later, Lynne—shared his new life and home.

Britain had no abiding interest in Tanganyika, a nebulous hunk of Africa stretching from the Indian Ocean to Lake Victoria. Covering an area the size of Texas and Arizona combined, the territory had been annexed by Germany during Europe's nineteenth-century scramble for African colonies; after the First World War, the League of Nations handed the country over to Britain to administer. Under the terms of the mandate, Britain was charged with steering Tanganyika to eventual independence. Lacking the colonial permanence of neighboring Kenya, Tanganyika attracted no more than a coterie of British administrators and a flotsam of war veterans, down-on-their-luck traders, and farmers from Germany,

South Africa, Italy, Greece, Poland, Scandinavia, Australia, and a dozen other nations. Tanganyika was the outer reaches of the empire and not very British as far as its neighbors in Kenya were concerned, but to my father, its very lure lay in being beyond the civilized fringe.

My mother certainly didn't have the outer fringes in mind when she settled in the bush outside the capital of Dar es Salaam. Our leaky house, which crawled with termites, mosquitoes, and snakes, was altogether too primitive for her London-born liking and she yearned for the comforts of home. But a trip back to the dreary weather, roaring traffic, and rationing of postwar England cured my mother's nostalgia for civilization. To her surprise, she found herself longing for the sleepy town of Dar es Salaam with its tranquil coconut-fringed harbor.

Dar es Salaam, or Haven of Peace, had changed little since the Germans had driven out the Arab slavers in the 1870s. Flat-roofed Arab houses and elegant mosques with tall white minarets mingled with imposing colonial mansions built by German colonials. British rule added nothing of note except drab Asian *dukas* (shops) and a suburban web of red-roofed bungalows dotted among bougainvillaea hedges and frangipani bushes.

I was three years old when we arrived in Mombasa after a month-long passage from England. My earliest memory, though dim and hazy, is of Mount Kilimanjaro seen from the train window across an endless stretch of thorn country as we traveled from Mombasa to Moshi in Tanganyika, en route to Dar es Salaam. The memory would lie dormant until twenty years later, when I sat staring in awe at the mountain outside my tent in Amboseli, wondering why it so perfectly matched my image of the archetypal Africa.

More vivid in my mind are images of lions and leopards prowling near our home. My father would dare me to walk around the house in the impenetrable darkness, and I can still recall my chest pounding with fear as I reached the dark stretch along the back wall where the wind whistled through the hatch and rustled the lantana bushes. Then came the ecstasy of turning the last corner into the light where my father stood laughing and impressed. After that the pandemonium of a leopard tearing through our neighbors' thatched roof to get at their dog wasn't worth more than a half-opened eye.

As Dar spread and the bush receded, Martin and I grew restless as we ran out of thickets to explore. My father, who had resumed hunting in his free time as soon as he arrived in Africa, decided the time had come for us to join him on safari. We loaded up our car with camping gear, guns, and food, took the ferry across Dar harbor, and ground up the steep concrete ramp on the far side. There we followed a sandy track snaking through the coconut groves until it petered out farther down the coast. At the end of the track stood a thatch hut, leaning precariously to one side in a sandy field of wispy cassava bushes and papaw trees. Mohamed, our local guide, would emerge from a derelict hut whose walls had collapsed under the weight of the roof, forming an A-frame shelter.

"Jambo [hello], Mohamed," my father greeted him. "When are you going to build a real house?" he joked. A building surveyor with a keen interest in African architecture, he loved to rib Mohamed about his novel design.

"Jambo, Bwana Mdogo," he growled down at me as if he had a stomachache. His stern wrinkled face and soiled linen turban wrapped around his grizzled head unnerved me. "Jambo, Mohamed," I whispered, scrutinizing the ground. Mohamed had a congenital smiling deficiency, of that I'm sure. Even when accepting an impala leg from my father, he showed his joy with a deep scowl.

The greetings over, Mohamed ducked under his fallen roof to collect his homemade knife for the hunt. Then, as if to punish Martin and me for our impatience, he, Dismus, and my father would squat under a mango tree and launch into small talk as only adults can—going on and on about where the animals were and what they were doing. In the meantime Martin and I pouted and grumbled, convinced that the animals would be gone by the time they stopped talking. The grownups took no notice.

As the minutes ticked by we grew restless and began fishing ant lions out of their sand pits with blades of grass. Wingless insects, ant lions build conical pit traps and lie buried at the bottom, waiting for a hapless insect, usually an ant, to fall in. When one does, the ant lion rears up, snaring its victim with its long recurved pincers. This wasn't exactly the hunting we came to Mbwamaji for, but at least the patience and skill needed to mimic a struggling ant with a blade of grass and extract the ant lion with a neat flick of the wrist took our minds off the long wait.

Finally, long after we were certain the animals had spread the alarm and hidden themselves in thickets, my father looked at Mohamed and said, "Tangulia," lead on, realizing how much time he had wasted.

Martin and I leapt up and ran ahead to a rickety wooden bridge traversing a narrow stream. There we sat with our legs dangling over the edge, watching the stream gurgle past, bombing water beetles with pebbles. Soon the adults caught up and filed across the bridge into the bush without a downward glance. Abandoning the beetles for bigger prey, Martin and I fell into line, elbowing each other for position. Up front was my father, followed by Mohamed, then Dismus. Wonk Eye, hired as porter to carry back meat, brought up the rear. No matter where I looked, there was no escaping that baleful white eye looking like some obscene maggot squirming in his head.

I witnessed my first shooting soon after the waterbuck hunt. It was a windless day: the birds and cicadas were silent, and I was deep in a daydream. Four warthogs exploded like cannons from a deeply shaded thicket a few yards from us and sped across a fire-blackened meadow, their tails erect like aerials. Three shots roared out, sending two of the pigs stumbling and skidding to a stop in a plume of gray ash. It all happened so fast I barely knew what happened.

Until then, the explosion of a gun and the sight of a dead animal had been separate events. Far from being repulsed by the scene, I found myself gripped by an unbridled desire to shoot animals and slash their throats as Mohamed did. The impulse came in such a primal rush that I could think of nothing else until the animals were dead. But no sooner were they dead than the urge passed and all the sadness and guilt I had felt over the waterbuck resurfaced stronger than ever, leaving me confused and angry. The emotional swing from an irrepressible urge to kill followed by the ineffable sadness of watching the life fade from an animal's eyes grew stronger with every hunt. At first I brushed off the contradiction by laughing at Wonk Eye's animated pantomime of the death scene, and for a while his lurid gyrations worked. Eventually, though, his mime became a macabre and grotesque mockery of death rather than a palliative. The crumpled carcasses filled me with a sadness so deep that every warthog squeal became my own inner scream.

For a while I fought off the sadness and revealed only my excitement about the hunt. After all, Mohamed and Dismus showed no misgivings about killing, and neither did my father; so why should I? I hid my feelings as best as I could, fully expecting to grow out of them. Years later, I realized how badly I had misjudged my father. For all his outward stoicism, the pity and shame were there in his drawn face each time he put an eland out of its misery and in his eyes whenever he saw the carnage of a poacher's camp littered with impala remains. As a boy I missed these subtle cues and tried to be as impassive as he was. Not until I was a teenager did I see that his repeated excuses for killing hid a deeper misgiving. He hated gratuitous killing and had little time for hunters who showed off their prowess by displaying stuffed leopards leaping out of houseplants and elephant-foot wastebaskets in corners. All the same, he loved hunting and always found an excuse to justify his passion. In the early days it was shooting for the pot, in later years saving African farmers and herders from marauding elephants and lions.

My mother was an unbridled sentimentalist when it came to animals. "Hunting is cruel," she told us when we handed her a butchered animal. Bea, as we call her affectionately, was always happier when we came back empty-handed. "Killing is wrong," she told us time and again. Her eyes flashed angrily when we tried to justify killing animals, however we did it. Auburn-haired and tanned from the sun, she was (and still is) strikingly beautiful and just as independent and strong-willed as my father. When it came to hunting, she was emphatic.

"The animals will get their own back someday," she warned. Her vehemence in siding with the animals against my father confused and annoyed me. Deep down I knew my anger over her sentimentality was an acknowledgment of my own guilt. As a family, we all loved animals. Dogs and mongooses ran freely around our household and we held them in deep affection, but I was still too thrilled with killing to let sentimentality stand in my way.

From the time of my first hunt I pestered my father to allow me to shoot my own animal. "No, you're too short to see the animals, let alone shoot them," he chuckled to my intense irritation, loving his joke and repeating it in Swahili to Mohamed and Dismus. "You must learn to live in the bush, track, stalk, and shoot before you kill," he added in his more serious moments. At eight, I had a lot to learn. So I worked feverishly on my bush skills, learning how to set up camp, spot animals, track, stalk, and skin. Bushcraft became a source of pride as my senses sharpened and I became attuned to the low rumble of elephant calls, the musty smell of lions, the slight scuffing of a hoof on hard ground, and the nipped-off twigs fresh with the saliva of a browsing rhino. By the time I was twelve, I could keep up with the adults on an all-day march and track and stalk an animal with the skill of our guides. My graduation came when my father asked Martin and me to take the wife of a hunting client to shoot a warthog while he went after buffalo with her husband. I had finally become an experienced hunter, even though I had yet to kill.

The more bush skills I learned, the less important killing became. Had that been my father's intention all along, having purged his own bloodlust at the expense of dwindling tigers and pigs in India? Or was he trying to purify me for the hunt and teach me the respect for animals that African hunters habitually teach their own children? Whatever the reason, the irrepressible bloodlust, the kill-anything-that-moves variety, drained away. Gratuitous killing became as loathsome, callous, and wasteful to me as it did to my father. Hunting, on the other hand, took on a deeper and richer meaning with my newfound bushlore. The joy of hunting burned steadily as an ember once we began tracking an animal and burst into flame the moment we began the final stalk. The flame died just as suddenly the second the shot found its mark.

A single magical encounter released my pent-up emotions and forever changed my view of animals. I was ten at the time, and walking in a line of familiar hunters, with Mohamed up front and Wonk Eye in the rear. Needing to take a leak, I dropped behind for a moment. Just as I unbuttoned my pants, a huge male sable antelope stepped out of the bush and halted ten paces away. A pair of long recurved horns arched high over his head and dipped downward like a pair of scythes. The antelope was ebony black except for a white muzzle, chest, and belly and thin cinnamon ears.

An imposing animal the size of a horse, the sable stood still as a rock staring down at me. I froze, both petrified and mesmerized by its beauty, until the antelope finally nodded its head as if challenging me to show that I too was real. Gradually my fear gave way to curiosity and wonder. There we stood, transfixed for what seemed like minutes until the antelope wheeled slowly around and paced off into the thicket.

Something ineffable happened in those few moments, something so wonderful and profound that it awakened my conscience and forever changed the way I felt about animals. What was it about that oddly human quality in those dark eyes? Fright at first to be sure, but then curiosity and fascination, too; perhaps even a touch of amusement at seeing a small boy peeing in the bush. The sable antelope was undeniably a sentient animal just like me. Did that imply a common thread of consciousness in all animals, not just in humans? In those few moments, the antelope and I discovered intimacy and understanding. During our fleeting encounter I felt we had seen into each other's souls and had bridged the evolutionary gulf between us.

"What's taking you so long?" my father asked as he hurried back along the trail.

"I saw a sable, Dad," I blurted out. "He was huge. He stood right there and stared, then walked off. Please, don't shoot him."

"I don't want to," he said, looking surprised that I should suggest it. He turned up the trail and walked on without another word. I never said anything either. How could my father possibly understand what had transpired if I couldn't understand it myself? Had the empathy been real or imagined? A couple of years later, I drew the animal so vividly from memory that the school judges awarded me first prize only after questioning me closely as to whether I had copied the antelope from a photograph. Whatever their doubts, the sable remained real to me as a unique sentient being. Killing became more painful than ever after that.

Until the sable encounter I had thought of animals either as pets or as objects to be hunted. Our mongooses and dogs showed humanlike emotions such as fear, hunger, affection, and even a modicum of personality and intelligence, and I loved their individual quirks of character. But wild animals? Well, they were different—more enigmatic and impersonal, creatures of the chase with emotional lives best ignored. Hunters waved off all that emotional nonsense like a bad smell, or so I thought until the sable antelope tripped some emotional switch and sent a widening ripple of awareness through me. Many years later, the curiosity and compassion triggered by my awakened sensibility found three targets: ecology, conservation, and the coexistence of people and wildlife, but as a ten-year-old my concerns were too primordial to merit such lofty labels.

Not long afterward I became aware of how animals affected African farmers and of the discrimination the farmers suffered from under the colonial game laws. We were camping in a village on a hunting trip at the time.

The villagers around Mbwamaji were typical of African bush farmers in the 1940s and 1950s. They barely sustained themselves on the anemic crops grown on the sandy coastal flats; few had more than a loincloth, blanket, and hoe. Even so, these farmers weren't poor in the conventional sense. If poverty is the pain of want and deprivation, then they were simply too cut off from materialism to want much or to feel deprived. The farmers seemed happy, easygoing, and self-contained in their small world. They seldom traveled far, but then there wasn't much to travel to or for in their world of look-alike villages separated by miles of bush.

My father's camp cot was set up under the stars, as usual, while Martin and I lay sweating unable to sleep, in an airless farmer's hut. I took no notice of the voices outside until I heard my father's nickname, "Bwana Wanyama." Then, I listened curiously.

"Why won't the Game Department kill the hippos around here?" someone was asking. "They're getting so bad we'll have to move. If we try to kill the hippos, they attack us. If we ignore them, they ruin our crops. Maybe Bwana Wanyama will do something. He's a *mzungu* [European]. He's allowed to shoot animals."

Not having thought much about the imbalance of the colonial game laws, I didn't understand the fear and resentment of the hippos being voiced in the dark, or why the farmers couldn't do anything about it. There could be no mistake about their hatred of animals though. Our trackers and guides evidently felt much the same as I did about wild animals and hunting. You could see the frenzy in their eyes and their chests heaving as we closed in on the quarry. They undoubtedly enjoyed the kill too, although for most of them animals meant meat rather than sport. Even the Swahili word for animals, *wanyama*, means meat. Having been sensitized by the sable antelope, however, I picked up an undercurrent of hostility. At first it was barely noticeable, a slight stiffening among peasant farmers and a tiny lull in conversation whenever the subject of wild animals came up in my father's presence, nothing more. As the years passed, though, the tension increased until it could no longer be ignored. Eventually the injustice at the root of African hostility to wildlife profoundly influenced my conservation philosophy.

The next day, the village headman revived the subject of hippos with my father. Always a good listener, he knew just how to bring the Africans out with thoughtful questions and a touch of humor. His fluency in Swahili drew admiration from the coastal Swahili-speaking people, who took pride in their language yet rarely met a white who took the trouble to learn it well. He listened hard that day as the headman explained the damage hippos were doing to crops and the risk to farmers confronting them in the middle of the night with nothing more than a spear. In Tanganyika, hippos killed more people than did lions or elephants, and several farmers died each year defending their crops.

The moment my father agreed to shoot the hippos I could think of nothing else and temporarily forgot about the sable. I was about to embark on my first big-game hunt.

The hippo tracks led into a dense thicket and down to a small lake not far from the sea. "Stay close, hippos can be dangerous if they catch you on their trails," my father warned us. More than a few hunters had been crushed by an oncoming hippo rushing for the safety of water. I watched my father load his sporting rifle, a bolt-action .375 magnum, with five hard-nosed bullets, doubtful that his marksmanship from his army days would suffice in the close confines of the dark tunnel bored into the dense thickets around us. The trail, worn four feet deep by generations of hippos, dropped precipitously. Even with our guns readied, I felt caged and nervous as we crept forward in the smothering heat and humidity. Dense undergrowth lined the tunnel walls, offering no escape from a hippo rushing hell-bent for water. The only sounds were the distant boom of the sea and the mournful descending "boop" of an emerald-spotted wood dove.

Up ahead, somewhere close, a hippo surfaced with a sharp puff. My muscles ached from the crouching and tension as we inched forward, trailing Mohamed through the undergrowth bordering the water's edge to a strangler fig where the farmers had constructed a shooting hide. We climbed slowly up the tangled branches and settled in. Lying flat on the hard poles we stared out over the lake. A few stretches of water opened up by the hippos punctured an otherwise unbroken mat of floating weed. African lily trotters high-stepped gingerly over the green rafts, searching for water bugs.

"They know we're here," my father whispered after a long wait. "Stay still. They can only stay under a few minutes."

After what seemed an hour, we heard another puff. I could barely make out the short rounded ears and gaping nostrils facing our direction. More heads bobbed up, this time higher and more curious. My father slowly eased his gun forward and clicked off the safety catch. A massive head surfaced a little closer. A deafening roar went off in my ear, and the acrid smell of cordite filled my nostrils. Water erupted in a great bow wave as the hippo lunged forward and sank. Then came the clack of a bolt and metallic clink of a cartridge as the hippo rose up and made two or three more charges through the water toward us, scattering lily trotters right and left. Another blast and the shot slammed home. This time the hippo rolled slowly on its side and sank. Several more hippos charged for the far shore and crashed into the undergrowth.

Minutes later the farmers appeared on the trail, shouting and laughing. "Wapi kiboko, wapi kiboko—where is the hippo?" My father pointed to where the hippo had sunk. "Aiy, aiy, the hippo is dead, the hippo is dead," they chanted, leaping up and down in a frenzy. "Come again, bwana, come again. You must shoot all the hippos. We hate them. They are our enemies."

Hippo hunts became a regular feature of our safaris after that and marked my father's first step from hunter to conservationist in a roundabout way. I'm sure he didn't think twice about killing hippos as long as he had the excuse of destroying them out of compassion for the villagers. Being compassionate about farmers rather than the hippos made vague sense to me too, despite my newfound sentiments for animals, for in those days it was the isolated and vulnerable villagers who needed protection, not the ubiquitous wildlife.

To say the least, I was thoroughly confused emotionally by all that went on at Mbwamaji. My heightened awareness and expanding sensibilities made me feel sorry for the hippos, sad about the farmers, and passionate about hunting. Sympathy, in fact, became my panacea for all the hurt, conflict, and baffling contradictions ranging from the spilled blood of the first waterbuck to the farmers' hatred of hippos. My sympathy solved nothing of course, except to make me feel virtuous.

The difference between whites and blacks when it came to hunting didn't occur to me as a boy. Back then, the similarities outweighed the differences. Hunters regardless of race killed for meat, trophies, and ivory;

game was plentiful enough to go around. Because African traditions held that God had granted wildlife free for anyone to use, no word for poaching existed in the Swahili language. Ownership fell to the person who killed an animal, and with that privilege came an obligation to share the spoils with hunting partners, family, and friends. But Africa's time-honored hunting traditions were soon to change.

My father's innocuous first step into game management led to more dangerous hunts for marauding lions, stock-raiding leopards, rogue elephants, and wounded buffalo. Game control as well as preservation began to preoccupy the Game Department in the 1950s, and the help of any hunter willing to volunteer his time, and risk his life, were welcomed. Most African farmers were glad of my father's efforts. But their gratitude changed to resentment when he took a second step, from game control to preservation, as the ranks of farmers swelled, commercialism spread, and Africans vented their feelings against wild animals with the approach of independence. Now it was the animals who were under siege.

After my father volunteered his time to game control work on behalf of the Game Department, I came to see the colonial game laws in a different light. Traditionally bush farmers built low watchtowers in the center of their shambas and stayed up nights beating drums, hurling stones, and burning fires to drive off crop-raiding animals. The farmers were stoical about the hardship they suffered from wild animals, but then protecting crops from animals was as much a part of their calendar as hoeing, weeding, and harvesting. It had its rewards too, for they ate the animals they killed.

This tit for tat had worked well for generations, but once human pressure on wildlife mounted and the Game Department began to enforce the game laws, the farmers grew angry at the injustice of favoring wild animals and Europeans over Africans. Their resentment fueled the backlash against wildlife which threatened its very survival in years to come.

Meanwhile Martin and I were sent to boarding school in central Tanganyika. Kongwa School lay 300 miles inland from Dar es Salaam in a harsh stretch of red-soiled bush two hours' drive from the nearest town, Dodoma. During the heyday of slave trading eighty years earlier, Kongwa had been a stopover for the caravans bound from Lake Tanganyika to Bagomoyo (Lost Hope) on the coast, where the slaves were crowded into dhows and shipped to Zanzibar, Arabia, and the Gulf states. Thousands died on the arduous 800-mile trek through waterless tsetse-fly infested country. The stumbling feeble survivors who reached the stop-off point earned the name Kongwa, the old people. Looking north from the school we could pick out the giant baobab trees reaching up from the bush like gray-robed headless ghouls with fat torsos and outstretched arms. Legend has it that the broad avenues of baobabs mark the caravan routes along which the hungry slaves chewed and spat out seeds as they staggered coastward under their loads of ivory.

Kongwa's notoriety faded with the slave trade but resurfaced after the Second World War, when the British government, desperate for vegetable oil, launched a colossal scheme to grow peanuts there. Tens of thousands of parched acres were cleared of all vegetation. A massive famine ensued. Environmentalists blamed the denudation for driving off the rain clouds. Climatologists blamed the catastrophe on project planners' miscalculations of rainfall reliability. The local residents, the Wagogo, had another answer. The crop failure was the curse of the ancestors on anyone greedy enough to annex and demarcate so much land, they said. And fail the harvest did, like no other agricultural scheme in history. After investing 200 million dollars, the British government abandoned Kongwa to a horde of European school kids drawn from all over East Africa. Our wild mien and ungovernable behavior marked the third and final phase of Kongwa's notoriety. The end came when the mud-brick buildings could no longer withstand the punishment of rain and unruly kids and began crumbling back into red earth.

Kongwa redeemed itself in my eyes as the world's premier school for bushcraft, with a modicum of attention paid to the three R's. The mud-brick houses were scattered too far and wide for the house masters to keep track of our activities. Had they known, the school might have been shut down far earlier. Remote from any supply center and often short of fresh provisions, food was always uppermost in our minds. The senior boys periodically went hunting with the staff to bag an eland or zebra for the school kitchen; I was among the wilder bunch that secretly hunted birds and roasted them over the wood-fired boiler at the back of our house.

Kongwa was decidedly Crusoesque when it came to food, and I fancy we had a good many more ways of knocking off birds than Man Friday.

My own preferred methods included a slingshot, homemade gun, and ground trap. I fashioned a gun by sawing the hollow legs from the school's aluminum chairs, turning an end plug on a metal lathe, and shaping a gunstock in the woodwork room. For explosives, I kept a supply of large red firecrackers, and for shot I used marbles or lead ballbearings, depending on the size of prey. Shooting a bird with this primitive firearm called for great skill. After a careful stalk, you had to snip the fuse to just the right length to take aim—but not enough for the bird to figure out where the huge hissing snake was. The hunt took practice and judgment, but for the persistent, a roasted bird offered a delicious reward.

The aluminum barrels began to swell after ten shots or so, which meant sneaking another chair out of the classroom. When seating became conspicuously short, and the early-morning bangs unnervingly loud, the headmaster threatened expulsion for any nimrod caught in the act. Loath to leave this newfound haven, I devised surreptitious ways of trapping birds. The dustbin-lid method called for ingenuity and patience, relying as it did on the insatiable thirst of doves and an odd assortment of hardware: a stolen dustbin lid, steel wire, rubber tubing, string, and a bucket of water. Staking out a stretch of bare earth close to where the doves congregated, I buried the dustbin lid, filled it with water, and hid, waiting for the doves to fly down in thirsty hordes. When the birds were tumbling over themselves in the water, I pulled the trip string, releasing the steel wire. The wire zoomed forward, propelled by the fully extended rubber tubing anchored to stakes on either side of the lid. In a single swift action, the wire decapitated a dozen birds or more. Our house mistress finally caught wind of our shenanigans when she found a row of headless birds on the veranda before I had time to pluck and roast them. That was the end of that method. Thereafter, the only alternative was to hunt beyond the range of the teachers' attention.

It was then that I joined a small gang of five like-minded kids—our bush gang, as we called it—each one of us named after a comic-strip character. My own nickname, Jonah, denoted someone a little on the wild side as far as the rest of the gang was concerned, and the name has stuck.

At age eleven, I began slipping off into the hills on my own, hell-bent on making the top of every hill in sight at the fastest possible speed. Once I tired of the closer hills, I started for the farther ones, often running and walking up to fifteen miles in a day; occasionally I would spend the night up a tree. On one trip, as I was heading back from rugged hill country, a band of Wagogo warriors dressed in finery found me parched and exhausted by the side of a trail. They led me to a brackish pond and gave me water in a gourd fashioned into a scoop. "Mzungu, you are not scared to walk alone in the bush," they said admiringly. "But be careful. The bush punishes mistakes, no matter who makes them." I took that lesson to heart, knowing I probably wouldn't have made it back to school without them.

The Wagogo look and live superficially like their neighboring Maasai cattle herders, except for their ear lobes. While ear-piercing with heavy plugs of wood or ivory is common among pastoral tribes throughout Africa, the Wagogo carry the practice to extremes. *Gogo* means a heavy log or tree trunk, which is more or less what they use to stretch their ear lobes down to their chest, much to the mirth of other tribes, who gave them their pejorative nickname—the people of the log.

Beyond Wagogo territory lies Maasailand and between them, a disputed boundary. One day when I was twelve, a band of about twenty Wagogo converged on a small trading post in this no-man's-land and attacked four Maasai warriors. Though greatly outnumbered, the Maasai killed several Wagogo and sent the remainder scampering for the bush. The Maasai—the lion killers and cattle raiders feared by every tribe in the neighborhood—already surpassed other tribes in Tanganyika in reputation and mystique. That day they soared higher than ever in my estimation. I most admired the Maasai for their fierce independence and ability to live entirely in the bush without any need of civilization. Later I would develop the same admiration for the Bushmen of the Kalahari Desert and the Pygmies of the Ituri Forest who lived in the wilds as no white man ever could.

Yet for all the independence and excitement Kongwa offered, it never quite matched the adventures my father promised us in the remoter reaches of Tanganyika. By the end of the first term when we returned to Dar es Salaam for the holidays, he had discovered Mikumi. "A place where I could die happy," he said. "The best game country you can imagine . . . lousy with game, stiff with buffalo and elephant. You'll see."

« 2 »

First They Took Our Animals,
Then Our Land

$\mathbf{M}$Y FATHER'S HUNTING
fantasies came alive in Mikumi.
At age fifty, he looked every bit the white hunter in his bush jacket and felt
hat, a double-barreled elephant gun slung over his shoulder. His hair had
thinned and grayed and his waist had thickened, but he was still strong
enough to outwalk a man half his age and regularly logged thirty miles a
day on safari. The long treks were not made by choice. The best elephant
country lay remote from the nearest roads and could be reached only on
foot. Elephant hunts meant traveling light with guns, blankets, water bot-
tles, and just enough safari rations to supplement whatever animals we
shot for the pot.

A low bank of hills rose to the south of Mikumi. To the north,
wooded thickets broken by small pockets of grassland stretched to an
expansive floodplain bounding the Mkata River, beyond which the land
rose like a rampart to the blue-forested mountains above Kilosa. Drier and
more open than Mbwamaji, Mikumi was a wildlife paradise. Zebra, impala, and warthog trotted away as we broke out of the tall grass onto the
fresh green stubble left by recent fires. And just as my father had promised,
the woods were stiff with buffalo and elephant.

The country looked as it must have to the British explorers Richard
Burton and John Hanning Speke as they followed the slave caravans
inland in search of the Nile a century before. Bush farmers and subsistence
hunters worked the land the way they had for centuries, blending with the
relentless bush and leaving no permanent mark on the landscape. The
small scattered shambas and makeshift grass huts nestled into the Doma

Hills were as fleeting as bush fires, the traditional hunters as mobile as the wild dogs they tailed in pursuit of migrating herds.

Elephants became my father's greatest passion in a region renowned as the last stronghold of the big tuskers and the retired hunters who had once preyed on them for a living. The small aging band of ivory hunters and former poachers, among them George Rushby, Ionides, and del la Bere Barker, had retreated to southern Tanganyika as civilization encroached inland from the coast and south from Kenya. At first my infatuation with these charismatic hunters ran so deep that I almost forgot about the sable antelope and set my sights on becoming one of them.

Professional elephant hunting was the exclusive preserve of a small, hardy band willing to traverse the inaccessible quarters of Africa in the late nineteenth and early twentieth centuries in search of big tuskers. The rugged professionals included Africa's legendary hunters, men like Jim Southerby and Frederick Selous, who had nothing but disdain for the white hunter who came later and stuck to the well-worn trails in the hire of effete clients insistent on a luxury safari and trophy heads to display in their dens back home.

Of all the professional hunters, the one who inspired most respect was George Rushby. By 1930, after crisscrossing interior Africa, Rushby ended up on the upper Ubangi River in French Equatorial Africa (now the Congo Republic), along with the last handful of professional elephant hunters who made a living off ivory. The profession slowly tailed off throughout the continent as the arriving colonial governments restricted elephant hunting licenses to six or fewer in an effort to curb the slaughter for ivory.

French Equatorial Africa still offered twenty licenses a year, just enough to make a living for those hardy and skillful enough to track down the biggest elephants in the remotest reaches of Africa's dense forests. Within a year, the Great Depression sent ivory prices tumbling, putting Rushby and the professional ivory hunters out of business. Intent on staying in wildlife and worried over the growing slaughter he had helped to instigate, Rushby signed on with Tanganyika's Game Department and, paradoxically, killed more elephants as a game control officer than he had as a hunter. His greatest exploit by his own account was destroying the man-eating lions of Njombe, a fearless pride that killed more than 1,500 people, far more than the infamous man eaters of Tsavo. By the time I met him through his son Jim, my wrestling partner at school, the ex-elephant hunter and self-admitted poacher was the deputy game warden of Tanganyika. Bushworn and impassive after thirty years hunting elephants, Rushby exuded a cool, granitic hardness not even John Wayne could fake.

Ionides and del la Bere Barker, eccentric and less sympathetic characters, fell short of Rushby's reputation and accomplishments but were no less engaging in their own ways. Misanthropic and reclusive, Ionides admitted to caring more for snakes than for Africans. He didn't care for kids either; I came to know him well only in my twenties, when as a frail old man he showed up in Nairobi shortly before he died.

De la Bere Barker, or Rufiji, as he was known, was altogether different and a legend of his own making. Whereas the older hunters like Rushby and Ionides were taciturn and modest about their accomplishments, Rufiji was affable, garrulous, and a braggart. Gaunt, with a weathered face and haze of white hair, he seemed as ancient as the river after which he took his name. One of his many Swahili nicknames, "Bwana Ziraili," alluded to the countless spirits he had plucked from elephants and other wild animals. Perhaps the spirits which returned to haunt him explain why, in his old age, he was obsessed with natural history. He loved to corner his admirers and run on for hours about the rare butterflies and beautiful birds of the Rufiji River, portraying a child's fantasy world where every imaginable color and shape blend in magical profusion.

My father, one of those admirers, brought him home, hoping in vain to garner more about the great elephant byways converging on the Rufiji River. After a week or so of Rufiji, my mother, who couldn't take his bragging and sponging, ordered my father to get rid of him. That was easier said than done, given my father's polite English disposition and a soft spot for aging hunters. After his years of living in the bush, subtle hints rolled off Rufiji's leathery hide like water. Eventually my father finally hit on the ingenious solution of setting him on to some other unsuspecting listener. Only later did we learn that another of his many African nicknames was "Jitu Masoga," the giant talker.

Despite his loquacious style, Rufiji was reticent when it came to elephants. Only once did he ever mention an elephant by name, and that one, Hamisi, made up for all the others. Hamisi was a legendary tusker who roamed the northern reaches of the Selous Game Reserve evading every hunter, even Rufiji, who knew the area better than anyone.

"Hamisi travels hundreds of miles a year," Rufiji told us. "Always on the move, guarded by a few younger bulls, sometimes by a big herd of females. The old fellow migrates north with the rains and south to the safety of game reserve in the dry season, as far as I can tell."

My father expressed his doubts, yet the mere mention of Hamisi brought a faraway look to his eyes, rekindling the hunting legends that had lured him to India in the 1920s and Africa in the 1940s. "I'm going to find him one day, mark my words," my father told us. At age eleven, I got caught up in his latest and greatest fantasy.

Months later, we were slogging across the Mikumi Plains in a hot withering wind, with Paulo, our guide, head-down in a daydream ahead of Dismus. Just then a young bull elephant stepped out of a thicket and raised its head menacingly. My father clicked at Paulo, who looked up in alarm and fell back behind him in a seamless movement. Up against the elephant, my father looked as small and vulnerable as a terrier facing off a bull. At that moment the elephant tossed its head in a cloud of dust and rushed forward in soundless flopping charge. My father stood his ground, gun at the ready, calling the elephant's bluff. At fifteen paces the bull came to a halt and swayed uncertainly from side to side before moving off pathetically in a stiff-legged shuffle with his tail curled up and his head half angled back toward us.

"Come on, come on," my father urged us, breaking into a fast walk, knowing the young bull would alert the main herd up ahead.

We caught up with my father as he struck the edge of a lightly wooded floodplain where the bull had vanished. Here, seventy or more elephants drifted slowly ahead, dwarfed by an outsized animal. I was momentarily puzzled, thinking the smaller animals were all juveniles gathered around a single adult. Just then the outsized animal veered right, displaying two enormous tusks angling into the grass. We were looking at a female herd dwarfed by a gigantic male.

My father, always decisive and sure as a hunter, hesitated, even though he could have loosed off a raking shot to the brain or heart. At that instant, the herd stirred like leaves in a gust and surged forward hesitantly. Seconds later they gathered into a chaotic rush of bodies and crashed off into the distance.

Was the elephant Hamisi? It is hard to say. He was certainly the largest tusker I have ever seen—far bigger than Odinga, a elephant with 130-pound tusks who became a familiar sight around my tent in Amboseli in the 1960s. Strangely, my father never spoke of the encounter. Neither did I, despite my anger and disappointment, for I didn't know what to make of his hesitancy and dreaded embarrassing him by raising the question. Had he been too caught up in his fantasy to react with his customary speed, or had he let the elephant go, in tribute to the legend? Whatever the answer, Hamisi evaded every other hunter as far as I know, unless he was the giant tusker shot in southern Tanzania in the 1970s, the second-largest elephant ever shot. After living down the disappointment, I fantasized that Hamisi outwitted all the old-time hunters and died along some remote stretch of the Rufiji River, where his tusks sank into the muddy waters, never to be retrieved.

Nothing is as thrilling as an elephant hunt, and no kill is quite as gripping as the first.

On the first hunt the tempo picked up the moment we located fresh spoor and began tailing a promising bull. The excitement rose to fever pitch when we heard the steady flap of elephant ears close by, only to be doused by the crashing sound of tall mteti grass being mowed down as the herd made a panic-stricken escape at a whiff of our scent. My second hunt began in much the same way, but ended in a kill.

We had struck fresh dung at dawn and tailed four bulls until midday, when they took refuge in the shade of a thicket. At the telltale sound of flapping ears, my father tested the direction of the wind with a touch of wood ash kept in his pocket. Satisfied with the wind direction, he crept off into a thicket on our left, leaving Martin and me with the porters. Ten agonizing minutes passed. Nothing. Had my father stumbled on the elephants in thick bush and been trampled? The steady flapping of ears halted abruptly, leaving an ominous silence. For a split second, I imagined the worst.

Then came the deep boom of the double-barreled .450, sending a flock of birds squawking from the thicket and the elephants crashing through the undergrowth. As the crashing receded, my father appeared tense and white. "Christ, that was bad. I had to get right on top of them to shoot. There was no telling which way they were going to go." His tenseness shook me. What right had he to feel fear, much less talk about it? He was a hunter, wasn't he? Confused, I searched his face for a hint of embarrassment but found none. Then he laughed, and the moment passed. "Let's go and look at the elephant."

He led us to a kigelia tree where the bull lay collapsed on its legs, its head propped upright on its tusks. The massive rough hide and sparse stubby hairs gave the animal an oddly prefabricated look and evinced not one twinge of sympathy or shame in me. Not, that is, until I walked round to the great domed head. There the elephant's ears hung like crumpled sails. Small amber eyes stared through long, delicate lashes. A thin trickle of blood meandered down the temple from a small puncture in front of its ear. Its heavy wrinkled trunk pointed at me like an accusing finger.

How cheap and sordid it felt, marching off, leaving those sad, gentle eyes and fifty years of memory to denature into nothing. Why had we killed the elephant and disfigured and defiled it by hacking out its ivory? For a pair of tusks soon to be numbered and stacked with thousands of others on the damp cement floor of the Dar es Salaam Ivory Room, ready for shipment to God-knows-where. And for what? Bangles or beads to adorn wealthy customers who couldn't care a damn about elephants or what happened under the kigelia tree?

"Not good," my father said, loading the tusks into the car after the long hike back. "Only fifty pounds or so, but I'm running out of time on my license. And it'll help pay your school fees at least."

If my father's intention had been to alleviate his guilt, selling the tusks to pay our school fees made me feel worse. We weren't wealthy, and three big tuskers a year worth $100 to $200 apiece in ivory did cover some of our school fees. The dead elephant wasn't about our school fees though. The truth was that my father loved nothing more than to hunt the animal he respected and feared most.

Raised to hunt, I saw no end to the hunter's ways and no end to the Old Africa either. In the vastness of southern Tanganyika, my fresh new world was impregnable to the encroachment Rushby, Ionides, and Rufiji evidently saw creeping over the horizon. Their evasion about past hunts riled me, as did their veiled talk about dark and sinister threats to wildlife. Why the evasion, and why had they given up elephant hunting for natural history and game preservation? Had they grown old, gone soft, or simply had one too many close shaves?

Even my father began to talk emotionally and reverentially about elephants, as if by ennobling them he sanctified killing them, much as the Maasai do in killing lions for sport. I didn't understand the changes in him at the time, any more than the softening of Rushby and Rufiji. I was too wrapped in my own dreams and had no time for all the conspiratorial talk about poaching and preservation. It made no sense to me. One thing was clear though: whenever the subject of preservation came up, Ionides' name was sure to follow.

A cadaverous man with a large, aristocratic nose, Ionides habitually wore baggy shorts and tennis shoes. Though widely known as a snake expert, Ionides was the man who masterminded the establishment of Selous Game Reserve. Named after the famous explorer and elephant hunter Frederick Selous, the reserve began as a cluster of game sanctuaries established by the Germans between 1905 and 1912. In a quirky tradition begun when Queen Victoria handed Kaiser Wilhelm a birthday gift of Kilimanjaro, Wilhelm himself gave the remote and scattered sanctuaries as a gift to his wife. Thereafter Selous and other reserves became known as "Shamba la Bibi," or the wife's farm, among Africans in the surrounding region.

As a young resolute game scout working for the Game Department, Ionides set about expanding the scattered parcels into a consolidated reserve covering 22,000 miles of wilderness the size of Ireland. His burning ambition was to create the largest protected area in Africa, a place where elephants could thrive unmolested. To this end, Ionides callously ignored elephant attacks on the scattered African shambas and pounced on an outbreak of sleeping sickness to evict the peasant farmers from the reserve. How they survived was none of his business. His job was saving animals.

To his credit, Ionides succeeded in protecting Tanganyika's elephants. By the time renowned biologist Iain Douglas-Hamilton conducted the first count of the reserve in the 1970s, Selous had more than 100,000 elephants, a tenth of Africa's total. Ionides had made up for the elephants he killed as a hunter and retired with a clear conscience to study his beloved snakes.

Ionides' success in creating Selous Game Reserve was not lost on the colonial government, even if his methods raised a few eyebrows. Emulating his success, colonial governments moved tens of thousands of peasants from their tribal homelands to make way for wildlife sanctuaries in the pre-independence years. Ionides, by virtue of his success with Selous, paved the way for the forced evictions and hard-line preservationism that put Africans and wildlife on a collision course.

All the same, it would be unfair to blame Ionides for the explosive conflicts to come, for in reality preservationism had its roots in nineteenth-century England, a time of unabashed Victorian sentimentality when concern for the well-being of nature and wild animals came to the fore.

As early as 1848, John Stuart Mill advocated zero population growth in Great Britain in the interests of protecting vanishing nature. By 1869, acceptance of wild creatures as beings in their own right, without reference to man or God, led to the first legislation to protect wildlife. Such an extraordinary switch in sensibilities from the medieval revulsion toward wilderness and Christian belief in the dominion of man over nature was transposed directly to Africa by the Victorian gentry, including Sir Harry Johnstone, special commissioner to the newly acquired Protectorate of Uganda. Johnstone, writing to the British foreign secretary in 1896, captured the sentiments of the time. "It would be melancholy to think that such glorious creatures as the eland, the kudu, the sable antelope and zebra were passing into extinction when they might be saved and perpetuated by our making a little effort in the right direction."

In adjacent German East Africa (Tanganyika), the administrator, Hermann von Wissmann, proved ahead of his time by trying to give local communities good reason to protect wildlife, an approach that would not resurface for another eighty years. In 1896 he created two game reserves and tried but failed to place wildlife under the stewardship of local chiefs, who were to be rewarded for their vigilance against poachers. He also believed that sportsmen had a duty to protect wildlife for science and succeeding generations.

Both Johnstone and Wissmann knew about the dangers of extinction. By their time the bison had been all but exterminated in North America, and in South Africa wildlife had been virtually eliminated from the southern Cape. The eighteenth-century Arab-dominated slave trade, in which slavers acquired ivory in the interior and used slaves as portage for the long march to the coast, had cleared much of the interior of both. The elephant slaughter raised colonial concerns over whether the elephant would survive at all.

The prospect of extinction prompted the British foreign secretary, Sir John Kirk, to call for a sanctuary big enough to cover several habitats in East Africa. In Kenya, his call led to the creation of the 13,000-square-mile Southern Game Reserve in 1899, and the 13,800-square-mile Northern Game Reserve in 1900. Both reserves gave complete protection to wildlife and indigenous peoples. Times were different then. According to the Victorian worldview, primitive man and wildlife had always lived in harmony and there was no reason to believe things would change if modern civilization could be kept at bay.

That colonial settlement and not indigenous Africans was seen as a threat to wildlife at the time can be judged from another step taken by the early colonial administrators. In 1899 the Queen's Regulations expressly prohibited commercial animal trade—except for crocodiles—to protect the interests of indigenous people and wildlife. A year later, in 1900, the first-ever international convention on wildlife was held in London. The purpose of the gathering was to bring together the eight European nations with colonial holdings in Africa to "prevent the destruction which has taken over wild animals in southern Africa and other parts of the globe."

By 1906 the Society for the Preservation of the Fauna of the Empire was urging the colonial government to set up reserves covering the migratory routes of wildlife before settlement made preservation impossible. In that year the British secretary of state, responding to what must surely rank as one of the first environmental lobby groups, wrote: "We owe the preservation of these interesting and valuable and sometimes disappearing types of animal life as a debt to nature and to the world—we are the trustees for posterity of the natural contents of the Empire—the reserves ought to exist not for the gratification of the sportsman, but for the preservation of the interesting types of animal life." This recognition of the need to set up reserves big enough to cover the migrations was remarkable for its time. It wasn't until the 1960s that the ecological needs of wildlife would begin to feature again.

The British official's high-minded and noble words were at striking odds with the ensuing colonial slaughter of wildlife and indifference to Africans. The short-lived aberration probably arose because the early colonial administrators thought of themselves as having an obligation to abolish the slave trade and protect the indigenous African—while furthering Britain's trading prospects, of course. Many of the early administrators were naturalists genuinely enthralled by the unimaginable wealth of wild animals and keenly aware of the threats posed to wildlife by incoming colonial settlement.

These remarkable sentiments were overtaken by the arrival of white settlers and commercial trade. With the influx of modern firearms at the end of the nineteenth century, the relationship between humans and animals in East Africa changed. In the first six months of 1888, more than 37,000 guns and one million rounds of ammunition entered the port of Zanzibar alone. The weaponry soon fell into the hands of Africans as well as Europeans. Ancient subsistence hunting practices expanded into vast commercial enterprises, threatening wildlife herds and the traditional hunters across Africa.

In an attempt to stem the slaughter, game laws were imposed on Africans too. From now on, only those legally holding a sporting rifle qualified for game quotas, and because Africans were denied guns on security grounds, hunting effectively became a European preserve. African antipathy toward wildlife can be traced to the colonial denial of their right to hunt.

At the same time that Africans were denied the right to hunt, a wave of land-hungry white settlers flooding into eastern Africa made a strong case for exterminating wildlife around their farms and dismantling the reserves for arable use. To a frightening degree, they succeeded. Without the fledgling Game Department and home government in Britain, which confined wildlife slaughter to the European settlement areas, hardly any wildlife would have survived. For the moment, though, East Africa's savannas were safe, protected by sleeping sickness and aridity.

The reprieve did not last long. The colonial suppression of the slave trade and tribal wars as well as development brought by the Europeans created a new threat. From now on the growth of African populations and farms would be the greater menace to wildlife, in the eyes of the colonial administrators. This is the threat that Rushby and Ionides saw approaching. As pioneers in the Game Department, they intended to preserve the last of Africa's wildlife, come what might. Ionides, the reclusive preservationist who ignored the indigenous rights the Victorian administrators had so scrupulously respected, led the way. However noble his intentions, he alienated the very people on whom the future of wildlife depended by putting the rights of elephants above those of Africans.

Influenced in part by hunters-turned-conservationists like Rushby and in part by elephants themselves, my father's views toward hunting and wildlife changed. Two particular incidents affected him deeply. In the first, he put a bullet through a marauding young female while on control duty and watched in anguish as the herd gathered around and buried her beneath bushes in a display of confusion and grief. In the second incident, he shot an older female who collapsed dying. The herd, trumpeting and bellowing, tried to raise her up.

These incidents, and others told by fellow hunters, eroded my father's carefully nurtured hardness. Though dismissive of the supernatural, he began to speak in awe of elephants' mysterious, even telepathic communication. How else, he asked, could one explain the silent alarm elephants spread whenever they sense the presence of a hunter?

Our safaris changed subtly. Game spotting and exploration gradually replaced hunting. Tanganyika abounded in remote and mysterious areas with evocative names like Itigi Thicket, Bohor Flats, and Malagarasi Swamp, places where one could walk for months without retracing a step. Bird book and camera became essential equipment alongside gun and ammunition.

By 1958 we spent more time game watching and photographing animals than hunting. Outwardly, there was little distinction; we still traveled on foot and lived off the land; we faced the same hardships and dangers in stalking big game, perhaps more, because we had to shoot them at closer range with a Leica and Brownie box camera; the final shot was just as thrilling, too, with none of the sadness of killing. Our photography was nothing to write home about, except for Martin's, whose aesthetic sensibilities developed early on. In later years he took up wildlife photography professionally and has won several notable awards in Britain.

Our switch from hunting to animal watching—like Ionides' switch from hunter to preservationist—subtly undermined our relation with

African farmers and led to the slow erosion of their trust. At Mbwamaji, the farmers had depended on us for guide fees, meat, and killing marauding animals. At Mikumi, things were different. We seldom heard complaints about wildlife at first, perhaps because we shunned settled areas. The few Africans we did meet were subsistence hunters who relied on killing animals and respected them deeply.

A chance visit to Momba, an abandoned village south of Mikumi, brought home a troubling and portentous message. While in pursuit of Hamisi, we had picked up a guide who, after a half day's walk, brought us to a dilapidated mud hut, the remains of an abandoned village where he once lived. One wall had been crushed by an elephant, opening a gaping hole to the smoke-blackened interior.

"The elephants come to Momba every night," our guide told us in a hushed voice, as if the marauders were still around. "They came when the mangoes ripened. We tried to drive them off but they became angry and attacked us. An elephant chased this farmer into his hut," he said, pointing to the collapsed wall. "Then the animal broke down the house and killed him. After that we fled Momba.

"We are poor people and live a long way from Morogoro," he continued, raising his voice accusingly at my father. "We told the Game Department, and they said they would come, but they never did. Why do the rangers care more about elephants than us? Do they ever come when an elephant kills one of us? No. But if we kill an elephant they do. At once. Then they raid our houses and arrest us as poachers.

"You help us. You're a mzungu. You can shoot all the elephants you want."

Villagers around Mikumi were polite and deferential to the point of subservience in their dealings with whites, making our guide's outburst all the more surprising. My father looked away embarrassed. "Not even wazungu can shoot elephants without a license or authorization. I'll report your case when I pass through Morogoro and get them to send out some game scouts."

The guide grunted in disgust. He knew nothing would happen. The *wazungu* (Europeans) were all like Ionides—they put elephants before Africans.

The farmers' fear and loathing of elephants grew as the herds protected within Selous Game Reserve proliferated and spread into the neighborhood. The Game Department, already stretched to its limits, did in fact ignore the farmers' pleas in the remoter areas, so long as the elephants themselves were not threatened. Another problem was adding to the conflict: much as Rushby and Ionides feared, new waves of immigrants from the Uluguru Highlands and the nearby town of Morogoro to the east settled in the Doma Hills and along the Mkata River. They were given encouragement by the colonial government to plant cotton and other cash crops in their new homesteads.

Hating the bush, the settlers blamed their failures on wildlife and urged poachers who sold their meat to the growing urban markets to eradicate the animals. By 1956 the blast of gunfire echoed around Mikumi, and vultures filled the skies in ominous wheeling columns.

"The commercial meat poaching is out of hand," Bill Dick grumbled. He was a small, wiry man with short cropped hair and baggy shorts. The district ranger at Morogoro, he was my father's closest associate in the Game Department. He could have been mistaken for a demure office clerk, but what he lacked in stature he made up for in gun. Nothing about the double-barreled .600 elephant gun he carried was vaguely sporting. As ugly and sinister as a sawed-off shotgun, it fired bullets as thick as a thumb with one idea in mind—stopping a charging elephant with the force of a five-ton truck.

Dick's words reverberated in my mind. "If we don't do something fast, God knows if there'll be any game left," he continued. "Too many people moving in, too many illegal guns. Ten years back we never had to patrol, never had to worry about the odd animal shot for the pot. Now it's all a racket to sell meat to the growing legions in Morogoro. The poachers are town people out for money, not traditional hunters living off the land. The gangs are big, well organized, and well informed. They know where the game is and where we are. We can't put a couple of scouts up against twenty men. It's suicide. It'll all be over in five years at this rate."

Not finished, Dick went on to say, "It's this bloody *uhuru* [freedom] business, you know. The damn Africans with primary school education think that as soon as they take over they'll be free to do anything they want. That's what freedom means to them. No African government's going to care tuppence about game."

Bill Dick spoke of a change that few whites cared to face. By 1955 the colonial government was contemplating handing over the reins of governance to Africans. What this would mean to wildlife was unclear, but there could be no doubt that the dividing lines were being drawn, with Africans on one side intent on killing off the wild animals they had come to hate, and Europeans on the other trying to preserve them.

"Perhaps you can help, Arthur," Bill Dick ended. "You come and go as you please; the poachers don't know your moves. And the farmers around Doma trust you. If you pick up anything on the quiet about what's going on in the bush, then I'd have a chance of moving in on them."

My father tried, but times had changed. The very farmers who had previously signed on gratefully as guides and porters now evaded him. Even my father's good-natured banter failed to win them over. Dismus, ever loyal, discreetly told Martin and me the reason why. "The porters now get more from the poachers than they do from your father. The poacher brings money and scares off the shamba-raiding animals, which is more than the Game Department does. So why should farmers turn them in?"

There was more to it than Dismus cared to tell. My father was no longer a genial white hunter. He now worked as a volunteer for the Game Department in his free time, and that—as far as the farmers were concerned—put him on the side of those who didn't care a damn about people. Even Paulo, our normally servile guide, turned nasty after Julius Nyerere, soon to be president of independent Tanganyika, told whites it was time to pack up and go home. "Rich wazungu come here and shoot buffalo for their horns," Paulo complained. "If we kill one to feed our family, we are arrested. You wazungu! You stop us hunting to save animals for yourselves."

Uhuru and game preservation got all mixed up in the days before independence, and not without reason. The game laws favored whites and made life intolerable for Africans. The colonial government justified its repression by claiming Africans would wipe out the game if given free license to hunt. The undercurrent of racism didn't bubble over until uhuru gave Africans a chance to vent their feelings.

In the poisoned atmosphere of agricultural expansion and political repression, Mikumi became a war zone. Poaching gangs along the Mkata River laid down miles of wire nooses and hunted with modern firearms.

On our first few encounters, the long files of meat-laden porters dropped their loads and fled into the tall grass when they saw us. But before long the poachers grew cocky and contemptuous, saying they were soon going to take over the country and kick the colonial officers out. On one safari, my father arrested a gang of seventeen poachers smoking dozens of dismembered impala carcasses on drying racks. He shrugged it off as luck; what if their guns had been in their hands instead of propped against a tree when he stumbled on the gang?

By now I was thirteen and hated poachers with a passion. I saw them as satanic figures moving furtively through the undergrowth, slaughtering the unsuspecting and innocent. The commercial meat poachers were mostly town people who swaggered around in fancy clothes, sunglasses, and leather shoes, bribing peasant farmers to kill game. Their wanton slaughter of wildlife and contempt of bush Africans infuriated me. Until then, I hadn't thought much about the distinction between bush and town Africans. But as the town Africans swarmed into the bush killing animals, I grew incensed and took sides. I developed a deep compassion for traditional people denied their voice and rights when it came to wildlife, and in time that compassion and recognition of local rights laid the foundation for my own conservation philosophy.

To its credit, the Game Department made the same distinction when it came to traditional hunters as opposed to the new threat posed by commercial poachers. Most game rangers turned a blind eye when it came to the *mwindaji,* as the hunter was known.

One traditional hunter we encountered was Salim, a quiet, dignified old man with the light skin and thin lips of mixed Swahili-Arab stock. Standing bolt upright in a black *kanzu* (loincloth), jacket, and fez, he looked like Tippu Tib, the legendary slave trader and elephant hunter of the 1800s. Salim proudly displayed his *kibori,* a hammer-detonated muzzle loader. Dating from the 1870s, the gun carried a black-powder charge tamped down with a ramrod. The old hunter informed us that he shot only impala and wildebeest these days. As a youngster he had gone after dangerous game, including elephants. He had to stalk within five to ten paces before blasting away at the elephant's side, then wait for the black-powder fog to clear. In the event of a charge, a single shot was all that stood between him and death.

The traditional hunters like Salim seemed to have boundless knowledge of wild animals and were undoubtedly part of the romance and mystique of the Old Africa in which I grew up.

It was during these turbulent times that I made my first kill and discovered my true feelings about animals. I made a careful stalk of a warthog rooting around at the edge of a dried mud wallow, held the gun steady against a sapling, and fired. The warthog slumped dead with barely a quiver. Everything about the kill was perfect, and my father was full of admiration. As for me, I felt nothing, neither pride nor satisfaction: I was a stillborn hunter.

With this realization my fascination for animals in and of themselves—rather than as objects of prey—awakened. The sable antelope, which had walked away unharmed, remained eternally alive and alluring, the warthog forever dead. I gave up reading hunting books and began opening my eyes to the world beyond the barrel of a gun. From then on I took satisfaction in natural history rather than hunting.

"Have you noticed how the zebra often hang out with giraffe in woody country?" I probed my father. To my mind, it seemed obvious that the association must yield a benefit to any zebra astute enough to use the long-necked giraffe as a lookout tower for lions. He seemed genuinely impressed and intrigued by my observation. The role elephants play in the savannas and the balance of nature caught my imagination. Why elephants should bash down entire groves of trees seemed totally enigmatic at first, but a close look hinted at their role in fueling fires in the dead groves, thereby preventing the plains from reverting to woodlands.

Much as I loved the challenges posed by biology, the troubling and turbulent times in Tanganyika left me confused and insecure. The word *uhuru* bubbled up all around us, with every discussion coming round to why whites had the right to hunt and Africans didn't. By 1957 the mood had turned distinctly hostile. When I returned to Dar es Salaam from school, I found the coastal Muslims raising their fists and taunting me with "uhuru, uhuru na kazi," freedom, freedom and work. Most whites tried to pass off the taunts as impotent protests, but deep down they feared the rage and resentment welling up around them.

My father handled the unrest by insisting that Tanganyika wasn't yet ready for independence and would fail. "Too few trained Africans," he insisted, with a shake of his head. "How can they run the country? Who'll run the railways, the factories, the offices? Show me a fully trained African engineer. And what about tribal conflicts? Look what happened in India after independence. Civil war. And India was a long way ahead of Tanganyika, I can tell you. If Tanganyika collapses, we're heading south."

At first, I accepted his opinion unquestioningly. He had, after all, spent fifteen years training Africans and was as sympathetic as anyone. In time, however, a wedge grew between parents and children when it came to who we were and where we belonged. Away at boarding school most of the year, we came to think of ourselves as white Africans rather than as Europeans. We had a distinctive East African accent and laid on our slang as thick as any first generation does to reinforce its roots in a new home. My father, in contrast, was a Briton to the core. He loved Tanganyika, but his remarks about the country going to hell after independence grated on us no end, partly because I feared he was right, more because being Tanganyikan had become a point of pride.

For the first time in my life, I saw doubt and apprehension in my father's face. He rarely joked now, and often appeared withdrawn and cynical whenever the subject of uhuru came up, which it did unceasingly. All his talk of heading south was an admission of defeat, a retreat to the over-civilized lands he had escaped in England, and that frightened me. Worse still, it frightened him.

As a result of the turmoil, my father got regular calls to deal with crop-raiding and marauding elephants and did what he could when he was in the vicinity. "Arthur," Bill Dick said to him in frustration one day, "there's a million head of game on at Mikumi. Christ, it's a second Serengeti. But the way things are going, they're doomed. Game laws mean nothing these days. There's more people, more elephants, more conflict, and more poaching. If we don't do something drastic soon, whoosh, it'll be gone just like that after independence," he gestured, flipping up his hands. "The only way to save Mikumi is to make it a national park. Then we can get rid of the wretched shambas and poachers and haul in some tourists."

Neither Dick nor my father can have had more than a hazy notion about national parks, although the first national park, Yellowstone, had been established in the United States some seventy-five years earlier. Monumentalism and public recreation, rather than wilderness preservation, were indisputably the motivating forces behind the formation of Yellow-stone and other American parks. Such justifications seemed irrelevant in Africa when the early colonial administrators set up the first reserves to maintain the natural harmony between indigenous Africans and wildlife.

Yet, with African antipathy toward wildlife on the rise and independence round the corner, not even Selous Game Reserve seemed secure enough to preserve wildlife forever. For some reason, the idea of a national park gave Mikumi an impregnability and permanence that Selous lacked in the minds of Bill Dick and my father. Whatever their thoughts, the creation of a park would be an uphill battle if the resistance by local white settlers to the formation of Nairobi National Park, the first in East Africa, was any guide.

As a last resort, Mervin Cowie, a resourceful preservationist, artfully planted a letter in a national newspaper siding with the farmers calling for all wild animals to be shot and for the Nairobi Commonage to be turned over to arable land. After a terrifying silence and implied agreement from the settlers, the ruse paid off. In 1946 a fusillade of public and international protest swung the government in favor of a park, with Cowie as its first director. Other national parks soon followed, including Serengeti, the first in Tanganyika, established in 1951.

"Just imagine," my father and Bill Dick fantasized, reinforcing each other's hopes. "A park. A place with nothing but wildlife. A place where tourists can watch animals as tame as cows."

I never did understand the distinction between a national park and Ionides' Shamba la Bibi and passed it off as ignorance on my part. Evidently Africans didn't either. Once they picked up the talk of a national park, the outlook for wildlife seemed bleaker than ever. If the marginalized bush farmer ever had any rights under the colonial government, wildlife preservation stripped them away. Time and again I heard the same sentiments muttered angrily out of earshot of the white game officers on the subject of Selous and the future of Mikumi: "First they took our animals, then our land."

Why any tourist would ever want to visit Mikumi anyhow escaped me. The animals were hunted and skittish, the woodlands head-high in grass during the rainy season, burnt black in the dry season, and infested with tsetse fly year-round. Lodges and game-viewing tracks were unheard of and vehicular access in the rains impossible. Tourism seemed a futile hope on which to pin the future of Mikumi.

A few years later, when a few real tourists arrived at Mikumi, my father felt vindicated, though not without some misgivings. Our anachronistic world of foot safaris and animal stalks vanished as a network of tracks sprang up across the Mkata Plains to accommodate the mollycoddled visitors, as he called them, who insisted on luxury camps and on snapping animals with huge lenses from the safety of a Land Rover. For all his scoffing, he saw the tourist as a God-sent answer for Mikumi and talked earnestly about venturing into the tour business himself. In December of 1957, we joined him on a trip north to Lake Manyara and Ngorongoro Crater to check out the prospects for tourism.

The narrow, alkaline Lake Manyara stretched along precipitous Rift Valley wall below the Ngorongoro Highlands. At its shore in the cool shade of an acacia grove we sat watching elephants sloshing around. In the distance, a pink band of flamingos danced in a mirage. "God, it's beautiful," my father muttered in the sort of dreamy half-voice I hadn't heard since his first days at Mikumi. "The elephants know they're safe. Look at them. Can you imagine driving a car up to elephants at Mikumi? This is what it could be like, you know."

A couple of juveniles stood idly in a wallow, slapping mud against their flanks. Could Mikumi ever really be like this, or was it yet another illusion? My father leaned out the window, gleefully pointing to a tiny baby hidden beneath its mother. I grinned at his impish enthusiasm. Despite his newfound pleasure in watching animals, he still looked more hunter than tourist in his heavy bush jacket and felt hat. It was hard to imagine him stomaching the soft life of a tour operator after all those years of big-game hunting. He was too independent for that, too much the old-style adventurer and explorer like Rushby to spend his time coddling tourists.

The next morning we drove across the open plains, pushing a gentle bow wave of wildebeest ahead of us. The animals continued grazing, scratching, honking, and mewing, ignoring us as they did the slow-plodding rhinos. Two lionesses crouched in a tuft of grass 100 yards away, intent on a waterbuck angling round a shallow depression. They barely stole a glance when we idled up ten paces away. "Surely they've seen us," Martin muttered, unable to comprehend their utter indifference. In

Mikumi we would have been greeted by a warning growl a couple of hundred yards off.

It was a gratifying time for my father. He felt confident that Mikumi would become a park and vindicated by the arrival of tourists. Perhaps he was right after all. Making Mikumi a national park would be a way of discouraging poachers and safeguarding wildlife, if Manyara and Ngorongoro were anything to go by. His entire future seemed to be brightening. Independence was a foregone conclusion, and the chants of "Uhuru!" became an exuberant show of victory rather than a sinister threat; we chanted back "Uhuru!" just as cheerfully. Thankfully there was no more talk of leaving Tanganyika either, and my mother began to enjoy the bush as much as we did, if from the safety and comfort of a car.

I was fourteen and back at school when my father wrote asking us to meet him at a village near Mikumi at the beginning of school break so we could head straight for the bush. I relished the thought and impatiently waited for classes to end. When the bus arrived at the village meeting point, an Asian storekeeper approached us with a letter. "Have gone down to Ifakara to deal with crop raiders. Will meet you back home. Dad."

Martin and I continued on to Dar es Salaam, where my mother, Sheila, and Lynne met us off the bus. Dar had expanded over the years and we no longer lived a Spartan life in the bush without running water or electricity. A large baobab heavily scarred by tusks was the sole reminder of the days when elephants had wandered by. How odd that enormous tree now looked among the pink and white flowers bordering the driveway.

A stranger pulled up. "Excuse me, but are you Mrs. Western?"

Bea looked puzzled. "Yes, why?"

"I saw you driving around town with your family and by the look of it thought maybe you hadn't heard your husband's had an accident."

I was stunned. Bea composed herself. "I haven't heard about any accident. Are you sure? He's up at Mikumi."

"Well, I'm not altogether sure about it. I'll tell you what: you hang on here, and I'll find out, if that's all right." With that the stranger was gone.

Bea shrugged it off. "I'm sure he's mistaken."

An hour later a police officer walked up the steps. He looked uncomfortable, dressed in his starched khakis and broad leather belt. "Mrs. Western, I am very sorry to tell you that your husband was killed by an elephant yesterday."

My heart pounded uncontrollably. He had to be wrong.

"I will be back tomorrow with fuller details and your husband's belongings," he concluded with a note of finality.

"He's wrong, he must be wrong," I told myself again and again, not wanting to cry for fear of admitting the truth. "A car crash, maybe, but not an elephant." We had been charged by two bull elephants in Hadza country on our recent trip to Ngorongoro, and my father had handled the episode with the coolness and skill of a bullfighter. How could he possibly have been killed by an elephant?

I clung to my belief, fully expecting to see my father drive up at any moment. Instead a steady stream of friends and condolences arrived, reinforcing the news. I heard Bea tell one visitor that you can't kill animals without their getting their own back, as she had quietly insisted all along. I knew it was her way of explaining the inexplicable and perhaps coming to grips with the hideousness of my father's death. All the same, it tore me apart to hear it, especially after learning he had died pursuing an elephant that had trampled two farmers.

"I want you to never go out in the bush again," Bea appealed in desperation. What could I say? What could I do? The bush was my life, and nothing else mattered.

The police officer returned with my father's belongings the next morning. He dumped a cardboard box of camping gear and clothes on the veranda. I stared in disbelief and went into a cold rage: a blood-stained bush jacket lay on top of the pile. I snatched up the jacket and trousers. "Christ, what the hell does he think he's doing?" I hissed at Martin as the officer walked in to see my mother. "Mum'll see it. We've got to get rid of it."

We ran to the back of the house and dropped the clothes on the cement laundry slab, desperate to know the truth, however devastating. A gaping tear under the left armpit showed where a tusk had entered, a smaller rip on the right flank behind the breast pocket the exit point.

"It must have been quick," Martin choked. The elephant had knelt on him, to judge from the scuff marks and heavy bloodstains over the jacket.

When we had satisfied ourselves that he died instantly and didn't lie around for hours suffering, we doused the clothes with methylated spirits and watched his jacket catch fire. The Old Africa of my youth and dreams drifted away on a pall of smoke.

‹ Part Two ›

Savanna Rhythms

‹ 3 ›

Amboseli

DECEMBER 4, 1967. TEN years have passed since my father's death, and I am camped alone in Amboseli Game Reserve. Waking at three in the morning chilled to the bone, I line the camp cot with newspaper and try to settle down again. Finally, giving up, I lie awake listening to the wind moaning through the guy ropes, a lion grunting in the distance, and a Verreaux's eagle owl booping mournfully in the acacias overhead.

Kilimanjaro slowly takes shape as the night sounds die, its glaciated peak tinged pink in the early light. A gray scree slope deeply incised by snowmelt falls steeply to a mottled heathland, then flares into a green bandana of forest. Below the forest, a grassy slope studded with dark bushes dips behind a broad belt of fever trees two miles south across an alkaline flat. A solitary wildebeest stares motionless as if mesmerized by the towering mass; a small caravan of giraffe drifts across the plain in solitary file, necks undulating to the slow rhythm of their gangling stride.

The African savannas evoke an inexplicable sense of déja vu, as if some subliminal memory is tweaked by the birthplace of our hominid lineage. No place on earth strikes such a resonance, and few places in Africa can rival Amboseli for the sheer vibrancy of its fever trees and the grandeur of its backdrop.

I open a black kitchen trunk, pull out a handful of bananas, brew some coffee, and sink into my camp chair to enjoy the view. Staring in awe at Kilimanjaro, I realize that an enduring memory of the mountain seen from the train twenty years earlier has lured me back. An African hoopoo pecking in the soil indignantly flicks its striped crest when I stand up and throw out the coffee grounds. Smiling at the bird's indignation at my offense, I stretch, ready to begin the day. Then I remember Sindiyo.

Daniel Sindiyo, warden of Amboseli, had caught me sneaking into the Maasai Amboseli Game Reserve a few weeks earlier. I had taken a shortcut through the bush and bypassed the entry gates. When I broke onto a stretch of asphalt near the headquarters, the road seemed oddly sticky. I put it down to the worn-out tires on my fourth-hand Land Rover and ploughed on. Things got even stickier moments later when a bristling official stepped in front of the car and flagged me down. "Look," he snarled, approaching the Land Rover window, pointing back at the telltale tracks furrowing the freshly tarred road. "My new tarmac road. How did you miss the 'No Entry' sign?" Bwana Kali, or Mister Fierce, as Sindiyo was commonly known, needed no introduction.

Cringing at the recollection, I zipped up the tent and climbed into the Land Rover. Sindiyo had sent word that he wanted to see me in his office first thing this morning. I took the curt summons as an ominous signal that he was about to kick me out of the reserve for flouting the regulations, ruining the nine years of slog that had gone into my carefully laid plains to study Amboseli.

It was neither my father's death nor uhuru that had sent me on the circuitous route from Tanganyika to England and finally to Amboseli, but a second tragedy. Rusty Thomson, a brawny school friend who had never seen the sea, joined us in Dar es Salaam during the school break of 1959. Fifteen at the time and at home in rough seas, I didn't think twice about going beyond the reef in a choppy southeast monsoon with visibility down to three or four body lengths. I churned ahead into the slapping waves and tugging current, knowing Rusty to be a strong swimmer. A few minutes later I turned to find him missing. I swam back, rising on the cresting waves on the lookout for his blue snorkel. Nothing. Wave after wave swept by. Still nothing. I began to panic.

I dove again and again into the murky waters, my lungs aching, my mind boiling with images of a lifeless corpse and how my mother would react. Finally, exhausted after hours of diving and in danger of being pounded against the cliffs by the high-tide surf, I made for shore and biked into town to call the police. Rusty's body washed ashore four days later, one arm severed by a shark bite.

My mother was mortified. "It's not your fault," she told me. "No one's to blame. Rusty's death happened a year to the day after your father died. It's a sign to leave Africa before there's another accident." There was no doubt about whom she had in mind. Spearfishing, like hunting, tempted the fates, as far as Bea was concerned, and maybe she was right in my case; I became fatalistic about death after all that happened at Mikumi and often took needless risks.

The drive to the airport took us past a group of African kids stripped to the waist, casting hand lines into the outgoing tide near Selander Bridge. A low crest of white breakers thudded against the reef offshore. Instinctively I looked for Rusty's blue snorkel, wondering whether my pending exile in England was punishment for my recklessness. Desperate for some reassurance, I picked out the tallest palm tree and whispered, "I'll be back."

The palm tree was still fixed in my mind when we landed at Heathrow airport on a cold foggy day in December 1960. Martin stared morosely out the window at the wet asphalt and soggy turf like a convict taking his last look at freedom. Fighting to keep Africa alive in my mind, I stepped off the plane in a daze and walked down the long arrival hall harshly lit against the winter gloom. London might well have been a jail.

Nothing about the hardship and loneliness of the bush had prepared me for a big city—not the heat, the dust, the mosquitoes, or the fear and confusion when Africans began shouting "uhuru!" There was no place free of traffic or hurrying crowds, no escape from the buildings, roads, hedgerows, and other transmutations of nature—or the freezing wet weather. How I longed for Africa and the wilds. I spent hours in London's Richmond Park watching the deer, pretending they were impala. For a fleeting moment, the familiar tingle returned when a red deer surreptitiously suckled her newborn calf tucked away in the bracken. All too soon the scream of an incoming jet or the wail of a kid who had lost his parents shattered my illusion. I was an alien in the land of my birth.

A month later, I landed a job with the United Africa Company, hoping to be sent back to Tanganyika immediately. My shyness and unsociability came as a shock to my boss when, on my first day at work, I sheepishly had to ask him how to use a phone. From then on, the beetle-browed taskmaster glowered at me malevolently and dressed me down as regularly as British tea breaks. My atrocious spelling was evidence of my retardation, he told me. "You colonials are all the same—too used to people slaving on you to do anything for yourselves. At best you'll make an export clerk, and we don't send them out to Africa." I was ready to crawl down the nearest hole.

Ironically, London brought me face to face with the very Africa and Africans I had spurned. The United Africa Company employed several Nigerian trainees, all well educated and infatuated with England. Despite my excruciating shyness, I was drawn by their infectious enthusiasm and felt more comfortable in their company than among the English trainees.

"London's beautiful, man. Goda du de sem for Aafrica," my Nigerian colleagues enthused in their lilting accents.

Their jealousy of the West irked me, but slowly their exuberance and optimism wore down my antipathy and made me face the changes sweeping across Africa. Peering into the Thames over a lunch of cheese-and-tomato rolls, we talked of Africa and independence. Finally, their message hit home: the Old Africa is dead, a New Africa is born.

Modernity came as naturally to these young Nigerians as it did to the English. With their help, I came to understand the worrying images of the past—the invasion of farmers, the spread of villages, the urban poachers, the growing racial strife, my father's death—and confronted the New Africa. To have grown up white in Tanganyika, to have lived through such turbulent times and radical changes and emerged ready to embrace an altogether different future, one had to be progressive and optimistic. I became both by conscious choice and force of will and have never had regrets. All the same, not even my optimism could will away the impact of modernity razing the bush and disrupting its people. To the Nigerians urging me to look ahead, the bush spoke of traditionalism and primitives, and neither had a place in their vision of the future.

By the time Tanganyika became independent on December 9, 1961, I had been in London for a year and saw uhuru more as a beginning than as an end. All the same, my expanding awareness brought with it a troubling contradiction. How could I embrace the aspirations of the new generation, knowing its impact on wildlife and traditional African societies? Surely the bloated carp, floating down the Thames among the spumes of detergent, oil slicks, and soggy condoms, were symptoms of development gone awry?

Where among the paved-over streets, ploughed-up fields, and polluted skies of Europe did there exist room for wildlife? Surely Africa, in modeling itself on Europe, damned itself to repeat the same mistake.

My future lay back in the emerging Africa, searching for ways to fit wildlife into the aspirations of the new generations. I had no one to share these thoughts with at the time—not my Nigerian colleagues, who had no time for wildlife, or even my own family. Bea had trouble enough settling back into England, and talk of going back to the bush after all that had happened visibly upset her. She had started a new job and still had Lynne to see through school. Sheila went into television advertising in London and established a new circle of friends, many from Africa. Martin dreamed of going back, but pragmatically felt it best to do so on holiday trips from the UK. He went into teaching, saying it would give him ample time off to go back to Africa. He fulfilled his ambition as I did mine.

Africa still ran in my family's blood, and looking back was hard. They needed time to settle into their new lives without my constant reminders. So I kept my plans to myself for the most part, knowing I would return to Africa alone. We were closer than ever as a family after my father died, and the separation would not be easy on any of us.

I regularly took the tube to the British Museum of Natural History to learn more about big-game animals. Visiting the fossil exhibits and dioramas, I was struck by an alarming message, one my London-born father must have read in the wheeling clouds of vultures over Mikumi: extinction. Less than 15,000 years ago, during the Pleistocene, Europe teemed with herds of mastodons, mammoths, woolly rhinos, lions, hyenas, giant elk, and bison. To stone-age hunters it would have looked much as Africa does today. Yet with astonishing abruptness, one-third of the mammals disappeared. What caused their sudden extinction?

Europe was not alone in losing its large mammals. Over 70 percent of the mammalian genera in North America, 80 percent in South America, and 90 percent in Australia vanished just as abruptly. The puzzling feature of these mass extinctions lies in their timing. The earliest extinctions occurred in Australia 50,000 years ago, the most recent in North America 12,000 to 15,000 years ago. Several theories have been advanced to explain the extinctions, ranging from climate change to vegetation succession and ecological competition. The most compelling is overexploitation by Paleolithic hunters. Termed the "Pleistocene overkill hypothesis" by Paul Martin of the University of Arizona, the timing of the extinctions does fit reasonably well with the known arrival times of Paleolithic hunters in Australia and the Americas and the influx of technologically advanced societies into Eurasia after the last glacial retreat. The fit is not perfect though, and the theory remains to be proved. For many scientists the term "Pleistocene overkill" is also a little too red-blooded and emotive for their liking.

Poetic license aside, what if Paul Martin is right? For a good many paleontologists the jury is already in: our Paleolithic ancestors caused a global mass extinction of large mammals long before the Neolithic age and Industrial Revolution transmogrified the face of our planet.

Why Africa escaped the Pleistocene extinction remains a mystery. Some paleoanthropologists subscribe to the view that Africa's population and technology never reached the levels of other continents, but the evidence doesn't bear them out. Mikumi—even before its invasion of farmers—sustained a higher population density of more technologically advanced people than North America's Paleolithic hunters. A better explanation lies in the long coevolution of people and wildlife in Africa, with prey animals adapting to each advance in hominid hunting behavior. Whatever the reason, Africa is indisputably the odd continent out, the last bastion of the Great Age of Mammals. Its herds, by a quirk of history, miraculously escaped the next spate of extinction beginning with European colonization in the sixteenth century.

The dodo, a flightless giant relative of the pigeon, became an eduring symbol of extinction when the last of its kind was hunted down on the island of Mauritius by European sailors in the 1660s. A half rotation of the Earth away a smaller relative, the passenger pigeon, a bird said to have darkened the skies of North America's deciduous forests with its countless millions, came to an undignified end at the turn of the last century. The bellowing restless herds of bison, which numbered upward of 60 million in the early 1800s, nearly met the same fate. So ruthlessly did the U.S. Army and commercial hunters massacre the bison to starve out the Indians and provision the hide and meat markets back East that barely 5,000 survived the final massacre in 1883.

Closer to East Africa, the first Dutch settlers in South Africa plundered the plains game of the open veldt. Within a century of the first colonial settlement at the Cape of Good Hope, all hope for wildlife was lost. The outcome? The quagga—dead as the dodo; the bluebok—a page in the history books; the white rhino—down to a pitiful two or three dozen; the springbok's heaving migrations quelled.

Had East Africa been colonized at the time of the Americas and South Africa, the Serengeti wildebeest would have gone the way of the bison and quagga. An accident of timing alone spared the East African savannas from colonial settlement—just long enough for the slaughter around the world to sink into western consciousness and for Victorian sensibilities to surface.

East Africa's herds evaded both the Pleistocene overkill and colonial settlement, but what of the latest threat, the mushrooming of African populations and hatred of wildlife induced by discriminatory game laws? Nothing, it seemed to me, could spare the wildebeest herds this time.

I had barely accepted the realities in the New Africa when Bernhard and Michael Grzimek's book, *Serengeti Shall Not Die*, appeared, cataloguing the threats Tanzania's Maasai herders, farmers, and poachers posed to the greatest wildlife spectacle on earth. A German zoologist of world renown and director of the Frankfurt Zoological Society, Bernhard Grzimek had the dramatic flare of a Hollywood star and commanded an avid television following like no other conservationist before or since. His account of the assault on the Serengeti shook the West.

"Tens of thousands of wildebeest and gazelle were ruthlessly being trapped in mile after mile of wire snares and butchered for meat," said Grzimek. The statistics were shocking enough, but the photos and film he showed to a mesmerized TV audience were positively gruesome. Serengeti was Mikumi all over again on a far grander scale. What worried me most of all was Grzimek's condescending conclusion: "Natives should realize that game preservation is a question of proper land use," he carped, as if they hadn't been practicing exactly that for thousands of years before the Europeans came and put an end to Africa's tested ways of living with wildlife.

Grzimek seemed oblivious to the deeper threat—the hardship that Africans had suffered under colonial game laws. What value had wildlife anymore, other than to white hunters, white tourists, white preservationists, and African poachers?

Viewed dispassionately from my isolation in London, the events at Mikumi, the winds of change sweeping across Africa, and Grzimek's alarm call brought home a point the colonial government had ignored. For wildlife to survive in independent Africa, it must become an asset to the African first and foremost. Why was it acceptable for the British farmer to reject the reintroduction of the wolf and bear and for the American rancher to gun down bison wandering onto his land from Yellowstone National Park, but wrong for the African husbandman to kill elephants and lions threatening his crop, stock, and life?

African intellectuals were quick to see through the double standard and accuse the West of trying to turn East Africa into a vast national park. Preserving Africa's wildlife salves the West's guilty conscience at having exterminated its own wildlife, they insisted. The more outspoken saw it as a ruse to thwart African development.

For the first time in my life, I felt that my passion for the wilds had a purpose. If Mikumi and Serengeti were to survive, the conflict between indigenous Africans and wildlife must be tackled with as much zeal and dedication as arresting poachers and creating parks. Africa's future wardens had to go beyond enforcing punitive game laws. The challenge ultimately lay in addressing the root cause of the conflict, in solving the problems facing the African farmer as well as wildlife.

Obsessed with this rudimentary vision and the burning conviction of an eighteen-year-old ready to save the world, I made a prescient decision to address the cause of conflict between people and wildlife in Africa. Serengeti seemed the place to start after all the publicity raised by Grzimek's book, but how?

Overcoming my reticence, I wrote to Peter Scott, famous British naturalist and son of the Arctic explorer, saying I was ready and available to work on behalf of African wildlife. His reply was polite but unhelpful: first, get a university education. I took exception to his suggestion. Having grown up in the bush among the greatest hunters and game wardens on the continent, surely I was already better prepared to tackle conservation than a university graduate?

I then walked across Regent's Park and into the library of the Zoological Society of London, certain they would be grateful for my eager young talent. An imperious silver-haired man, who it transpired was the famous primatologist Solly Zuckerman, hustled me out the door when he found me browsing among the book racks. He wasn't interested in people like me, he told me curtly. The Zoological Society wanted people with degrees, good degrees. So would I kindly get out of his library at once?

A dozen rejections later, my frustration turned into sullen resolve. I drove myself relentlessly, enrolling in correspondence courses, supplemented by three or four evening classes every week in zoology, botany, and chemistry. I eagerly quit the United Africa Company when offered a lower-paying scientific assistantship at the Museum of Natural History, recognizing the chance to get some practical experience with animals, however menial.

My job at the museum was to organize the extensive tapeworm collection in the Platyhelminths Department. The pickled creatures filled thousands of glass jars in the aptly named Spirit Building overlooking Imperial College. Every day I peered at limpid worms sloshing around in alcohol strong enough to make a drunk gag. It certainly put me off the stuff for life.

Cestodes, as tapeworms are formally known, aren't everyone's idea of a charismatic animal, but one has to admire their evolutionary genius in selecting the warm, moist vertebrate gut for an ecological niche. Feeding and breeding is a cinch for these flat-segmented worms, which clamp onto a gut wall with their powerful octopus-like sucker and miniature grappling hooks. Food gurgles past them predigested every mealtime and sex is on call: being hermaphrodites they have it all the time and both ways. Sewage disposal is equally ingenious and parsimonious; the worms pirate the plumbing system of their host. In fact, the tapeworm's only singular failing is in public relations; but then they were never meant to see the light of day.

I owe a lot to tapeworms. They gave me a chance to dabble in biological research, peruse the museum exhibits, and browse in the library to my heart's content. There in the vaults of the Spirit Building, I stumbled on the joys of science to complement the natural history that had so gripped my imagination in the bush. The new assignment meant learning the basics of taxonomy, adaptation, and evolution, a task which not only indulged my passion for animals, but opened up new and endless horizons of discovery.

I was seldom home before ten at night and invariably up before five, a safari habit I still retain. Weekends saw me dissecting dogfish, rabbits, and frogs on the roof of my mother's flat to avoid stinking up the house. During the balmy summers the smell of freshly cut lawns and lime blossom wafted away the stench of formalin. During the winters I continued my dissections with frozen fingers, the scalpel jerking wildly in my hand like a conductor's baton. Sometimes I went through three or four frogs before I laid out the arterial system without slashing the blood vessels to shreds. In the process I discovered the rewards of determination and hard work.

To my surprise and delight, I began getting straight A's in biology. The greatest boost to my newfound infatuation with biology came when I happened across a copy of George Clarke's *Elements of Ecology* in a London bookstore. Thumbing through the red-jacketed book, I felt my life coming together. The diagrams illustrating food webs, energy flow, nutrient cycles, plant succession, population oscillations, migrations, and ecosystems lit up like landing lights on a runway, guiding me to a whole new vision of the African savannas. In this vision animals were integral parts of an ecosystem, both dependent on it for their survival and contributing to its overall health. I could see in a flash that East Africa's national parks did not encompass entire ecosystems or provide the food webs and nutrient cycles needed to sustain the migratory herds. Ecology. The word was like magic. It indulged my passion for biology and held the key to wildlife survival. I was going to need that degree after all.

Within eighteen months I had won a place at Leicester University, in no small part as a result of my grasp of natural history learned at the museum. Filled with conviction that ecology had the power to save wildlife, I studied zoology and botany with an intensity that came easily after the hard slog of evening classes.

Three years later, in June 1967, I graduated with an honors degree in zoology and began casting around for a grant to work in Serengeti. The heterodoxy of my ideas—that the survival of wildlife depends on the well-being and support of the African farmer and herder—didn't dawn on me until it came time to apply to doctoral programs. Time and time again I was told, "You can't study people and wildlife. If you want to study people, you're talking human geography, not ecology. If you're interested in ecology, fine, but then you need to study areas without human disturbance."

Having taken Peter Scott's advice, I hadn't expected another obstacle. I had done well academically and participated in biological expeditions to the deserts of the Near East and the Sahara to study the adaptations of lizards to extremes of heat and aridity. The work had caught the attention of several prominent biologists, and, like any other aspiring graduate, my head was turned by offers of fellowships at first rate universities—provided I undertook ecological research in areas free of human disturbance. Once I regained my equilibrium, I turned down the offers at the risk of alienating senior figures in the scientific establishment. I had come too far to turn back. The answer lay in putting humans back into the ecological picture, not denying their presence.

Eschewing all advice, I took a calculated gamble and applied for a prestigious Leverhulme Travel Fellowship. With only six awarded annually for all subjects, the odds were against me. Yet against all reason, I felt supremely confident and breezed through the interview with uncharacteristic effusiveness. A week later I tore open the envelope. Yes! The gamble had paid off.

Heady with visions of working in Serengeti, I boarded a plane to Nairobi to join the Zoology Department at the University of East Africa. Freedom to follow my instincts and a commitment to the New Africa weighed more heavily in my decision than academic allure. In retrospect it was the right decision, not only because the university had established a graduate course in conservation biology fifteen years before the new discipline caught on in North America, but because it gave me contacts with up-and-coming Kenyans.

Bea was reconciled to my return by now. The bush wouldn't pose the dangers she worried about, so long as I wasn't out hunting animals. Saving them was an altogether different proposition as far as she was concerned, a cause worth fighting for. It would be hard leaving the family in England. The only consolation was that they took some delight in telling me they would be out regularly for a visit.

I arrived in Nairobi in July 1967, overjoyed to be back on East African soil. The palm tree had been my constant guide all these years and still appeared as clear as ever across the mangrove flats beyond Selander Bridge. My anxiety about independence, about getting back, and about what the future in Africa held was gone. The future lay ahead, wide open and challenging. Four years after uhuru, Nairobi stirred with life, and the vibrancy

and optimism were palpable. Kenya had overcome the strains of its liberation struggle under Jomo Kenyatta and was moving forward. The same exuberance my Nigerian colleagues in London had felt about the future
gripped Kenya's up-and-coming generation. It was easy to feel at home in
this newly liberated and liberal atmosphere; the University of Nairobi was
the right choice. But much as I enjoyed the almost carnival-like atmosphere that still pervaded Nairobi in its halcyon days after independence,
this was not my ultimate destination.

Intent on returning to Tanzania, I lingered just long enough to register
at the university before setting off on a reconnaissance trip to Serengeti.

The Serengeti Research Institute, set up to continue Grzimek's pio-
neering work, lay in the heart of the park. SRI, as it was known, had attracted the best and brightest scientists from Europe and North America.
Funded by the Ford Foundation, the institute had a mandate to study the
Serengeti ecosystem and collect data vital to its conservation and management. When I arrived, fifteen scientists from Oxford, Cambridge, the Max
Planck Institute, and a handful of other research institutions were busy
studying lions, elephants, zebra, wildebeest, and several other species. The
sprawling labs, library, workshops, and comfortable rows of suburban bungalows appeared oddly out of place among the timeless granitic kopjes and
stately flat-topped acacias bordering the open plains stretching to the distant Ngorongoro Highlands.

Referred to as a neocolonial bastion with a distinctly Oxford accent,
the epithet wasn't far off the mark. Not a single African worked at the institute, except as a bottlewasher or mechanic. Even the field assistants were
European and American students. "We're studying Serengeti as a natural
laboratory," Hugh Lamprey, the director, said when I inquired about
studying the conflict between the Maasai and wildlife. "There aren't any
people in the park. That's why we set up the lab here."

The myopia at Serengeti was puzzling. Were humans not part of the
ecosystem, and had they not been so from the dawn of humankind in
Africa? Treating Serengeti as a natural ecosystem when its human occupants had been turfed out seemed perverse. Bitterly disappointed, I left.

There had to be a better site, one steeped in conflict. The search took
me to most of Kenya's prime wildlife areas, from Tsavo in the east to Samburu in the north and Mara in the west. If nothing else, the safaris served

as an introduction to the problems Kenya's national parks had faced since the Royal Nairobi National Park was created in 1948. There was one place not on the list.

"Hell, if you're looking for problems, Amboseli Game Reserve's the place for you," Bristol Foster, a gangly Canadian in the Zoology Department at the University of Nairobi advised me with a wicked grin. "The Maasai are killing off the famous yellow-fever trees and turning the area into a dustbowl. No one gives Amboseli a chance unless the Maasai are kicked out soon."

Foster was right about Amboseli. There wasn't a single conservation problem it didn't have bigger and better than any other place in East Africa. It offered the ideal study area. Located in Kajiado District of southern Kenya beneath the slopes of Kilimanjaro, Amboseli was one of the country's most spectacular reserves and the only one still occupied by people.

"This little piece of Africa is second to none for its wildlife and its scenic charm," D.E. Blunt had written in 1955 for *Country Life* magazine. The founding director of Kenya National Parks, Mervin Cowie, had considered Amboseli the crown jewel of Kenya's wildlife sanctuaries and a tourist paradise. By 1966, drawing more than 60,000 people a year, the reserve was the most popular spot on the East African tourist circuit. The inevitable conflicts between tourists and livestock had begun in the late 1940s, when British efforts to make Amboseli a national park were thwarted by the resident Maasai. From then on, the battle lines were drawn.

The colonial view was summed up in Blunt's article. "Today, two-thirds of the reserve is frequented by a tribe with their countless herds of livestock. Wherever one looks, there is desolation and practically desert. What will the rest of the nations say in a few years' time when they arrive at Amboseli reserve (it is not a national park and therefore has no permanency) to find a dust bowl? What will they think of Britain's responsibility for preserving wildlife for the rest of the world? Natives live only for the present. Weakness and appeasement seem to be our watchwords."

Within a few years of Blunt's article, visitors from other nations arrived in Amboseli and were alarmed. The renowned anthropologist Louis Leakey, whose pronouncements on any subject carried inordinate weight, blamed the Maasai herds for turning the area into a dustbowl. Leslie Brown, a highly respected raptor specialist and former director of agriculture in Kenya, was blunter still. If anyone needed evidence of Maasai stupidity and short-sightedness, he insisted, they need look no further than the desert called Amboseli. Nothing short of national park status would do for Amboseli as far as Leakey and Brown were concerned.

Most conservationists agreed. Few saw any hope for wildlife unless Amboseli was set aside as a national park. For their part, the Maasai rejected a national park as assiduously as they had in colonial days. Amboseli was, in their eyes, more important to them than wildlife.

The standoff took a turn for the worse shortly after the 1,259-square-mile game reserve was handed over to the Maasai Kajiado County Council in 1963. The council administered the 8,000 square miles of Maasailand east of the Rift Valley. Leslie Brown complained that under the council's lax management, cattle herds had proliferated like locusts and devastated the Amboseli reserve, threatening tourism and wildlife alike. But with three-quarters of its income accruing from Amboseli tourists, the Kajiado County Council was not about to cede the game reserve to anyone. The real question was whether the council could resist the combined weight of government and international conservationists agitating to expel the Maasai from Amboseli. Given the forces aligned against them, the chances that the Maasai would avoid the fate that had befallen Serengeti, Ngorongoro, and Tsavo seemed slim.

All that stood in the way of studying the conflict in Amboseli was Sindiyo.

I pulled up at a derelict thatch-roofed cottage at Ol Tukai, the reserve's headquarters. Calling out "Hodi," hello, I went in, hoping Sindiyo wouldn't recognize me. A young fresh-faced warden dressed in a khaki safari suit looked up. "Come in," he muttered gruffly.

Sindiyo rose. "We have met before, Mr. Western, haven't we?" How could he forget? The tire tracks were there in the asphalt to remind him every day.

"Please, sit down." A handsome man with the slender build and light skin of a Maasai, he had the dark, brooding eyes of Omar Sharif and a moustache trimmed in the fashionable President Nyerere style. Leaning back in his chair, he looked me over. Making no mention of my tire tracks, he asked in perfect English, "Tell me, what do you have in mind for Amboseli, Mr. Western?"

I shifted uncomfortably. The tone of his "Mr. Western" unnerved me. How much should I tell him? If I were honest, he would probably kick me out for meddling in political matters that didn't concern researchers. If I tried to pull the wool over his eyes and he saw through me, I would be back in Nairobi before dark.

"I'm interested in the migrations, the woodland destruction, and how the problems between the wildlife and the Maasai can be resolved, Mr. Sindiyo," I muttered, throwing in a few technical terms like ecosystem dynamics to obfuscate my intent.

"Good, good," he responded enthusiastically. "I took a diploma course in wildlife management myself, you know. At Colorado State. You're talking about the sort of information I really need here."

Sindiyo leaned forward, amused at my bewilderment. "The reserve is run by the Kajiado County Council, as you know, but the Maasai are totally opposed to handing over the area as a national park, despite the pressures. I'm here myself to see if I can sort things out." He half turned and waved his arms at a stack of files piled high on a shelf behind him. "All these files go back years. Not a single animal count. Nothing about migrations. Nothing about the cause of the woodland problem except overgrazing. I'm worried. There's a lot of pressure on Amboseli. The government's not going to stand by and see it destroyed. I'll do what I can to help you, but I'll need some answers from you soon if your research is going to be of any use."

He stood up. "One thing before you go. I'm sending a ranger along with you, if you don't mind. His name is Kibori. He'll show you around until you know the place."

A few moments later, a short stocky corporal dressed in starched khaki shorts and shirt several sizes too large appeared at the door. He snapped to attention and saluted. "Jambo bwana. Corporal Kibori. I have arrived," he barked out in Swahili.

That afternoon Kibori joined me on a reconnaissance. The plains were silent, the herds gone with the arrival of the rains. Where had they vanished and why? Before answering that question, I had to get the lay of the land and sketch out a vegetation map.

Kibori led me to the top of Observation Hill, a small lava plug rising 100 feet above the Amboseli flats. Twisted shards of black lava covered the hillside. "The Maasai call this hill Nomatior," he explained. "The name means broken pottery. That's what the black stones look like."

The promontory overlooked a flat expanse of country rising gently from the foot of Kilimanjaro to a range of mountains marking the threshold of the Kenya highlands sixty miles north. "That is Osilalei," Kibori added expansively, whistling the *s* gently through his missing lower incisors. "Osilalei is the common thorn tree found in the bush country."

Most westerners think of East Africa as endless Serengeti grassland, with scattered flat-topped acacias breaking through teeming herds of wildebeest, zebra, and gazelle. In reality, most of East Africa is covered by thick brush and broken woodland. The large migratory herds occupying Serengeti, Ngorongoro, Tsavo West, Samburu, and Amboseli are the most famous of the wildlife concentrations occupying the grassy islands. The islands owe their existence to volcanic activity, hot fires, and shifting Maasai settlements.

Osilalei, the commiphora tree scrub north of Amboseli, is typical of the vast stretches of thorn country enveloping the inland plateau stretching from central Tanzania to northern Kenya. The Swahili word *nyika* refers to this thorn scrub; Tanganyika is the great stretch of scrub country lying inland from the coastal trading port, Tanga.

East Africa's national parks cluster around the wildlife herds congregated on open plains and dry-season watering points. The wildlife congregations are no coincidence. The migratory species wander widely during the rains when grazing is plentiful, following the green flushes. As the rains slacken and the earth turns dusty and dry, the herds home in on the few permanent sources, gathering in large aggregations.

The assemblages attracted the eye of East Africa's pioneer preservationists. For the most part the national park boundaries circumscribe the dry-season concentrations, ignoring the all-important wet-season dispersal areas. The few exceptions include Tsavo East National Park and Selous Game Reserve, protected areas carved out of scrub and woodland marginal for human occupation. Grzimek's study of the migratory wildebeest, for all its shortcomings by modern census methods, identified the glaring deficiencies in Serengeti's park boundaries.

Evicting the traditional occupants from the dry-season range of an ecosystem and ignoring the wet-season range secures only half the ecosystem for the wildlife migrants in most East African parks. The land annexations have stirred up animosity toward wildlife among the traditional occupants of the land, creating enemies at the threshold of migratory pathways.

In Amboseli there seemed no way out of this conundrum without knowing the ecological needs of the wildlife and the people living side by side.

After taking in the enormity of the task and the beauty of the land, I sat down at the top of Observation Hill and began rifling through a stack of aerial photos bought in Nairobi. The glossy black-and-white images showed the dark band of swamp bordering Observation Hill. Starting from this point, I sketched in the habitats spread out below like a patchwork quilt.

To the north stretched the alkaline grasslands like a miniature Serengeti. To the south, a band of flat-topped tortilis trees looking like overgrown toadstools separated the basin from the slopes of Kilimanjaro. A broad belt of yellow-green fever trees wound east–west across the basin, dividing the tortilis trees and plains. Two slashes of dark green swamps— Longinye behind the Ol Tukai headquarters and Enkongo Narok looping around Observation Hill—gave the arid flats an oasislike appearance. Below me, the long sinuous Enkongo Narok swamp meandered north before curving west and discharging into Lake Conch, an enlarged marsh stretching onto the seasonal floodpan of Lake Amboseli.

The first three days were spent roughing out the habitats and another three exploring the basin, refining the map, and collecting plants for my herbarium. Kibori, no longer the tour guide and informer, sat glumly watching me squash plants between pages of newspaper and strap them into a plant press. "You don't have to squash the plant to learn its name," he told me in earnest. He looked unconvinced when I explained the need to preserve the plants and have them assigned a scientific name at the herbarium in Nairobi. What good was a name no one around here understood? he wondered. He grinned with relief when the plant collecting was over and he was free to return to his lucrative tips scouting lions and cheetahs for tourists. But beforehand, I added, I wanted him to track down the migrations.

Our first trip took us south to Lemomo, one of several cinder cones clamped like a barnacle to the base of Kilimanjaro. We clambered over loose lava rocks and brushed through a tangle of thorns to reach the summit. Scanning the plains below through binoculars, I picked out a few aimless herds of zebra dancing in the amplified heat haze.

The next day we drove north to Osilalei, where the scrub country had grown lush and green after heavy rain. A purple sea of ipomeas and delicately arched heliotropum flowers carpeted the barren red soils. Three-inch long buprestid beetles with iridescent wings of purple, green, and red hummed noisily around wait-a-bit thorns in bright mating clusters. Droves of white colotis butterflies with red-tipped wings drifted lightly along on the breeze like eddying snowflakes.

"It's beautiful, isn't it?" I asked Kibori.

He shrugged, unimpressed. "No animals here. Let's go."

We were well outside the northern boundary of the game reserve when we came upon the first migrating herds. Resting the binoculars on the steering wheel, I squinted through the eyepiece with mounting excitement. Herds of zebra, wildebeest, eland, and oryx stretched into the distance along the Kejuado floodplain, their feet melting in the mirage, tails swishing metronomically to beat off the clouds of flies. A long line of cattle filed slowly north, trailed by a lone Maasai herder. "What about the rest of the migrants?" I asked Kibori.

"I don't know, bwana. I've never seen big herds in Osilalei. Here the animals are scattered, some here, some there, depending on the rains."

Kibori's statement stopped me short. If the migrations spread erratically over a huge area north of Kilimanjaro, as he suggested, mapping them with any reliability would take years of aerial surveys. All I had was an aging Land Rover and a year's funding.

Struggling to absorb the enormity of what he said, I turned my attention to the grasses attracting the migrants: *Chloris guyana, Eragrostis tenuifolia, Cyperus obtusifolia,* all highly palatable species. The herbivores obviously preferred these soft, broad-leaved grasses to the thin wiry grasses of Amboseli's alkaline soils, otherwise they would still be in the game reserve. But if the grasses were so palatable and so widely distributed, why did the migrants return to Amboseli at all? What could possibly drive them back? Lack of water?

If this line of reasoning were right, the permanent swamps in Amboseli acted as a choke chain, limiting how far the grazers could forage from water in the dry season. That in turn would mean that the size of the migratory population was regulated by the amount of forage within reach of the Amboseli swamps. And if that were the case, surely the dry-season range in the Amboseli basin was the main arena of conflict between Maasai and wildlife?

Sindiyo still clung to hopes of a compromise between the Kajiado County Council and the government of Kenya, but with overgrazing and the pressure for a national park on the rise, time was not on his side. An innovative solution had to be found soon.

The time had come to feel the pulse and learn the rhythms of Amboseli to understand how it functioned. How did the Maasai fit into the scheme of things and coexist alongside wildlife? If these questions could be answered and the threats to Amboseli understood, there was still a chance to conserve the entire ecosystem.

With so little time left and so much to learn, I had decided to cut myself off from all distractions and bury myself in Amboseli. My reasons for choosing voluntary isolation were more pragmatic than spiritual or romantic, though the romance of being alone had its appeal, too.

« 4 »

The Pulse of an Ecosystem

LEARNING THE RHYTHM OF Amboseli meant finding a secluded spot beyond reach of the roving minibuses to immerse myself in the daily ebb and flow of animal life. The ideal spot lay under an elegant avenue of trees filling an ancient swale extending from the northern arm of Longinye Swamp. Here I pitched tent and settled in. Discreetly hidden in a thicket of Sodom apple, the site commanded a stunning view across the open plains to the tortilis woodlands banked against the Eremito Ridge to the north. Fifty miles farther on, the outlying massifs of the Kenya Highlands rose up in a broken wall. A dusty elephant trail wound erratically south across the plain into the Salvadora thicket behind the tent, and from there through the avenue of trees into the swamp. On an evening's walk I could take in a microcosm of Amboseli's varied habitats and follow the progress of the migrants day by day.

My small buff-colored tent squatting behind a fallen fever tree was protected from sun and rain by a thin fly sheet and veranda draped over a long ridgepole. With a camp cot and worktable arranged along one wall and a small gas stove, black kitchen trunk, bookshelf, herbarium, plant press, vegetation quadrants, and other odds and ends along the other, the tent walls bulged so ominously that I kept the flaps open to ease the pressure on the canvas and gain a few extra feet of working space under the front awning.

I was not alone by any means. A superb starling with iridescent blue wings and a vivid yellow-and-red chest dropped down from the tree overhead to investigate the goings on. Its bright reptilian eye scrutinized me carefully and saw an easy touch. Within a couple of weeks the starling learned to squawk insistently for food and pick crumbs from my hands. Hundreds of striped rats scurried through the undergrowth like miniature tapirs. Skinks crawled into every nook and cranny of the tent in search of insects. The boldest and most endearing visitor was a crested francolin that padded across the plastic groundsheet as I sat on my camp cot reading early one morning. Nonchalantly it pecked at my toes and pattered on through the tent.

All animals were welcome in my tent, except the huge hunchbacked rats that chewed a neat hole in the groundsheet and scurried around the tent like an eager mob of bargain hunters. At first I tolerated them too, despite the ruckus. After all, Amboseli was a game reserve, and animals had right of way. My temperance broke down when I awoke in the middle of the night to a gnawing sound and a dull ache in my head. Throwing up my hand, I dislodged a huge rat determinedly chewing hunks out of my scalp. From then on I exercised more discrimination and less restraint in evicting unwanted guests. Still, the fading yellow tent became a conspicuous homing point for every animal in the neighborhood once the migrants returned.

Charlie the elephant was the first to find the new landmark. A middleaged bull, he was like no elephant I had ever met. I was busy working on my notes when he lumbered by in early January 1968. He formally introduced himself with his thick bristly trunk, which snaked under the tent flap and groped its way across my desk. The trunk stopped inches from my face, sniffed inquisitively, then dropped away toward two massive legs rising up in front of the awning. I slid out of my chair petrified, ready to bolt through the back flap, until I noticed Charlie half-framed by the tent calmly champing on a broom handle. Totally habituated to visitors, he found human intruders more curious than frightening, a stark contrast to the hunted elephants of Mikumi. Charlie became a regular visitor and spent hours ripping up the bushes around my tent and probing the smells from my kitchen trunk.

The intimacy of tent life grew as the animals became accustomed to the yellow curiosity in their backyard. Within three months my guest book bulged with photos of rhinos, lions, lesser kudu, bushbuck, snakes, lizards, miscellaneous smaller creatures, and a solitary human being.

Amboseli outside the reserve was another matter. I often took long walks beyond the basin to escape the tourists and feel the crunch of hard soil after bumping around in the Land Rover all day. Here, where professional hunters and poachers shot big game and several Maasai lost their lives to wild animals each year, walking unarmed called for alertness and skill.

I found myself mimicking the hesitancy and alertness of a gazelle walking through the thickets. Every sense strained itself to the limit, one playing off one against the other in an integrated harmony of sight, smell, sound, and touch. Ten thousand years of agricultural living cannot obliterate the exhilarating symphony of the senses attuned to the wilds—and there is nothing quite so exciting as walking alone and unarmed in the African bush. Being truly alone, on the other hand, is not a part of the human condition.

"Upweke ni uvundo," loneliness is disgusting, goes a Swahili saying, expressing the horror Africans have of living alone—of being an outcast. I had never given much thought to loneliness as a child, but as weeks stretched into months, an unfamiliar despondency stalked my late-afternoon walks and crept into my tent at night. As primates we are intensely social creatures and find idle chatter as reassuring as grooming in monkeys and apes. I missed the small talk over a meal and the joy of sharing a sunset with my friends and family. Most of all, I missed the banter and delight in new discoveries that came with intellectual life at university.

At first I yelled out involuntarily at each new revelation and talked to imaginary friends. No one answered. Gradually I learned the joys of being alone and reveled in the thrill of each discovery with no need of social reinforcement. Eventually there was no longer any need to share my world and thoughts with anyone, and I found happiness in my own company. If I had been shy and reticent before cutting myself off in Amboseli, I became positively withdrawn during the time alone, with painful consequences when it came to actively promoting conservation. Shy, reticent, reclusive, secretive, independent, a loner—these were some of the tags used to describe me during the early years in Amboseli.

My fascination grew as my familiarity with Amboseli deepened. I loved the freedom to explore the land at will and to discover things for myself. Oddly, no matter where the search began, whether with the geology, soils, hydrology, plants, or animals, it inevitably led back to Kilimanjaro.

Several million years ago, Kilimanjaro burst up from the magma deep below the earth's surface and dammed the headwaters of the ancient Pangani River running from the Kenya highlands to the Indian Ocean. Seeking another exit, the river swung east, gouging out the soft young lava at the northern foot of the mountain. Older, more viscous flows blocked the river's exit to the sea, forming a shallow lake. Over the eons, ash fall and erosion from the mountain filled the lake with the fine white dust, which billowed off the exposed surface whenever it dried out.

Today the highest solitary mountain in the world dominates Amboseli like a hunched giant stretching fifty miles from head to toe and 16,000 feet into the sky above the dead-flat plain. Were it not for Kilimanjaro's tumultuous past, Amboseli's short-grass plains would resemble the flat monotony of Tsavo's tangled bushland. Were it not for the mountain, Amboseli's distinctive white soils and rich alluvial deposits would be indistinguishable from the sterile red soils of the surrounding lands. Amboseli is cradled in the rain shadow of Kilimanjaro. The great extrusion attracts the monsoon rains, which fall on the forested slopes and bubble up as a series of springs. The steady underground discharge of water feeds the swamps and elevates the water table close to the surface of the ancient lakebed far below.

The depth of the water table varies according to the microtopographical relief, giving Amboseli an extraordinary variety of habitats, ranging from desert to woodland and short-grass plains to tall papyrus swamps. The migrant animals—zebra, wildebeest, hartebeest, gazelle, buffalo, and elephant—move in and out of Amboseli with the seasons, across its rich tapestry of habitats. Late in the dry season the returning migrants end up in the ever-green swamps after depleting the grasses of the scrub and basin.

Of all the intriguing features of Amboseli, none proved more fascinating than the migrations. This seasonal mystery taxed my imagination as it undoubtedly has countless generations since the emergence of our species. Hunter-gatherers down the ages survived on getting the seasons right, on knowing when and where the herds moved and the best time to harvest and kill. Survival and successful childrearing came down to an attentive mind and good memory. Our abhorrence of the unexplained, perhaps even our very curiosity, is the outcome of natural selection for predicting how to beat competitors to food.

I decided at the outset to focus on a few big questions concerning the migrations. In Amboseli, each species has its own characteristic migration. Only once each season, when the first curtain of rain falls, do all species head in a rush for new pastures like theatergoers breaking for the exit. Thereafter they spread out erratically while the rains last, before heading back to the basin in staggered formation, elephants first, then zebra, wildebeest, and gazelle. Why the semblance of a formation, with the bigger species returning first and the smaller last? Why do impala barely move and buffalo only to the outer reaches of the basin? More fundamentally, what governs the diversity and numbers of species and, ultimately, the balance of nature in Amboseli?

Similar questions have intrigued and baffled humanity long before scientists took up the quest for an answer. In ancient mythology the creation of the universe and the elemental forces governing our planet were attributed to spontaneous acts of creation. In Indian, Chinese, and Greek traditions, the earth developed from an egg. African creation myths revolve around a similar theme, with God sending man down from the sky or up from the earth. The world is perfect and harmonious until man falls from grace and learns evil.

Myths are sacred explanations of the inexplicable, a way of making sense of the origins, identity, order, expectations, and, ultimately, the very being of peoples and the world around them. Balance if not harmony is assumed to be the natural state in all ancient myths. The balance is often explained by a discordant harmony, by war between the gods responsible for such elemental forces as thunder, lightning, and rain, sometimes through the opposition of heaven and earth, water and fire, love and hate, peace and war. These discordant forces maintain the natural balance even in monotheistic religions like Christianity, where good and evil face off as God and the devil.

Early myths uniformly take a metaphysical view of the world, a world in which creatures are imbued with spirits, emotions, and motivation. The gods display human emotions and traits ranging from love and anger to fallibility and purpose. Animals, if lesser beings, are imbued with feelings and purpose, too. In African fables, animals are typically our alter egos used to convey a social message in poignant and enthralling stories. Aesop's fables—told to the ancient Greeks by African slaves—are full of humor, passion, cunning, and intrigue, with animals acting and talking like humans. In short, myths the world over teach us that our social and natural world is organic and dynamic.

New myths replace old as knowledge and beliefs change. Divine explanations of nature supplanted the organic and dynamic beliefs when the great religions rose out of the Middle East. One of those beliefs, Judeo-Christianity, had profound repercussions on nature and the wilds through its association with European colonial expansion. Instead of seeing humanity as part of the great web of life and intimately connected to nature, Judeo-Christianity views man as separate from nature and as having dominion over other creatures. Nature is seen as immutable, a manifestation of God's great design for humankind. Even the exquisite design of the leopard's spots is seen as evidence of divine inspiration, as are the superlative adaptations of the giraffe's neck, the elephant's trunk, and the bird's wing.

Changing beliefs have a fundamental bearing on the way we view and affect nature today, much as we would like to believe we are immured. Western beliefs, for example, altered when scientific explanations of nature arose to challenge the prevailing divine view. From Kepler's explanation of planetary motion based on Newtonian physics to Descartes's belief in animals as automata lacking feelings and emotions, science has characterized nature as a machine rather than an act of God or an organism. The machine metaphor emerged supreme with the spectacular success of the industrial age, paradoxically reinforcing the divine view of balance and harmony in the natural world. Energy and mass were the new reality, rather than the spirits and free will of ancient mythology or the hand of God in Judeo-Christianity. Ecologists, full of "physics envy" and eager to make a hard science of their birds-and-bees natural history origins, adopted the laws of thermodynamics and mathematical models to describe nature in precise terms. And, as in physics, the hunt was on for order, regularity, equilibrium, and homeostasis amid the chaotic jumble of life forms and processes crowding the earth.

The 1960s were exciting times for ecologists and had a bearing on my ecological beliefs and expectations about Amboseli. Many ideas which had kicked around in conceptual form for half a century were being quantified and formalized in elegantly simple analogue models, algebraic equations, and Newtonian calculus. Everything from population growth and regulation to plant succession, the structure and dynamics of ecosystems, and the diversity of life forms was being studied quantitatively in the lab, field, and computer models. I had the distinct feeling of being on the front line of a brilliant new synthesis, with a rare opportunity to study an ecosystem using an objective methodology capable of reducing the complexity of Amboseli to a few simple equations.

For example, ecologists were beginning to ask such basic questions as, What limits the growth of a population, and what determines the mix of species in a community? Higher levels of ecological organization were also falling into neat, predictable patterns. The sequence of plants colonizing bare ground or disturbed sites, for example, no longer appeared as some inchoate tangle of weeds, bushes, and trees, but as a neat and orderly succession. Amboseli, with its gradual colonization of receding lake waters and eventual establishment of mature woodlands, was sure to provide an ideal model of plant succession.

At a higher level yet—the ecosystem—order was appearing out of chaos, too. The concept of an ecosystem, a term coined in the 1930s, began as a convenient label ecologists used to reduce boundless nature to manageable units with some degree of integrity, such as a pond or lake. No ecologists pretended for a moment that ecosystems had cookie-cutter boundaries, but the precise laws of physics were considered applicable all the same. In 1959 Eugene Odum, in his classic college textbook, *Fundamentals of Ecology,* concluded that ecosystems are determined by basic laws of physics. Like plant succession, they progress from simple communities of animals and plants to diverse assemblages of species—the climax state. The mature ecosystem is in perfect balance and resists further change, like the governor on a steam engine.

Describing nature as a steam engine might take away the old mystique, but I had to admit an ecological training gave one a godlike power when it came to explaining creation.

The only area in which I disagreed with the prevailing scientific views lay in my ideas about humans in relation to nature. Having grown up in the bush of Tanganyika, I shared the African perspective that wilderness does not exist as a separate entity, a place where nature achieves perfection and harmony in the absence of people. In keeping with the African belief, I fully intended to study the Maasai as an integral part of Amboseli, rather than regarding them as an artifact as the Serengeti scientists were doing. This was the basis of my search for coexistence between people and wildlife, rather than the alternative of dividing ecosystems between the two—the apartheid approach to conservation.

It was easy to get carried away by the intellectual fever of the times. Doing so called for hard data and proof about how Amboseli worked, rather than feelings and intuition.

A look at my newly pieced-together vegetation map showed that Amboseli's rich diversity of habitats stacked one above the other like a giant layer cake. Starting from the south was the strip of woodlands, then swamps, open plains, and dry scrub, all conveniently running northwest in a parallel series. The migrants returning from the dispersal areas to the north nibbled their way slowly through the habitat layers from the outer belt of scrub to the inner band of swamps and woodlands as the season progressed. The layer-cake effect made it comparatively easy to study the vegetation preferences of the migrants by running a series of sample transects across the habitat grain. By counting every animal within a 400-meter transect and extrapolating the sample area to the whole basin, it was possible to estimate the population size of every species from elephants down to Thomson's gazelle. Finally, by simultaneously recording habitat, pasture, water, fire, and any other conditions that seemed relevant, it was possible to go a step further and infer how the elephant, Thomson's gazelle, and every other species moved in relation to environmental conditions and to one another.

The sampling regimen would help quantify the obvious—that elephants favored woody habitats and gazelle the short-grass plains—as well as myriad subtler factors governing the seasonal migrations beyond the grasp of casual observations. Repeated over several years, it would allow me to record large-scale changes in habitat, such as the woodland decline, and their consequences for Amboseli.

The beauty and simplicity of the monitoring program was a source of intense satisfaction, but I worried about my ability to keep up the five grueling days of dawn-to-dusk driving it took each month.

Locating the beginning of the first transect, I drove by compass bearing and map, stopping every 100 meters along a five-mile strip to record the pasture conditions and animal numbers. By midday I was sweltering with my shirt off, tense with concentration, and yelling in anger whenever the vehicle crashed into an aardvark hole or a hidden log. By evening I was all done in and ready for early bed after a hurried supper.

Before sunup I was at it again, huddled in a sweater against the cold air whipping through the open-sided Land Rover. Quantitative science as opposed to natural history calls for rigorous quantification and routine, but this was more than I bargained for. The strain gradually took its toll on the aging Land Rover and my temper. Eventually the metal cab cracked and grated with such nerve-screeching intensity that I couldn't take another day of it. The problem was solved by bracing the cab with a cedar fencepost and whacking it back into place with a mallet whenever it wobbled loose.

The impersonal nature of the counts was far harder to take than the physical strain. Each animal represented a data point logged onto a computer form. There was no time to idle about during the counts, or any opportunity to follow the impulses that had been my joy and inspiration in the first few weeks. I missed the spontaneity and freedom of watching a troop of baboons and a family of jackals vying for a young Grant's gazelle calf, or a pride of lions trying to bring down a full-grown giraffe. The sampling regime called for rigorous scientific procedures, and meant sticking to a predetermined schedule.

For all its strain and frustration, the monitoring program was a small price to pay for the insights that came tumbling from the accumulating stack of data sheets and graphs. The first revelation came from graphs showing the number of animals moving back into the basin through each habitat. The rising graphs left no doubt that larger species such as elephant and buffalo were the first into the woodlands and swamps, followed by the medium-sized zebra and wildebeest, and, finally, tiny Thomson's gazelle. Was the sequence a regular feature of the migrations, and, if so, what explained it?

If Amboseli seemed timeless in these formative weeks, the world and Africa were changing at an accelerating pace to the sound of environmental alarm calls. In the West, Rachel Carson's *Silent Spring* was the first publication to alert the postwar generation to the dangers of industrial pollution, agrochemical residues, and radioactive waste. The bald eagle, symbol of the United States, was slipping toward the brink of extinction along with dozens of other birds species, all victims of eggshell thinning due to the concentration of DDT residues through the food chain. Killer fogs in London, the Torrey Canyon oil spill, a dying Lake Erie, ailing Bavarian forests, and the blackened and pitted monuments of Europe could no longer be written off as the price of progress now that Carson had underscored the threats to our own health and survival. Dying eagles and blackened monuments became symbols of an ailing environment and harbingers of worse to come—perhaps the end of humanity itself.

Carson's *Silent Spring* still left a loophole for the cynical and wealthy to escape the industrialized West for a slow-paced life under the unpolluted skies of Asia, Latin America, or Africa. Paul and Anne Ehrlich's *Population Bomb,* published in 1968, firmly closed off that escape route by casting an even greater shadow of doom over the entire planet, especially the Third World. The specter of runaway growth had first been raised by the British economist Thomas Malthus in 1798, in his *Essay on the Principle of Population.* "It is difficult to see any check to population which does not come under the description of some species of misery or vice," he wrote, stating that geometric growth in population invariably outstripped the arithmetic growth in food production.

Europe didn't founder under misery and vice, of course, but the Ehrlichs raised afresh the prospects of an apocalypse, this time in the Third World. "Some time between 1970 and 1985 hundreds of millions of people are going to starve to death. That is, they will starve to death unless plague, thermonuclear war, or some other agent kills them first." India, the basket case of the teeming, poverty-stricken Third World, was already beyond reprieve as far as ecologists were concerned, and Africa was soon to follow. Within a year of Barry Commoner's 1971 *The Closing Circle*'s hitting the media headlines, ecology and environment leapt out of the academic closet to become household words.

The environmental concerns sweeping the Northern Hemisphere

were viewed as remote and bourgeois in the East Africa of the 1960s. Kenya was enjoying a postindependence boom, stimulated by President Kenyatta's free-enterprise policies. Although I avoided Nairobi, each visit saw new shops, businesses, and high-rise buildings spreading at an unnerving pace. At first glance, things seemed to be going well for wildlife too, confounding the colonial skeptics and dampening my own earlier misgivings. In Tanzania, President Nyerere embraced wildlife conservation in the widely quoted Arusha Manifesto. President Kenyatta struck an equally reassuring note in an address to a conservation conference in 1963: "The natural resources of this country, its wildlife which offers such an attraction to visitors from all over the world, the beautiful places in which the animals live, the mighty forests which guard the water catchment areas so vital to the survival of man and beast, are a priceless heritage for the future. The Government of Kenya," he concluded, "pledges itself to preserve them for posterity with all the means at its disposal."

It didn't take long to realize the futility of that promise and how little had really changed in East Africa. If anything, the animosity toward wildlife ran deeper than ever. Ecologists blamed runaway population growth for the mounting environmental threats. Health care had cut East Africa's death rate and quadrupled its population since the turn of the century. At 4.1 percent a year, Kenya's population growth was the highest in the world and land chronically short. The consequences of too many people on too little land showed up in the crowded slums of Nairobi's Mathare Valley, on the brutally rilled farming lands of Ukambani, and across the denuded rangelands of Kajiado.

Although the population problem posed a real and growing threat to wildlife too, the bigger problem to my mind lay in the resentment of wildlife, however many or few the people on the land. Despite all the education, political freedom, land reforms, and rising prosperity—perhaps because of them—wildlife had become an unwelcome reminder of Africa's backwardness.

The promise of restoring the importance of wildlife in rural African economies evaporated after independence. Wildlife still belonged to the government, notwithstanding the promises and expectations of uhuru. The same European wildlife officers ran the parks. The same white hunters and their clients shot the big game. The same foreign tourists, only more of them, used the national parks. Not one cent of the money generated by hunting or tourism went into the pockets of African landowners. And with hunting and tourism booming, the newly independent governments were more loath than their colonial predecessors to shoot marauding animals. More than ever before, wealthy urbanites made all the profits, and the rural poor paid the price. Wildlife remained a white man's preserve and a black man's burden.

Outside Africa, the international conservationists stood aloof from these underlying problems, stridently insisting that Kenya had an obligation to save its magnificent heritage for the world at large. In doing so, conservationists deliberately played on African sensitivities, knowing the new political actors on the international stage were too insecure to confront the hypocrisy of the West, which had eradicated its own wildlife. So African politicians went along with the sham and paid lip service to preservation. Few apart from Kenyatta had real conviction. Consequently, a change of government did nothing to change perceptions in the bush. A Shamba la Bibi simply became a Shamba la Serikali—the government's shamba—and the resentment smoldered on.

Foreign researchers inadvertently reinforced African resentment. However well-intentioned in drawing attention to the threats facing Serengeti, Bernhard and Michael Grzimek had made the park's neighboring Maasai herders and Kuria hunters into criminals and villains. An influx of new researchers became the postcolonial European heroes of the African bush, replacing the dead and aging hunters like Ionides and Rushby. *National Geographic*'s coverage of Jane Goodall's chimp research narrowed the gap between humans and animals. Joy Adamson's best-selling books on Elsa the lioness portrayed a deeply moving and poignant picture of lions threatened by the callous and furtive African poacher. By the late 1960s, George Schaller was working on lions, Iain Douglas-Hamilton on elephants, Dian Fossey on gorillas, and at least one scientist on every charismatic species.

The media perpetuated the romantic notion of East Africa as a vast, untouched wilderness, the last vestige of unspoiled nature. In countless wildlife films, animals became personalized, Africans dehumanized. When they were mentioned at all, rural Africans lurked in the background as some impersonal destabilizing force in an otherwise harmonious Eden running out of time.

Back in Amboseli, these concerns seemed remote at the time. The end of the rains and the beginning of the dry season had been serene, so serene that nothing could conceivably go wrong, whatever the environmentalists said. As for me, I had achieved my life's goal—to live and work in the bush. I could die happy. Only the daily crash of falling branches and the thinning groves of trees screening Kilimanjaro hinted at the problems ahead.

‹ 5 ›

The Ilmodiok War

JANUARY 1968, MESHANI
Hill. The pacific blue of Kilimanjaro
looms high above the emerald-green swamps flowing sluggishly across the
basin toward the lava promontory where I sit overlooking Lake Amboseli.
A month ago a ten-mile stretch of shin-deep water stretched south to Tanzania. After the rains petered out, a velveteen fuzz of green grass spread
across the receding floods like an algal growth, attracting thousands of
zebra, wildebeest, and Thomson's gazelle.

A light wind carried the faint metallic clink of cattle bells. Looking
down from the rocky promontory and across the acacia mellifera thickets,
I picked out the long column of animals heading onto the lakebed. A few
minutes later another herd followed, then another. Half an hour later dust
billowed up from 5,000 cattle filing across the flats to the swamps, driving
a wedge through the herds of zebra and wildebeest. "Christ, there're thousands of them," I exploded angrily. My resolve at objectivity collapsed at
that moment. The invasion of cattle at the start of the dry season triggered
a visceral outrage I could neither control nor explain. Shaken by the sheer
number of cattle flooding into Amboseli, it was easy to see why conservationists felt that overgrazing threatened wildlife and the very future of the
Maasai themselves. My search for a harmonious solution suddenly seemed
naive in the extreme.

Back at camp that evening, out of sight and earshot of the Maasai, the
selfishness and bigotry of my outburst dawned on me. Those months of
freedom and bliss in Amboseli made me resentful of any intrusion. My
objectivity had been overwhelmed by protective instincts the moment the

Maasai invaded the personal piece of Africa I had carved out for myself. I lay awake for hours, wrestling with the question of objectivity and emotions. Who was I to resent the very people who had shared their land with wild animals? Did I have any rights over their ancestral home? Wasn't I here to resolve the conflict, not to defend my freedom?

Once I had reined in my emotions, the morning's scene no longer seemed so threatening. I could see the Maasai ambling alongside their animals, red *shukas* (robes) fluttering, polished spears glinting in sun. In retrospect, the cattle appeared more benign and less disruptive as they eased through the herds of zebra and wildebeest barely bothering to make way. Count animals, study their movements, and understand the ecology of Amboseli before jumping to conclusions, I told myself; check every emotion, question every assumption before blaming the Maasai for destroying Amboseli.

Despite my resolve, the sight of cattle in the dusty wastes of Amboseli set me off all over again. Instead of confronting my ambivalence, I began to resent and avoid the Maasai. It was the Maasai themselves who finally made the first overtures and got the better of my curiosity.

I had just finished the last transect of my monthly count and put down my binoculars when a voice caught me by surprise.

"Jambo."

I glanced up to find a dandified warrior festooned with jewelry standing beside the car. He was stocky and heavily muscled, with a finely chiseled jaw and high cheekbones. Ignoring me, he ducked to admire himself in the wing mirror.

"What are you doing?" he asked in Swahili. "I saw you looking at my cattle with binoculars." I could see he was too preoccupied with his own appearance to take offense.

"Counting animals. Looking at what they eat," I told him.

He stuck his head in the cab, inspecting everything minutely. Leaning over, he daintily picked up the binoculars between his thumb and index finger and peered intently into the eyepiece from several inches away with the prisms pointed to the ground. Feigning curiosity at some distant object, he talked nonchalantly about his herd with a herding stick jutting up between his legs like a giant phallus.

He handed back the binoculars with bored indifference. "Kuja," come, he insisted, beckoning me with his palm turned down, Maasai style. "I will show you what cattle eat." Curious, I followed his long loping stride across the bush.

We entered a shady grove, the warrior's bright crimson robe contrasting with the verdant greenery. Cattle pushed forward all around, snuffling in the herbage to the melodic tinkle of metal bells. A cloud of white butterflies flitted up momentarily from a fresh dung pile.

"Here, you can see what cattle eat. They like this," he said, pointing to *Sporobolus kentrophyllis,* a broad, soft-leafed grass. "Cattle give good milk when they eat it. Buffalo and zebra like it too. And here," he added, pointing to a tall clump of wiry *Sporobolus consimilis.* "Elephants eat it in the dry season. Cattle don't—unless there's nothing else. It's hard on their teeth."

Sensing my intrigue, he ran on and on, pointing to nearby plants with his herding stick, naming each species and detailing its use. "The gazelle and goats like this one, and this—well, cattle don't eat it, but women do, when they start feeling sick with child."

"You know all the plants," I asked, half surprised, half dubious at his fund of knowledge.

"Yes. I know them all, and what eats them too."

Then he was gone, running to catch up with his herd.

The warrior had piqued my interest, but I still wasn't prepared to face the Maasai or tourists after the blissful months alone in Amboseli. Weeks passed before my guard dropped again, this time to an elder. I was scouting around in the acacia woodlands, angrily looking for the fence wire someone had stolen from an enclosure set up to test the evidence for overgrazing by livestock. A Maasai elder tending his stock sauntered up, trailed by two kids. I barely acknowledged his greeting.

"Who stole my wire?" I demanded. The two kids bolted. The elder stood his ground and looked at me contemptuously. He walked round the fence ignoring my question, inspecting each post minutely like a sniffing dog.

"I know nothing about your wire," he told me in a level voice after finishing his inspection. "Who are you, anyway? What are you doing here? Building a house? or an animal trap maybe?" Short and muscular, he wore the red-checked robe of an elder and had missing lower incisors—a practice common among East African tribes, who fear lockjaw. I had committed the unpardonable gaffe in African customs of ignoring the formal greetings expected of a stranger.

I smiled to allay his suspicions. "No, I am not building a house or a trap," I responded, amused at how small he thought a house should be. "I want to see what happens when I get rid of the animals, to see how the plants change."

He stiffened as if I had spat on him. "Why? Do you intend to get rid of all our cattle and make Amboseli into a park, like the government wants?" He leaned forward, scrutinizing me. "Are you government?"

He had caught me treating him like a fool and being evasive. "No, I'm a student," I sputtered, still trying to pacify him, "not a game officer."

He snorted, throwing back his head. "Then you don't need a cage to tell you what will happen. I can tell you that. My cows eat the same plants as wild animals. I know about these things. I will show you," he added, marching off in a jouncing Maasai stride, slapping the dusty soils with heavy-duty tire sandals. "Look," he said, poking his herding stick at a clump of green star grass. "See this grass? It's called *nyaru*. It grows tall when there are no animals. And those bushes over there," he added, pointing out a clump of *Azima* and *Lycium*, "they will eventually grow everywhere."

The elder, like the warrior admiring himself in the Land Rover mirror, certainly knew his plants. Though I had picked up a good deal of bush lore from Mohamed Mbwana and our hunting guides in Tanzania, the Maasai knew far more. I tried to reassure the elder by giving him my version of the migrations.

"Shye!" he grunted. "You know these things? I didn't think wazungu knew anything about animals, except how to shoot them." Stumbling over the Latin name for nyaru (*Cynodon dactlyon*), he laughed at himself. "Hiya, if you are a student and want to learn, good."

He extended his hand. "My name is Ibrahim. Come, let's go to my *boma* [settlement] and have some milk. We can talk there. I can tell you a lot about Amboseli and wildlife, if you really want to know."

The boma was hidden in a grove of tortilis trees. Ibrahim pointed out a small break in the impenetrable thorn fence. "My gate. Each elder has his own." Some twenty identical loaf-shaped huts hugged the inner wall of the stockade. The huts were fashioned out of saplings crudely bound with bark and daubed with cattle dung which had dried and cracked in places, exposing an underlying wooden frame. Fresh dung filled the deeper cracks. Three or four small children, flies swarming over their faces, rushed to greet us. "Mzungu, mzungu!" they shouted, alarmed and excited at the novelty of a white man in their boma. They dipped their heads in respect at Ibrahim; he touched them each as gently as the pontiff does his subjects. One kid hugged his leg affectionately. Giggling, they trailed us across the spongy dung floor of the stockade, past smaller sheep and goat pens to a shoulder-high hut. Ibrahim ducked and entered a dark tunnel which traced the rounded inner contour of the wall into the pitch-black interior. I entered, then hesitated, half crouched and totally blind. A hand reached out and grasped my wrist. "Here, an *olorika*." I was handed a small wooden stool and sat down, trying to make out the inky interior.

The inner hut was stuffy with smoke from a three-stoned hearth. My eyes, stinging from the smoke, picked up a thin spike of light piercing the blackness through a tiny vent. A wisp of gray smoke drifted up the silver shaft and eddied through the hole. As I fingered away tears, shapes began to emerge: first a central pole bracing the roof, then two low beds made of sticks overlaid with a grass mattress and cowhides. A grass mat laced with leather thongs screened off a small recess beside the entrance where three or four calves snuffled in a pungent mound of grass.

Ibrahim's right hand reached out of the dark and took a long-necked gourd from a slender arm fleetingly bathed in light and jingling heavily with copper bracelets. I could make him out now, vigorously shaking the gourd. He paused, rotated it, and shook again. Satisfied that he had mixed the watery whey and lumpy curds, he pulled out the wooden stopper to the pop of fermented gas and filled an enameled pint mug. "Drink," he said.

I took a long gulp. The mixture had the consistency of soft putty and tasted cool and smoky. Small clumps of charcoal floated in the milk from the burnt stick used to clean the gourd. The acidic liquid tasted pleasantly refreshing. I thrust a finger through the screen behind the entrance. A calf sucked expectantly, its rough tongue wet and sensual. "The calves are kept here for safety," Ibrahim explained. "Otherwise they would be crushed by the adult stock in the corral. When they are older and stronger, we put them in calf pens outside."

Ibrahim taught me more in two hours than I had learned in weeks of research. A born teacher, he brimmed with astute observations and delightful metaphors. "We must become good friends," he insisted. "You visit me and I will drive with you to look at animals."

Ibrahim found me at camp a few days later. "Let's go. You said you would show me the lions."

He called himself Peter this time, obviously still too distrustful to tell me his real name. Weeks passed before he did so. Until then he regularly changed his name, forgetting what he had called himself the last time. Stoical by nature, he tendered friendship slowly, and it ran deep with him as it did with me.

We located a pride of lions sprawled on their sides next to the zebra's favorite waterhole. I positioned the lions on Peter's side and cut the engine ten yards short. "What do you think?" I asked as a lioness rolled over and stared at us through the open cab. Silence. I looked over. Peter was cringing against the back of the cab, petrified. He had never seen a lion so close, except on the end of a spear. I laughed to reassure him.

"I am not scared. Why should I be? I am a Maasai."

He forced a warped grin and feigned hide-and-seek, as if he had been playing a game all along. When I looked back a few moments later he was at ease, making little thrusting actions with his spear hand. "Ai, ai. I was great warrior. I killed two lions myself and went on many hunts."

Peter came by several times, then migrated north with the rains. He returned weeks later when the first straggling herds of zebra and wildebeest appeared on the bleached plains of Amboseli. Greeting me effusively, he plunked himself down in a safari chair. "Yonah," he said, softening the J of Jonah, "you tell me you want to learn about the Maasai, but you are always too busy. Take me to my boma, and I will teach you." He had a habit of snorting gently through his nose when he was emphatic. "Let's go now." I glanced at his heavy bag of supplies and chuckled to let him know I understood his ploy to get a lift home.

We drove across the shimmering bleakness of Lake Amboseli, picked our way along the narrow cattle tracks through the bush, then forded the sandy gullies draining the volcanic tuft close to his settlement. It was stinking hot when we reached his herd, and Peter got out and greeted two young boys. "Come," he signaled. I followed as he slowly wandered through the herd, whistling over his bottom lip, thwacking sluggish cows with a thin herding switch. "Sidai oling," very beautiful, he kept saying in Maasai. "Look at this bull. See its horns. So long and curved. Sidai oling. We have our favorite animals. This is mine," he added proudly. A broad ridge of raised skin arched artistically round the bull's bulging stomach from its penis. Warriors decorate their favorite animals as they do their own bodies. The slow, painful process involves pricking the animal's skin with thorns and rubbing in euphorbia latex to raise the snaking line of cicatrizations.

I trailed Peter through the herd, absorbing his world. He pointed out the plants cattle ate, the best milkers, and the drought-hardy animals, naming every one and recalling its birth date with the familiarity and affection of a doting father.

"Why only a few bulls?" I asked him.

He gave me a nod of appreciation. "We separate bulls and milking cows in the dry season. The milking cows stay close to the settlement. It's less strain on them. We herd the bulls and dry females farther away."

The intimacy of the herd was unexpectedly tranquilizing. The snuffling noses, the steady wrenching of grass, the languid swish of tails, the buzz of flies, and the scrape of hooves resonating to the rhythmic clink of bells were oddly hypnotic. I ran my hand along a short black coat and affectionately stroked the soft skin behind a cow's ear. A few small herds of zebra and wildebeest straggled by a stone's throw away. Time slowed to the seductive tempo of an ancient pastoral world, and my anger at the cows melted in the soporific haze. I turned to Peter. "Why are you not grazing your cattle in the swamps, where there's more grass?"

"Grazing is better here, Yonah," he responded. "There is not much of it, but it's better. My cows are healthier and give more milk than they do in the swamps. The swamps are wet and have a bad disease carried by buffalo." The disease, I later learned, is East Coast fever, a virulent protozoan disease transmitted by ticks.

"What about water?" I continued. "It must be twelve miles off. Isn't that a long way for cattle?"

"Yes, but we only water them every two days," he said, pointing south to where the swamp merged into the lake. "Cattle every two days, sheep and goats every three or four. *Maape ngare,* or go-to-water days, alternate with *ngaruni,* or go-grazing days. The herds leave at dawn and graze until they slow in the midday heat. After resting in the shade they head back, grazing all the way. The women milk them before we let the calves have their turn."

He also told me about his seasonal migrations. Occasionally he moved his herd south to catch early showers on Kilimanjaro. For the most part he followed the zebra and wildebeest herds north with the rains, to Osilalei.

"Let's go back for tea. Nothing will happen now the cattle are shading. There's something I want to show you at my boma."

Two elders were clacking stones in a wooden bao board under the shade of a tortilis acacia when we reached his boma. An old man lay stretched out in the heat like a corpse, his face covered by a shuka against the flies. In the distance, dwarfed by the emptiness of the dry lakebed, four women were driving a train of donkeys laden with bulging water skins toward the boma. They walked with liquid smoothness, quite unlike the jouncing stride of men. Their legs dissolved in a shimmering heat haze, and their sarongs bustled sharply in the wind.

Peter followed my gaze. "Donkeys aren't only used for the migrations, you know. We use them in the dry season to carry water to the boma—for us and the young animals too small to walk to water."

A junior elder walked out to greet us. Rail thin and prematurely lined, he was no more than his mid-thirties, I later learned. Peter introduced us. "This is my friend Mashakio." The elder offered me a frail feminine hand and greeted me in carping voice, nodding deferentially to Peter. Peter nodded back and ducked into a hut, returning a few moments later with a small tin box. "Here's what I want to show you. Come."

We sat under a balanites tree heavily pruned by giraffe while he unclasped the box, which was gaudily painted with primitive motifs popular among Nairobi's street artists. Sorting through a batch of loose papers, he drew out a small notebook. "Here. You asked me about my cattle. Well, these are my records. This is the name of the cow here. And here's when it was born. This is when its calves were born."

He turned page after page of records scrawled in the slow, unsteady hand of a fourth-grader. His methodical entries and willingness to reveal them to an outsider surprised me. Few Maasai reveal their cattle wealth, least of all to Europeans, who in colonial days imposed a head tax on their herds.

Like other literate Maasai, Peter was nonchalant about his education. Many Kenyans barely able to write their name try to impress you with their education. Not the Maasai. They take education in their stride, like so much else about the outside world. Peter, it turned out, had gone to primary school in Loitokitok for several years before returning to his traditional life. Nothing revealed his worldliness except his ear lobes tightly wrapped up and hidden to avoid the taunts of other tribes when he went to town.

Peter turned the pages with the reverence of a historian poring over an ancient text. "Look! Most calves are born at the start of the rains. We take the bull to the females late in the rains and separate them in the dry season. Most years we get enough milk to see us through the dry season."

His strong, handsome face had warm, searching eyes. Crow's feet were barely discernible on his shiny black skin. Time and the elements would weather his face the way his cattle had rilled the earth around his settlement. I watched him leaf through his precious book with growing respect and affection.

"Unafahamu, unafahamu—do you understand?" Peter kept asking. I nodded mechanically.

"No. I can see you don't," he answered, exasperated at my inattention. "Wazungu don't remember things unless they write them down in books. Write! Write! Write it in your book, then you will remember."

The Maasai can recall observations and conversations in vivid detail, aided by no more than a meditator's concentration, inane-sounding grunts, and repeated half-sentences. The eehs, oohs, grunts, and snorts, far from being the moronic impersonations aped by white settlers at Nairobi's Norfolk Hotel bar, are the Maasai way of memorizing things. Sometimes they repeat an entire sentence or a key phrase to capture crucial points. The responses reassure the speaker too. My ignorance of Maasai mnemonics—my dumb silence, in other words—rattled Peter. It took time and immense concentration to became an avid listener like him and to appreciate how much the literate mind misses.

I entered a vast uncharted land with Peter, a land wholly new to me scientifically and emotionally. Until meeting Peter I had seen the bush as a place of wild animals where people featured peripherally. Peter held a similar image, but in reverse, of the village and its rollicking children in the foreground and cattle pastures in the background. Wild animals filled his pastures, and he accepted them as naturally as he did plants and insects, except when they attacked his herd. To him, nature existed not as a separate entity, as the wilderness does in western culture, but as part of his very existence. When he grew too old to follow the settlement, he would be left behind for the hyenas, ready to recycle in the living realm rather than being buried ignominiously in the dead earth.

Although I regarded human beings as a part of nature, Peter helped me understand in concrete terms how people and wildlife coexist. For him, there are not two worlds, one pristine and harmonious, the world of Adam and Eve before the Fall; the other, a land of degradation and decimation brought about by civilization. Human impact came in all grades, from benign to positive and negative, depending on the type and level of activity. His broader view of humans and environment convinced me more than ever that wildlife can survive in the modern world without dividing the land into two unbridgeable entities.

Peter represented one segment or age grade of Maasai society, the ruling elders. Collectively the elders, who range from about thirty to sixty in age, make decisions for the Maasai clans. Every male Maasai belongs to an age set, each of which is given a distinctive name. Peter belonged to the Nyankusi age set. A Maasai moves with his age set through each age grade during his lifetime. A boy, or *laioni,* becomes a junior warrior when he is circumcised around puberty. In his late teens he becomes a senior warrior, then a junior elder. The junior warriors have little authority or social responsibility—other than defending the villages and learning about Maasai culture from a group of instructors, the firestick elders. Senior warriors take on more responsibility socially, build up their herds, prepare for marriage and attend elders' meetings, but don't yet share their full authority.

Warriorhood is a time to explore Maasailand, raid cattle, and chase young girls, *nditos.* At twenty-four I was still a warrior in Maasai terms and, like them, still testing myself and others. I spent most of my time with the elders at first; their gentleness did not prepare me for the brittle egos of the warriors, or the dangers of challenging them.

On the way back from Observation Hill late one morning I encountered the dandified warrior who months earlier had peered through my binoculars. I couldn't help but admire the beauty of his finely chiseled face and high, aristocratic forehead. Girls clearly thought the same, to judge from his tangle of armlets, anklets, necklaces, and earrings. He eyed the .22 rifle cradled between us and clicked in disgust. "That's a mzungu weapon. Even a boy can kill a lion with a gun. With us it takes a man to kill a lion."

I laughed, telling him I could throw a spear as well as he could. Having thrown a spear since childhood and trained with the British javelin champion in England, I thought it was a fair bet. He was too macho to believe that anyone but a Maasai could throw a spear. "If you are going to live among the Maasai, you should learn to throw like one. I'll teach you," he added condescendingly.

True to his promise, Lochokop, as he called himself, showed up at my camp in the company of two finely dressed warriors. His eyes immediately fell on my red javelin sticking out of the paraphernalia in the corner. "What's this? Is this what you throw?" he asked me mockingly. Grabbing the javelin, he went outside onto the open plain, curled his fingers round the yellow cord, drew back his arm, and snapped his wrist at the end of an arch-backed fling. The javelin sliced the air and thudded quivering into the ground in a puff of dust.

"Shye! this feels good. Let me throw it far." He pushed his shuka to one side, danced forward, drew back his arm, arched his back gracefully, and let out a heavy grunt. The javelin vibrated with a gentle zing. "Aiy, aiy, aiy. Look how far it goes. Let me try again," he insisted, enormously impressed with himself. After a few more throws he turned to me full of his prowess. "Now you have seen what a Maasai can do, it's your turn."

I started farther back than Lochokop and accelerated into a fast sprint. At the release point I anchored my left leg and whiplashed over it. The javelin soared way ahead of Lochokop's mark. He clucked in disbelief and made me throw again and again until he was satisfied. "You can throw better than a warrior," he yelled, laughing at my odd style. "Let me bring someone who is really good. I want you to beat him. He is always boasting."

The warrior whom Lochokop brought round was surly and humorless. He lost badly and made a lame excuse about a sore arm. Lochokop exulted in the warrior's defeat, and that didn't improve his mood.

After that my spear arm gave me easy access to the warriors but no inkling of their irrepressible rage. I learned the hard way why the Maasai warriors are so feared and reviled by other tribes. I was dropping goat dung in plastic bags and storing them on the seat of my Land Rover ready for dietary analysis in Nairobi when a warrior strolled up, picked up a bag, and sniffed it as he would a dead rat. Disgusted, he tipped the pellets onto the ground. I shouted and ran up to stop him. He stiffened as if hit in the chest and turned on me.

"What's this?" he shouted, ditching more pellets.

"Who do you think you are, going into my car?" I yelled back. We faced each other two paces apart. A second Maasai stood behind him.

"Whose sheep shit is this, then?" the warrior screamed back. "It's my *ilmodiok* you're stealing."

His friend sniggered. I was too angry to see the funny side of it.

"If you want a fight, here, take this spear and fight," the warrior screamed, snatching at his friend's spear.

The warrior's friend held on tight, trying to push him away. "Stop, stop. You can't kill each other over sheep shit. Don't fight. Take this row to the elders. They will sort it out."

Somehow we all bundled into the Land Rover and made for a nearby settlement. A crowd of elders quickly gathered around the warrior as he stood in the middle of the settlement, screaming insults. A tall elder approached me hesitantly. "You stole his sheep shit. Is that what he's saying?" he asked, raising his eyebrows quizzically. The other elders began to grin at each other, then to snigger uncontrollably. That only made things worse, and the warrior began yelling louder than ever, demanding a fight or retribution.

The elders took us to opposite sides of the boma and shuttled between us, trying to arbitrate our row over the sheep shit. They were clearly torn between laughter and worry that things were getting out of hand in the ilmodiok war, as they called it.

An hour later, the elders arrived at their decision. I would pay a fine of 100 shillings, they said, and my shoes. The warrior had astutely worked out his demands in the middle of his tirade and yelled all the louder to make it stick. I had cooled down enough to realize the absurdity of the situation and gladly settled for the sneakers rather than a spear fight. When I left moments later, a lot wiser about Maasai honor and anger, the warrior shot up to my Land Rover door. "You may think this is the end of it, but it's only the beginning," he yelled. Fortunately, we didn't meet again for several years. By then my position with the Maasai was too well established for him to make good his threat.

As the weeks went by, I saw more and more of Peter, but although our friendship deepened, his mistrust remained. It took a nearly fatal accident to cross the threshold. He knocked on my door at midnight, deeply agitated. "My brother has been mauled by a lion at Tinga Tinga and will die unless I get him to Kajiado hospital quickly. Can you help?"

I had one of Sindiyo's drivers take Peter and his brother to Kajiado immediately. The next morning Peter was back, saying his brother would be just fine apart from a few scars and a bruised ego at having been rescued from the jaws of a lion. "You saved my brother's life, and I want to tie our friendship. My name is Parashino Ole Purdul," he told me appreciatively, purring the *r* in a deliciously feline way. "Among the Maasai we exchange sheep and call each other *supen* when friends become as close as we are. You have no sheep, but you can lend me your Land Rover when I need it."

"Fine, but what can I do with a sheep in the middle of the reserve?" I asked.

Parashino grinned. "Let's eat it. Let's have a meat feast."

So we loaded a plump sheep into the Land Rover at his settlement and drove to camp. As host, the killing fell to me. After instructions from Parashino, I bound the sheep's legs, gripped its mouth with my fingers, and blocked its nose with my palms. The animal struggled halfheartedly at first, then frantically as its eyes bulged. Try as I might, I couldn't choke off my emotions. Parashino seemed indifferent. Despite an inordinate fondness for his animals, he had no compunction about slaughtering them when the time came. Tenderness and stoicism blended without seeming contradiction in the Maasai's relationship to their animals.

The Maasai have been portrayed as a proud, even disdainful people who survived colonialism virtually unchanged. In bygone days they reputedly raided and ravaged other tribes with cruel indifference. Whatever their past, the Maasai are sensitive and intensely social within their own circle. Children and families are held in great affection. Age mates form a tight clique, and elders are highly revered.

The first white man to cross Maasailand, Joseph Thomson, like the

British settlers who followed, was awed by the Maasai and their ferocious reputation. Fortunately for the Scots explorer, the warriors were raiding down on the Tana River when he entered Maasailand in August 1883. Even so, it took all his considerable guile to win over the cantankerous elders. At one point the embattled Scot desperately removed his false teeth and clacked them at the astonished Maasai, threatening to pull out his eye unless they stopped harassing him. Henceforth known as a white *laiboni,* a spiritual leader, Thomson became much revered but no less troubled. One admiring elder brought his doting young wife along and expressed his wish to have a little white laiboni just like him. Thomson, a Victorian gentleman and resourceful to boot, brewed up some Eno's fruit salts and gave it to the trembling women. The elder departed with lingering doubts about the way white men make babies.

The Maasai nation Thomson crossed stretched from Lake Turkana, in northern Kenya, to Kongwa, in central Tanzania, an area the size of Great Britain. Half a millennium earlier, the Maasai had snatched the East African plains from an assortment of Bantu and Nilotic tribes. They had no inkling they were occupying the richest wildlife habitat on earth, or that the wild herds would someday threaten their own survival. That realization came far too late for the Maasai to do anything about it. By independence, the colonials had usurped huge swaths of their land for farms. By the time the Maasai learned to use political leverage rather than spears to retain land in the postindependence years, their nation had been whittled down to half its original size.

When I first began to discuss things with them in the late 1960s, the Maasai blamed most of their troubles on land loss and drought, but beneath their dogged insistence lurked another, more pernicious factor few Maasai understood or acknowledged—population growth. Mashakio, Parashino's friend, was not alone in being poor. Fewer and fewer warriors could expect to raise as many cattle as their fathers. With a ballooning number of youngsters surviving to adulthood and the option of rustling neighboring herds no longer available, individual cattle holdings were falling steadily.

Their vulnerability to these changing circumstances first became apparent in the protracted drought of 1960, when over three-quarters of their cattle died and the Maasai were thrown into the lap of famine relief.

British and American aid teams trucked and airlifted in thousands of tons of food to relieve starving Maasai. As if conspiring to finish them off, the floods which followed the drought killed scores more enfeebled cattle, destroying the wealth and subsistence herds of Mashakio and countless other families. Cattle poverty weakened their traditional lifestyle and sapped their self-esteem.

By the end of the 1960s, the Maasai herds had rebounded, giving rise to renewed claims by livestock experts that the proliferating herds were turning Maasailand into a dustbowl. Several highly regarded ecologists argued that the destruction of Maasailand was self-inflicted, resulting from the unrestrained growth of the herds after the inoculation campaigns launched by the colonial vets in the 1940s. The most immediate culprit, alleged to have contained the herds within the carrying capacity of the range, was rinderpest. Rinderpest is a highly contagious bovine pneumonia responsible for destroying millions of wild and domestic animals at the turn of the century.

The evidence for rinderpest eradication leading to tripling of the livestock herds and dustbowl conditions seemed altogether unconvincing to me. If the pandemic had kept livestock numbers so low, why had the colonial vets grumbled about the overgrazing problem in the 1930s, long before the inoculation campaigns began?

Data amassed from my own research pointed to a different explanation for the growth of herds. Before the arrival of the colonial government, large tracts of land lay unused in the dry season, either because they were vulnerable to tribal raids or because they lay too far from water. The suppression of tribal wars and construction of dams and wells by the British in the 1940s roughly tripled the available dry-season pastures in the southern Maasailand, accounting for a similar increase in livestock. Heavy grazing, once a localized phenomenon, expanded in all directions. The Maasai, responding to the growth in their herds and improved health care, flourished, their numbers roughly doubling between 1930 and 1950. Their numbers doubled again by 1970, cutting per-capita livestock holdings in the process. How could a Maasai family survive on four head of cattle when it had taken eight or more to keep them alive in their traditional economy?

The projections of a faltering subsistence economy preoccupied my thoughts. Surely the Maasai way of life was doomed. Tragically, few of them had the faintest idea about overpopulating the range. All they could think of was building up their herds for the next drought, as they had always done.

Parashino evaded the subject of too many people for the land. "Our problem has always been loss of land, first to the colonial settlers, then to the national parks, and now to the Kikuyu farmers around Loitokitok. The next drought? Huh. We will look after ourselves. It's the only way. The Kikuyus are our enemies. They ignore us more than the wazungu did. Now that they are on top they call us primitive."

The newly independent governments in Kenya and Tanzania found the Maasai an embarrassment. Their policy was to settle and clothe the Maasai as soon as possible. Such feelings were fueled by media portrayals of the Maasai in events such as the *eunoto* ceremony held on the slopes of Lemi Boti Hill north of Amboseli in 1968. The press had gathered to watch the colorful pageant of the junior warriors graduating to senior warrior-hood at a ceremonial settlement built for the occasion. Presiding over the event was Stanley Oloitiptip, a Maasai who had risen from a medical assistant in the colonial days to an assistant minister of health in Kenyatta's government. He was also reputed to be Amboseli's biggest poacher.

Oloitiptip was unmistakable. His huge gut burst through his shirt and spilled over a brightly beaded belt. A jacket several sizes too small barely reached around his bull-like neck and barrel chest. He was an altogether grotesque intrusion in this world of lithe muscular warriors and beaded finery.

"Look at these warriors," he bellowed. "These are the real Maasai. In Tanzania President Nyerere is treating us like primitives, telling our warriors to hide their buttocks and wear shorts when they go into town. Why? We are not ashamed of our nakedness. We are proud to be Maasai. And that is the way we will stay. Here is my answer to Nyerere."

Oloitiptip lifted a shuka to expose a warrior's bare buttocks. The warriors screamed their approval. Pressmen crowded round, popping flash cameras and snickering nervously. Oloitiptip, reveling in the media attention, threw a final taunt. "We will not be turned into city people. Tell Nyerere that."

Whatever his shortcomings, Oloitiptip was one the few Maasai in a position of power and alone among the top politicians in brushing off the intimidation and sycophancy which characterized Kenyatta's government. Yet for all his bravura, Oloitiptip knew that the cattle raids and the lion hunts were heroics of the past. Progress in Kenyatta's modern republic was measured by gross national product, annual growth rates, educational enrollment, and housing starts, not cattle raids conducted by half-naked warriors. If the Maasai featured in Kenya's developmental thinking at all, it was as a constraint on the commercialization of Kenya's rangelands and beef exports.

The Maasai for their part had scant regard for the Kikuyu government. "We are going to Kenya," they would say when leaving for Nairobi, as if it were some foreign country. Despite their disdain of the Kikuyu, every Maasai, including Oloitiptip, feared for the future of his people under the governance of their age-old enemies.

What would happen a decade from now, when human mouths outstripped the milk supplies of their herds? What would happen to the new generation of warriors unable to make it on the land? Already a trickle of uneducated and ill-prepared youngsters were seeking work in town. Few made it farther up the ladder than a ranch hand, a night watchmen, or a security guard. Sindiyo was an exception in successfully straddling Maasai and western cultures.

Daniel Sindiyo, an educated Maasai, was an intriguing product of contradictory worlds. Born in a Maasai settlement, he had received a college education and was outwardly westernized, sophisticated, and articulate. He lived in a modern house filled with plastic plates, vinyl-covered settees, and family pictures on the wall. Like other educated Kenyans, his large extended family included traditional and cosmopolitan members, some still in shukas, others in trousers, most of them young, optimistic, and in a hurry to catch up with the West—like the young Nigerians at the United Africa Company in London.

Through Sindiyo, I gained a strong sense of the problems confronting wildlife in Kenya. His concern for wild animals was genuine, but he worried about the wedge colonial policies had driven between them and his people. He knew the risks of putting the interests of wildlife first, especially among the truculent Maasai. The Maasai would not tolerate a loss of livestock or land to wild animals without fighting back.

Sindiyo's was a lone African voice at a symposium on wildlife management and land use held in Nairobi in July 1967. In a vain effort to call
attention to the need to address the rising animosity between people and
wild animals, he quoted a Samburu elder who spoke with wisdom and
authority for his people: "We Maasai have to share our land with wild and
dangerous animals. We have to learn to give way to the elephant, the rhi-
noceros, the lion, and this has not been our way of life. Many of us have
lost children, others have lost relatives and stock to these animals which
belong to the government. The government has value for these animals,
but they are of no value to us any more. The use we had of wildlife is
quickly becoming a thing of the past. This value of wildlife being gone, we
know of no other value whatever."

Sindiyo argued perceptively that the clash of interests must be solved
by participation, not alienation—that offering education and tangible
benefits to those afflicted by wildlife was the only way ahead for conservation. Nothing came of his appeal at the time. One of only four African
papers among the fifty-five presentations, Sindiyo's voice was too earthy
for the high-flown rhetoric about land-use models, economic cost-benefit
analysis, and ecological objectivity.

Convinced of what he preached, Sindiyo worked with the committee
of elders he set up in Amboseli to discuss their grievances and win them
over to the cause of conservation. True to his own traditions, he handled
the growing conflicts with extraordinary finesse and understanding,
respecting the ways of the elders and working toward consensus, no matter
how long it took.

My first trip with Sindiyo to resolve one of his many crises taught me
a great deal about how to handle conflict in Maasai style, through dialogue
and consensus.

We drove up to a settlement at the base of Il Marishari Hill, where a
leopard had killed several goats. A large and agitated group of elders came
out to greet us. Sindiyo shook hands with each of them. "I'm here to listen," he told them with a genial smile. The elders squatted in a circle flanking Sindiyo, exchanging pleasantries and expressing their appreciation of
his interest. Before long their geniality turned to anger as they harangued
him about the leopard.

"The leopard came last night. It killed six goats. We know this is not an Amboseli leopard—they don't behave like this because they are scared of our warriors coming after them. So tell us, Bwana Warden, where did this leopard come from? If you don't take action, our warriors will."

Sindiyo listened intently, repeatedly expressing sympathy. When he responded, he spoke to the elders as equals, allowing each one to speak his mind until he had vented his feelings. He knew full well that the Game Department was dumping stock-killing leopards into Amboseli from the Kikuyu settlements, as if the Maasai were lesser people.

Sindiyo's quiet, firm diplomacy was a lesson in patience and perseverance. Time is not a limiting commodity among the Maasai. Discussion, trust, and consensus are everything. Every view is voiced, carefully weighed, and finally arbitrated among the elders. And if one thing weighed heavily on their minds in 1968, it was the fear of losing Amboseli to wildlife.

‹ 6 ›

In the Dust of Kilimanjaro

T HE FORD FOUNDATION hall, tucked in between the East African Herbarium and National Museums of Kenya, is small as lecture theaters go, its upper floor rising steeply toward the ceiling. The auditorium was packed and the atmosphere noisy with anticipation as I waited to give my findings on Amboseli at the request of the East African Natural History Society. It was eighteen months since I had begun work, and a newly released film titled *The Death of Amboseli* had put the reserve back in the international spotlight.

I felt hedged in and nervous after so long in the bush. Only a handful of black faces looked out from the crowd. Several prominent hunters, tour operators, and preservationists sat waiting to pounce. Researchers were a highly suspect bunch among the old wildlife hands, and my degree labeled me a boffin—a scientific egghead—regardless of my upbringing. It didn't help, knowing that a failure at today's function could scuttle my plan for Amboseli.

Flicking on the first slide, I began to describe the ecology of Amboseli, stressing the erratic pattern of migrations extending well beyond the reserve boundaries. Slide after slide showed large herds of zebra, wildebeest, buffalo, and elephants, dispensing a subliminal message that far from being dead, Amboseli was very much alive. To judge from the murmurs of approval, the message was hitting home, but the provocative point was yet to come.

"The Maasai fit into the picture much the same as wild species—and have done so for centuries," I hurried on, trying to quell the reaction to cattle and lay the ground for the conclusion.

miles of the Amboseli basin. The congestion caused conflicts, running the gamut from the amusing to the grotesque, from an elephant charging furiously through a bucking herd of donkeys, to a large python that swallowed two goats and terrified the Maasai. A Maasai elder horned by a rhino had dragged himself several kilometers homeward, only to be trailed and killed by a lion. Lions had also broken into the cattle camps up on the Eremito Ridge, killing several animals. Exacerbating the already volatile situation, the Maasai warriors, irate over rumors of a government takeover of the reserve, speared several rhinos in a show of protest. *The Los Angeles Times* ran an article decrying the killings and calling for action.

Conflict had become a way of life in Amboseli, and, for many, a way of death.

Tempers flared all round, with the government threatening to crack down on the Maasai, the tourists grouching about the invasion of cattle, and the Maasai angry at anyone who sided with wildlife.

Sindiyo ran himself ragged, trying to restrain the warriors from killing animals and animals from killing livestock. Oloitiptip made a bad situation impossible for the warden by brazenly poaching zebra and daring the rangers to stop him. Sindiyo fought hard to keep the Maasai out of the small wildlife sanctuary around Ol Tukai. The Maasai resented Sindiyo for banning cattle from their favorite swamps and accused him of caring more for wild animals and foreigners than for his own people. The Kajiado County Council came in for its own share of resentment for allocating the thirty-square-mile sanctuary to wildlife and tourists without consulting the Maasai. In fact the Maasai felt doubly cheated by this latest slight, having resisted the efforts of the national parks only to fall victim to their own council.

The final straw came when the government banned tourists from photographing the Maasai under the pretext that it was tantamount to treating them like wild animals. In truth, Kenya's progressive government was embarrassed by the half-dressed Maasai warriors. The latest stricture meant the Maasai couldn't earn money from tourists, and thus deprived them of their only source of wildlife-related income. The resentment bubbled over when fresh rumors of a government takeover reached the Maasai. A warrior watering his cattle couldn't take any more and vented his fury on a tourist who snapped a shot of his cattle, then sped off in a plume of dust. Running after the vehicle, the herder hurled his spear through the rear

"And what about the destruction of Amboseli's woodlands? I am sur
this is what you've all come to hear about." I waited, letting expectation
mount. Made famous by countless photos and tourist brochures
Amboseli's fever trees growing at the foot of Kilimanjaro had come to epit-
omize the African savannas to countless people around the world. Nothing did more to infuriate conservationists than to hear that the elegant
trees were being destroyed by hungry hordes of Maasai cattle.

"Well, the Maasai are not destroying the woodlands. Overgrazing is
not the cause of habitat loss."

"Look at the trees here," I continued, raising my voice above the shuffling. "This slide was shot in the center of the stock-free area. No cattle,
but plenty of dead trees. And this shot? It was taken at the edge of the
basin where there are thousands of cattle. Look. No dead trees. Why?"

The shuffling died down, and the room went quiet. I had no explanation for the loss of trees, but evidence did point to earlier treeless cycles.
"Let me read the first written account of Amboseli made by the Scots
explorer Joseph Thomson in 1883. 'Conceive of yourself standing in the
center of the plain. In your immediate vicinity there is not a blade of grass
to relieve the barren aspect of the damp muddy sand, which, impregnated
with various salts, is unfavorable to the growth of any vegetation. Here and
there, however, in the horizon are to be detected a few sheets of water, surrounded by rings of green grass, and a few straggling trees or scrubby
bushes . . . In spite of the desolate and barren aspect of the country, game
is to be seen in marvelous abundance . . . The question that naturally rises
in one's mind is, How can such enormous numbers of large game live in
this extraordinary desert?' "

I projected slide after slide to accompany the text, illustrating a con-
temporary Amboseli resembling the scene Thomson described eighty years
earlier rather the intervening years. "So what are the implications for conservation?" I continued with rising confidence, expanding on a plan hastily
sketched in the dust a few weeks earlier.

❮ ❮ ❮

THE PLAN BEGAN to take shape at the tail end of 1968, a year after
starting my research. In August of that year I had counted 20,000 cattle,
6,000 sheep and goats, 5,000 wildebeest, 3,700 zebra, 800 buffalo, 450 elephant, 60 rhinos, and 15,000 other animals packed into the 150 square

window and skewered the tourist through the shoulder. News spread among the Maasai like wind through the grass, tempting other warriors to follow suit, if that's what it took to get attention.

Tourists were no less resentful of the Maasai intrusion into their pristine African wilderness. "We've paid good bucks to visit a national park, not a cattle ranch," they groused over drinks at the lodge bar after a day's game drive. By 1968 conflict saturated the game reserve like a leaky gas tank about to explode.

The germ of a new conservation plan came to me during an evening's walk. I had set out from the tent when the first weary lines of zebra and wildebeest began filing out of thickets onto the plains. The evening light slowly restored rich hues to the sun-scorched pastels, and deep shadows crept through the woodlands until only the upper branches of the trees caught the waning sun. On the plains the bleached grasses turned deep amber, and the eroded soils of Eremito Ridge warmed to a deep crimson.

The migrations are finally making sense, I told myself. During the rains the Maasai and wildlife range over an area five to ten times the size of their dry-season range, covering an ill-defined tract stretching around Amboseli like the penumbra of a waning moon. During the dry season the boundaries contract and sharpen as the migrants return to the basin, slake their thirst, and feed on the pastures within cruising range of the swamps.

"How can such enormous numbers of large game live in this extraordinary desert?" Joseph Thomson had wondered. The explanation lay in the seasonal migrations. Block off the herds migrating to the wet-season pastures, and their numbers would dwindle by half. Close off the swamps, and the entire ecosystem would die like a city denied water. Reduce the complexity of habitats to Tsavo's homogeneous bushland, and Amboseli would be as drab as the thorn scrub tourists thunder through on their way from Nairobi. I turned to watch a string of wildebeest thread its way through the scattered mswaki bushes, following a geometrical path precisely defined by the midpoint between the thickets. The burnished yellow of the fever trees had faded to gray as I headed back to camp. A year's work didn't amount to much, but enough to realize that what the national park conservationists had in mind would be as ecologically ruinous as tearing up a dollar bill. Dividing the Amboseli ecosystem in two was not the answer for the Maasai or wildlife.

The game reserve boundaries made no ecological sense either. The map of Kenya's parks gave the illusion of space and protection for Amboseli Game Reserve. In reality the western two-thirds of the reserve supported few animals and lay off the migratory routes which stretched to the north, far outside the existing boundary. Doubling the area of the reserve would add some protection, but not enough to secure the ecosystem. Such a huge expansion was inconceivable in any event. No independent African government in its right mind would entertain the political fallout of the mass deportations involved. The days when Ionides could move Africans like chess pawns to make way for elephants were gone. Every extra inch of conservation land came at the expense of an African family and created new enemies.

There had to be some better way to protect the entire ecosystem. Western preservationism behind the national parks movement stems from a legacy of extermination, stretching from the extinction of the mammoths to the passenger pigeon. Africa's far richer wildlife legacy rested on millennia of coexistence rather than segregation. So why not try coexistence?

Coexistence if not harmony was a fact of life, seen through Parashino's eyes. Any lion bold enough to attack his herd became sport for the warriors, reestablishing fear at the root of mutual tolerance between predators and African peoples. But what of the herbivores? His cattle outwardly grazed benignly alongside wildebeest, and zebra mixed freely with his donkeys. What lay behind the mutual tolerance? Such equanimity made no sense in the face of intense competition between wild and domestic herbivores during the dry season. Why, before the colonial laws and tourism turned the Maasai against wildlife, had the Maasai tolerated wild animals consuming half their pasture and spreading disease to livestock?

In Maasai mythology, recounted jokingly by men, wildlife belonged to the womenfolk who attended them so poorly that the animals wandered out of the boma and into the bush. As a solitary voice opposing the rising clamor that the only way to conserve Amboseli lay in a national park, I needed a hard explanation.

Halfway back to camp, I glanced up at the dying acacia branches starkly silhouetted against pink-tinged snows of Kilimanjaro. Soon the trees would be dead, exposing my fading yellow tent to the sun and minibuses. That's when the contradiction hit me. How could I have been so blind? Here in the wildlife sanctuary, where livestock were banned, the trees were either dead or dying. Around the Maasai settlements, trees flourished. Whatever else was killing the trees, it couldn't be the Maasai. The wildlife sanctuary was a natural experiment exonerating them.

Gathering the incontrovertible data needed to vindicate the Maasai would be easy enough. All I had to do was show that the condition of trees across the basin bore no relationship to the presence of Maasai encampments or livestock. When I eventually did so, the results were utterly compelling. The condition of the woodland trees was in fact inversely related to cattle activity; the healthiest trees were associated with the highest density of livestock.

Whatever the cause of woodland decline, it wasn't the Maasai, so there was no longer cause to evict them on the grounds of habitat destruction. If I were willing to be perverse, I could go as far as to say that, if anything, the Maasai preserved rather than destroyed the woodlands. At the time, that claim seemed so farfetched as to court ridicule; so I dropped it.

Try as I might, I couldn't get around the need for some protection of the swamps. If farmers turned the Amboseli swamps into shambas as they had in Kimana Swamp ten miles to the east, wildlife would disappear. The newly irrigated shambas and rows of thatch huts at Kimana had driven off the last of the rhinos and elephants and cordoned off the swamps, blocking wildlife access. So why not keep the protected area to an absolute minimum, just enough to secure the swamps and tourist game-viewing circuits? Coexistence rather than segregation could then prevail in the rest of the ecosystem.

Ideas of coexistence bolted through my mind like some Arcadian vision until checked by the reality of population growth and cultural disintegration destroying Maasai traditions. All the same, the Maasai would surely be better off with Amboseli than without it—and wildlife better off in their hands than anyone else's. Either the mutual tolerance of old would survive, or Amboseli would perish. I squatted excitedly in the dirt track and began roughing out a plan, using a stick to trace a rudimentary map in the dust of Kilimanjaro.

First I sketched out the protected area around the swamps and central surrounding woodlands. With the swamps safe from drought and settlement, wildlife would continue luring tourists. Why not call it a Maasai park, making the local community rather than government or county council the custodians of its wildlife? Under this scheme, tourism would provide money and jobs, diversifying the Maasai economy and preventing the pitfall of poverty and landlessness arising from their faltering subsistence lifestyle. The land outside the Maasai park could continue under pastoralism. Amounting to some 3,000 square miles, or some 90 percent of the ecosystem, the land had no arable potential anyhow. Provided with additional water points, the dry-season range could be expanded to make up for the loss of pasture in the Maasai park. New incentives to conserve wildlife outside the protected area could also be explored, perhaps by giving the Maasai a percentage of hunting revenues. And there was no reason why tourism could not be expanded over the entire ecosystem, giving the Maasai additional revenue and reducing the visitor pressure in the park.

The light had faded, and the map sketched hastily in the dust was barely visible. Straightening up, I made for camp, anxious to write up the details while they were still fresh. Coexistence had all the right appeal. Not only did it explain the historical survival of wildlife on the continent, it also offered the only hope of perpetuating open ecosystems and large-scale migrations in modern Africa.

For over a century wildlife around the world had been preserved by government decree, by the establishment of game laws and national parks in the interests of society at large. Preservationism was a triumph of compassion over greed, a noble commitment to save endangered species and set aside the Yellowstones and Serengetis for the world and for posterity. But however well-intentioned, preservationism failed more often than it worked. Usurping rights to wildlife and land from its traditional owners and vesting them in the state didn't provide any assurance of preservation. All too often the well-heeled hunters, tourists, and preservationists won out over the rural poor—whether American Indian or Maasai. Disfranchising the people controlling the fate of wildlife was no recipe for its survival.

The time had come for a new approach, an approach resting on fairness and local involvement rather than on alienation and enforcement. Why should local communities not become the principal beneficiaries and ultimate custodians of wildlife, as they always had been, without sacrificing the larger interests of society?

The idea, however appealing, had a major flaw. Local participation challenged a century of governmental control and vested interest. There was sure to be resistance. Why should governments voluntarily give up their authority and commercial interest to tribal people who openly despised and threatened wildlife? What could the uneducated Maasai, who couldn't stop their own cattle from destroying the land, possibly know about conservation? How could they stop poaching and address their own population problem?

Persuading conservationists, the government, and the Maasai themselves was certain to be an uphill task, but I was undaunted: fairness and logic would prevail.

The tent loomed against the darkening sky as I made camp. The sound of wildebeest shuffling across the plain and a heavy hide scraping against an acacia tree reached out from close by. After savoring the night sounds and the cool breeze a few moments longer, I ducked under the canvas to jot down my thoughts.

❬ ❬ ❬

THE APPLAUSE died down in the lecture hall after I concluded with a description of the new plan. The questions were unexpectedly sympathetic, even encouraging. Exonerating the Maasai of the woodland die-off had momentarily silenced the argument for a national park.

"I take your point about the reserve boundaries being all wrong, and about the need to conserve the entire migratory area," a voice spoke up from the rear. "But are you saying that we should only protect a small area, hand it over to the Maasai and write off the rest? If so, you're advocating helping the Maasai at the expense of the animals."

I hedged, knowing that the mention of a Maasai park, indigenous rights, and social responsibility would smack of communism to the conservative white settlers in the audience. "What I'm trying to say," I continued cautiously, "is that we have to think about the entire ecosystem, not just the dry-season range. To conserve the ecosystem we must win Maasai support by accommodating their interests. We don't really have any alternative. Besides, we know that coexistence worked in the past, so why not now? My ideas are admittedly tentative, but there's reason to think the Maasai could be persuaded to preserve Amboseli if they got a share of the tourist revenues, social services, and jobs."

"Excellent, excellent." A short, balding man grasped my hand and pumped it enthusiastically as I left the hall elated by my unexpected success. "My name is Emil Rado, director of the Institute for Development

Studies at the University. I was intrigued that you touched on the social issues. Do conservationists really think they can save animals and ignore people?"

We drifted outside with the crowd into the night. "Look," Rado continued, "how would you like to give a more detailed lecture on these ideas at IDS? You would have an enthusiastic group, I assure you."

Buoyed by the success of the lecture and the promise of an enthusiastic reception, I met Rado and his staff in downtown Nairobi shortly afterward. "Well, of course, I'm a sociologist," Rado began the introductions. "And this is Frank Mitchell, economist. Over there, Tim Aldington, livestock specialist. And Alan Jacobs, anthropologist. He worked on the Ilkisongo Maasai in Tanzania for his Ph.D., so you should have a lot in common." Rado continued round the table. "And finally, Dr. Leonard, a political scientist specializing in administration."

"I hope you don't expect too much," I responded. "Frankly, you're the people with the answers, not me. Amboseli is a tough problem, full of emotions. It needs the sort of social and economic approach you can bring to it. The professor of the Zoology Department told me I should think about a social science degree if I wanted to study humans. Seems I've come to the right place," I joked.

Mitchell, the economist, smiled and eyed me through steel-rimmed glasses. "The trouble with you biologists is that you never consider economic or social factors. You're a bunch of birdwatchers. That's why wildlife is in trouble. What I heard you say is different. Downright exciting in fact. We'd love to help with ideas."

Mitchell leaned forward, a lock of dark hair falling across his temple. "Seems to me that you need to state and quantify your arguments clearly. Tourism is the key to integration, right? So what do the visitor stats and income projections look like? Who benefits and who loses from wildlife?" The writing pad in front of him was filled with elaborate inked-in doodles around the margins. "Let me put it more simply. If you want to save wildlife you have to sustain the tourist industry and include the Maasai. That means pumping money back into tourist management and covering the opportunity costs of wildlife to the Maasai . . ."

He caught my blank expression. "Sorry. By opportunity costs I mean the costs the Maasai incur through loss of grazing, disease, and so on from

the wildlife migrating out of the park onto their land. You know, this lais-
sez-faire approach to tourism is a damned disaster. It'll destroy Amboseli,
but the conservationists just can't get it through their heads. The days
when the colonial government could draw a line round Tsavo and kick out
the Wakamba are over. We have to start dealing with the human problems
or lose the parks."

Under Emil Rado, the institute had attracted an assortment of social
scientists and economists from North America, Europe, and East Africa,
most of them liberal, intellectual, and critical of the conventional economic models for transferring wealth from the developed to developing
world. Few bodies anywhere in the late 1960s could have rivaled the institute's dedication to dismantling disciplinary barriers, challenging conventional modes of development, and trying out new ideas for incorporating
the social and economic dimensions of change. The atmosphere in the
institute fairly sizzled with ideas and acid humor about development
schemes gone awry. All the institute lacked in fact was a focus for its rare
collection of talent—and a touch of ecological reality. Amboseli provided
both.

So began an association that over the next few months fleshed out
details of the rudimentary plan sketched in the dust weeks before. Apply-
ing economic, social, and ecological models to Amboseli proved to be an
innovative and exciting collaboration. We all sensed that we were breaking
new ground, but none more than Frank Mitchell. He talked with great fer-
vor about interdisciplinary studies, integrated conservation and development, and the social dimensions of change, but not even he anticipated
that our team effort would help launch a new paradigm of integrated conservation and development in the 1980s.

Nine months after our collaboration began, I summarized our findings to an enthusiastic crowd in the institute's seminar room. This time the
analysis focused on the economic and social implications of conserving
Amboseli. Mitchell, who reveled in economic forecasts, had generated
reams of figures on the opportunity cost of wildlife to the Maasai and the
benefits they stood to gain from tourism and hunting. The analysis spoke
overwhelmingly in favor of an integrated use of the land, rather than a separation of wildlife and livestock. Even under assumptions of heavy capital
input, intensive management, and favorable markets, livestock would gen-

erate only some $600,000 if free to use the entire ecosystem. If, on the other hand, the entire ecosystem were turned over to wildlife use without any livestock present, income from tourism and hunting would amount to $8 million. The highest revenue of all came from combining both uses and excluding livestock only from the small protected area around the swamp. Under this scenario, revenues would rise higher still, avoiding the horrendous economic and social costs of evicting the Maasai from their traditional homelands.

Three conclusions came out of the collaboration. First, if the Maasai were cut in on Amboseli's wildlife proceeds, they would end up several times better off economically than if they relied solely on their herds. Wildlife, the livestock women had so inattentively let wander all over the countryside according to Maasai myth, had become more valuable than the men's herds! Second, the total number of wild animals and the ultimate volume of visitors would be far higher under ecological integration—a technical euphemism for coexistence—than under segregation. Third, the coexistence of wildlife and livestock would generate greater wealth for the Maasai than either option alone.

After the seminar, Mitchell walked me to my car. "You know, Jonah, you have a golden model here. You're onto something. Stick with it. Make sure you publicize it. Those crusty colonials who can only think of parks or nothing have their heads in the sand, and the wildlife biologists aren't much better. This is bigger than Amboseli. Make sure you pull out the general principles. I'll help you with the next stage, too, if you like."

Mitchell's admonition and help gave me a badly needed boost to push ahead with the plan. The next step was to win the approval of the Maasai, the county council, and, finally, the conservation community and government.

◄ ◄ ◄

THE DETAILS, it turned out, meant everything to Parashino. Mistrust flickered in his eyes the moment I laid out the plan. "What you are saying is that you want to turn Amboseli over to the animals and throw us out. Is that it? I thought you told me you were not Game Department? Well, are you on their side or ours?"

Parashino's anger caught me off guard. "No, no," I told him defensively. "Don't you see that Amboseli would be a Maasai park, not a government park? A Maasai park would not only prevent a government takeover, it would also make Amboseli's wildlife valuable to you. Wouldn't you want to preserve wildlife if you got money out of it?"

"You think you are helping the Maasai, don't you," he interjected. "Well, you're not. Wild animals are useless to us. Nothing but trouble. The British took our land in Serengeti and Tsavo, then in Mara and Samburu. Next it was the Kajiado County Council, which claimed our land in Amboseli. Now it's the Kikuyu government which wants it, and you're helping them.

"Listen to me," he went on, "to the way we Maasai see it. Wild animals are government cattle. We are told to look after them for the tourists. And even though we have, it's not enough. The government wants our land too. If we kill their animals because they eat our grass and kill our livestock, we are arrested. The Kikuyus want us to keep quiet while they steal everything. Why should they care about the Maasai or listen to you?"

I had never seen Parashino so angry. Far from winning his approval, I had betrayed his trust. "No matter what you say, Yonah," he added with finality, "a park means the Maasai lose."

I tried everything I knew to win his approval, or at least get a hearing, but he would have none of it. He perceptively saw that in vindicating the Maasai of the woodland destruction, I had spiked the argument for a national park. "So why do you still want a park if we are not to blame?" he demanded.

"Why?" I shot back angrily in frustration and defeat. "I'll tell you why. Aren't the Maasai already pushing government to scrap the reserve and turn it over to ranches? What then? Shambas like Kimana, then fences and houses? And after that? The wildlife will disappear, and you, the council, the government, and everyone else in Kenya will lose."

I was not going to let the plan get shot down without a fight. "Do you think the government will stand by and see Amboseli destroyed? Tourism is too important to Kenya for that to happen. And what of the Maasai in the future? Won't they need money, schools, and clinics? Won't you need jobs when your cattle can no longer feed your children? Surely it's better to make Amboseli your own park rather than let the government grab it."

Parashino's anger subsided as mine mounted, but frustration and distrust still showed in his eyes. I was looking ahead, to the dangers of population growth and a collapsing subsistence economy, he to the past and all the injustices the Maasai had suffered. We were talking at cross-purposes, I about threats and opportunities he barely grasped, he about memories and fears incomprehensible to an outsider. I had yet to grasp the full significance of space and mobility to the pastoral mind, or the significance of the swamps the Maasai would lose. Unwittingly, I interpreted all Parashino's fears in strictly ecological terms, as if he were herding wildebeest and zebra. What the ecological interpretation missed was psychology, the pathological fear of land loss and faltering Maasai power, which clouded everything else. Our mutual ignorance lay like a gulf between us, a gulf that only time, trust, and exposure to each other's experience would bridge.

Parashino's myopia and intransigence put me in a moral dilemma. Should I press ahead with the plans in the Maasai's long-term interests, or accept their decision as paramount, whatever the consequences?

Sindiyo had no such qualms. The worldly Maasai had an obligation to persuade the more traditional. The greater moral crime lay in seeing the threats and walking away, leaving the Maasai to their fate. But then, Sindiyo was a Maasai—and they his people. I was an outsider and had no pretensions to being a Maasai.

It was Simon Salash who persuaded me to put conviction above paternalistic guilt, though he never knew it: I met him only once.

The day, June 22, 1979, was hot and windy. The long rains had been indifferent and the grasses had wilted prematurely, leaving the animals short of grazing. From the top of Kitirua Hill I sat watching small dust flurries billowing off the barren ground as a lone figure came tramping up the hill. He had the short-cropped hair, red-checked shuka, and *rungu* (knobkerrie) of a traditional elder and the battered raincoat, black patent-leather shoes, and holed socks of an urban Maasai. Shaking hands, he introduced himself as Simon Salash and said he was a farmer from Loitokitok who had cattle out this way. Our discussion quickly came round to Amboseli.

"The Maasai will never accept a park," he told me emphatically. "Why should they, when it stretches all the way to the Chyulus and Namanga? Where would the Maasai go?"

I laughed. "What do you mean? The park goes only from here to

Kalunyet and up to Eremito, not to the Chyulus—only around the swamps and part of the woodlands."

He looked at me in disbelief. "Honest to God? But the Maasai here tell me Oloitiptip said it was 200 miles long."

"Two hundred miles long? That's wrong. Its 200 square miles, not 200 miles long."

"What's the difference? Two hundred miles is 200 miles, isn't it?"

I laughed again, unable to believe the damage done by a simple misapprehension. The local Maasai had adopted British measures and talked of distance in miles and area in acres. How could a mile possibly be square? I explained the distinction to Salash.

He laughed too. "Well, if it's as you say, then it's not such a big park, is it? But Amboseli will not survive even if the Maasai are given the park. They don't know what land titles mean. When they get a title deed they sell for it money and think they can still keep the land. Look at Kimana. The Kikuyus and Wakambas have already moved in. Why should Amboseli be any different? These Maasai don't see what's happening to them.

"And look at this place. Dry and dusty. The cattle are already showing ribs. How will the Maasai survive the coming drought?"

Salash's experience in the larger world gave him the foresight Parashino lacked. "They will have to change or lose everything," he had concluded. The words went round and round in my head for days and convinced me that Sindiyo's paternalism was morally the better course. Surely a touch of paternalism was better than letting the Maasai and wildlife go marching blindly up the path of mutual destruction.

Even if Salash's words had not made up my mind, an article in East Africa's *Standard* newspaper on July 4 certainly did. "The Money Locked Up in Amboseli" read the center-piece spread. The article detailed the report I had prepared for the Institute for Development Studies and Mitchell's economic analysis. "So far Amboseli's potential as a money spinner has hardly begun to be realized," the article went on. "Given proper management as a wildlife area, Amboseli could look forward to a gross tourist revenue of between $8,000,000 and $14,000,000 a year by 1980."

The press coverage would have been welcome but for one omission: Maasai participation. Far from drawing attention to the need for Maasai involvement, the article mentioned only the economic profits at stake, giving the government a new excuse to step in to protect national interests. Sure enough, in Nairobi the promise of Amboseli's wealth glinted like a torch beam in the government's eyes. To make matters worse, conservationists promptly substituted national economic interests for the discredited dustbowl argument and pushed even harder for a national park. At a wildlife workshop, one conservationist accused me of suffering from Maasaiitis, as if it were a deadly disease.

"Some conservationist!" was how he put it, as if excommunicating me from the honorable fraternity. I was mortified at the slight but too young and timid to tell him that I cared more about Amboseli and wildlife than he ever would.

Frank Mitchell's hide was thicker than mine, and he relished the rebukes. "That makes it 460 so far," he bubbled, ticking off another bird on his Kenya list as we skirted Lake Amboseli on his first tourist survey. "Jonah, don't take it so hard. The old farts shouldn't get you down. There's more than a little hypocrisy and racism in their reaction and it's downright irresponsible of them to slam you for taking up the Maasai side. Fine, we all love to save elephants, but conservation won't work unless it benefits the guys who get saddled with the bill. Conservationists couldn't care a damn about disfranchising the Maasai."

Mitchell's caustic comments and encouragement always bolstered me, and at no time more than now. Sindiyo's response was just as emphatic when he read the *Standard* article. "We have to act immediately or lose Amboseli," he told the committee of Maasai elders. He had a particular idea in mind.

Royal Little arrived a month later. A lean, hard-driving American businessman who had built a multimillion dollar business conglomerate, Little was a man in a hurry who let nothing stand in his way. He had become passionately concerned about wildlife on his many safaris to Africa and jumped into conservation with his legendary business zeal and acumen. He wanted the best for the wild, and if his famed guide and ex-hunter, Sid Downey, said Amboseli should become a national park, then Little would see to it.

Sindiyo and I met Little and his retinue in a small clapboard guesthouse at the back of the Kilimanjaro Safari Lodge, where elephants grazed on the well-tended lawn. Little wasted no time on formalities. "I hope my plan for the park and offer of money through the New York Zoological Society is still alive," he kicked off. He had earlier offered the government $90,000 to provide alternative water sources if the government removed the Maasai from 200 square miles of central Amboseli and turned it into a national park. The informality of his khaki safari suit and languid appearance couldn't disguise his corporate impatience.

Sindiyo responded diplomatically, omitting Oloitiptip's acerbic comments about Little's plan and his insistence on a Maasai solution to Maasai problems. "David Western—Jonah—whom I introduced earlier, has an alternative plan we think will work, though. He'll explain it to you."

I was irked at Little's bombastic style and his assumption that anything he said went, even in Amboseli. "The plan you want to support will never work," I told him abrasively, "not for wildlife, not for the Maasai. The boundaries are wrong ecologically. Now that the Maasai have rejected your plan, we have to start from scratch." I went on to describe my own plan for conserving the entire ecosystem. "A small core park makes sense," I concluded, "but only to protect the swamps from agriculture."

Little stared at me coldly after the presentation. He did not take kindly to a twenty-four-year-old whippersnapper telling him his plan was no damn good. "Fine, if you think this plan of yours will work, I'm all for it," he growled. "I want to see it work for the Maasai too. The new ecological information makes sense. What matters is that we save Amboseli from going down the tubes."

He abruptly turned to Sindiyo. "This is your baby, Mr. Sindiyo. But if you want my money—and it's still available—you're gonna have to get approval from the Ministry of Tourism and Wildlife and New York Zoological. We'll only deal directly with government."

Much as I resented the put-down, Royal Little's offer could make all the difference to the viability of the new plan. Money, a lot of it, would be needed for Maasai water points outside the park. Sindiyo lost no time in taking advantage of Little's offer. Swallowing his pride, he called on Oloitiptip, who he knew would be the power broker in persuading both the Maasai elders and the Kajiado County Council. Once persuaded, Oloitiptip called a meeting of Maasai elders on August 2 to deliberate the threats and opportunities facing Amboseli. The member of parliament for Kajiado North, several county councilors, Sindiyo, and representative Maasai elders attended.

The elders, like Parashino, were decidedly cool, but Oloitiptip was nothing if not a master persuader. "You have to think about the future, not the past," Sindiyo later reported him as saying. "We must change or die. The park will be our bank. What will our children think of us if they look at the park and say it was their fathers who gave it away?"

No agreement was reached that day, but Oloitiptip—like Royal Little—was not a man to give up. "Don't forget what we thought of the British when they insisted we send some children to school for our own good, the good of our future," he argued when the meeting resumed the next day. "We resisted, didn't we? We thought they were wrong. But where would we be today without our educated Maasai to represent us, to fight for our interests? I should know. I was one of those children, and I am now fighting for your interests."

After two days of anguish, debate, and Oloitiptip's incessant haranguing, the elders adopted the plan to make Amboseli into a Maasai park. Everything had fallen neatly into place—a plan acceptable to the Maasai, a prospective donor who would provide money for the new wells, and the beginning of a new era in ecosystem conservation. The ecological surveys, time spent with the Maasai, the interdisciplinary work with the Institute for Development Studies, and my close relationship with Sindiyo had paid off. The rest was up to others.

I could finally return to my privacy and research. There was so much more exploration and research to do, and, having done my bit for conservation, I felt I deserved the luxury of doing it.

My mother, Beatrice Western, at nineteen, as strong-willed and independent as my father.

My father, Arthur Cyril Western, who joined the Indian Army as a passport to adventure.

Right to left:
*David (age nine), Martin (age eleven),
and tracker Mohamed Mbwana (age sixty)
on a hunt.*

Arthur Western with a large tusker which helped pay our school fees.

*Having shot my first warthog at age thirteen, I lost the trigger itch
and gave up plans to become a big-game hunter.*

A secluded spot where I set up camp to learn the ecological rhythm of Amboseli.

With Parashino Ole Purdul, who insisted I see Amboseli through the eyes of a cow.

Elephants seeking refuge from poachers flooded into Amboseli,
where they quickly destroyed the woodlands.

Six years after building an electric fence around my house
to exclude elephants, the fever trees are thriving.

Kerenkol Ole Musa (left), a leading spokesman for conservation, dressed in traditional regalia on his wedding day.

In the 1970s and 1980s poachers almost wiped out Amboseli's rhino population. Of the seventy animals I counted in 1967, only eight remained ten years later.

Peter Matthiessen paddles a pirogue, or dugout canoe, across the Sanga River in Central African Republic in search of the mysterious pygmy elephant.

My wife, Shirley Strum, whose studies of baboons have helped change prevailing views of primate society, observes baboons at her field site in Kenya, accompanied by our two children, Guy and Carissa.

*Traditional and western cultures blend at the wedding ceremony of
my close friend and long-term field assistant, David Maitumo.*

*A Maasai elder awards me an orinka, a ceremonial stick
of authority, as John Marinka looks on.*

◀ Part Three ▶

Through the Eyes of a Cow

‹ 7 ›

Not One More Inch

FIFTEEN MONTHS OF SUN, rain, and wind took its toll on the faded yellow tent tucked into the receding thickets of Kampi ya Western, as the rangers called my hideaway. Acacia sap had eaten holes in the fly sheet and the side walls of the eleven-by-nine-foot tent bulged to bursting with the paraphernalia of my expanding research program. Much as I loved camp life, the tent could no longer house all my gear. Worse, the thinning woodlands and thickets no longer screened my tent from the prowling minibuses. The time had come to move on. What I had in mind was a small banda, a mud-brick house with a thatch roof, secreted among a grove of fever trees accessible to the plains and swamps where I could continue following the daily progress of the migrants.

In a turn of good fortune, the Kenya Game Department began to take an interest in the Amboseli work. The head of the research division sent down a tiny fabric-covered aircraft each month to help count animals in the basin and secured $1,000 for a house cum research lab. Sindiyo, who fretted about my remoteness, chose a quiet spot in a stand of trees lining the game trails filing into Longinye Swamp close to Ol Tukai.

Sindiyo became a close friend as well as a keen supporter, despite our first encounter. To start with, our meetings in his cluttered office under a grove of dying fever trees close to his house were strictly business. His brusque manner didn't invite informality, but as the weeks went by he began to chat more amiably and invited me over to his nearby house for tea to meet his wife, Zippy, and four young children. Full of fun and laughter, they became a surrogate for the family I missed. When a fever tree fell and destroyed his office, Sindiyo worked at home for a while, giving me more opportunity to see his family. Soon I became a regular caller, especially on Sundays, when they sat down to roast goat at the large family table beneath a plaque declaring "God is the Head of this Household." When my tent disintegrated after eighteen months, Sindiyo asked me to move in for a couple of months until the banda was completed. He graciously treated me as family, joking that I would turn into a weirdo living alone.

When the banda was completed I dumped a bedroll, kitchen trunk, small worktable, a few books, and field equipment onto the bare cement floor of the living room. The tiny dusty pile looked pathetic against the stark white-washed walls of the new quarters. I slumped into a tattered camp chair, filled with misgiving about giving up the intimacy of the francolin padding through the tent, the lions resting under the fly sheet, and Charlie the elephant chomping on the broom handle.

The walls of the banda rose up like a fortress. Cut off from the animals and land I loved, I wandered out onto the open plains outside and cried, knowing the carefree days were over. Naively, I had expected a return to the joys of research and exploration, leaving the drudgery of hustling through the plan to others. Instead, I was writing reports, attending meetings in Nairobi, and coaxing the plan from office to office in Nairobi to win over the Ministry of Tourism and Wildlife. It irked me that no one in the government seemed willing to do these things. But why should they, given the skepticism about a Maasai park? So, despite my ineptitude and frustration, I did the chasing up, knowing that otherwise the plan would falter.

I wandered down the game trails crisscrossing the plain, trying to sort out my feelings about the banda. Never had I felt so alive and free as living in a tent close to the animals. This is all I had ever wanted—until a sense of purpose crept into my life once the Maasai park was adopted by the council of elders. Obliged to do the follow-up, I felt torn between freedom and responsibility, with research pulling one way and conservation another. Rationally, I knew there could be no freedom without the wilds and no wilds without solving Amboseli's problems; but I was not in a rational frame of mind.

The herds of wildebeest staring curiously at the human being distractedly wandering down their winding trails finally brought me back to the beauty and vulnerability of Amboseli. In the end, I resolved never to give up the daily contact with animals or abandon their defense. Why not enjoy the beauty and freedom of the African savannas and find fulfillment in conserving them?

By the long dry season of 1969, the ecological monitoring was paying off. The large-scale migrations fell into place, along with an explanation of Amboseli's biological diversity. Contrary to the stability and predictability announced by Odum's equilibrium theory, the ecology of Amboseli changed continuously. The neat succession of plants, from simple colonizing communities to complex habitats, was continually thrown off track by countervailing forces like a cork bobbing on the water. The mix of species varied, depending on rainfall, soils, animal activity, and human impact, never settling into one state before shifting to another. The number of animals also fluctuated as the migrant populations tracked the erratic rains and changing vegetation patterns. Change rather than constancy emerged as the ecological refrain in Amboseli.

At first I took Amboseli to be exceptional among savanna ecosystems in flouting equilibrium theory, but stability, it transpired, was proving just as elusive to researchers in Serengeti, Tsavo, Queen Elizabeth, Murchison, Meru—in fact, in every national park in East Africa. If habitats shifted erratically throughout the savannas, surely animal communities had to be equally unstable?

Oddly, despite the evidence of change, few ecologists seemed unduly worried at the time. Nature's equilibrium drew support from a distinguished line of ecologists. Exceptions were chalked up to human disturbance, the unsettling force in nature's otherwise harmonious balance. The first person to document the unsettling force was George Perkins Marsh, U.S. ambassador to Italy and Egypt and later fish commissioner in Vermont. In *Man and Nature*, written in 1864, Marsh catalogued a distressing list of destruction to forests, soils, waters, and the atmosphere. In his account, humans wantonly destroyed the perfect harmony of nature on an unprecedented scale, endangering species and threatening nature. Marsh's views were finally taken seriously in the 1960s, a full century later, when ecology, the science of the environment, was erroneously cast as the doomsday discipline behind the environmental movement spawned by Rachel Carson, Paul Ehrlich, and Barry Commoner.

Amboseli challenged both Odum's theory of stability and Marsh's man-the-destroyer imagery at every turn, pointing to change as the rule and to the Maasai as a positive no less than a negative force. Change was universal, from the long, slow, concatenated events triggered by the eruption of Kilimanjaro to the apparently whimsical migrations and grazing succession. And, challenging Marsh's belief in humans as an unnatural and destructive force, wildlife abounded in the East Africa savannas and no species had gone extinct since the arrival of pastoralists several thousand years earlier.

The perpetual change cried out for an explanation. Could it not be that ecological change rather than stability was the rule? Surely the whole string of disruptions set off by geological upheavals, climatic change, even human activity, made it impossible for any ecosystem to stabilize for more than a fleeting moment? If so, disturbance was the dominant perpetual force, rather than a fleeting aberration. And, if that were true, could it possibly be that change rather than stability explained Amboseli's wealth of species?

Seeing Amboseli in a new light, I returned to Observation Hill clutching a batch of 1950 aerial photos. The change was staggering. Twenty years earlier, fever trees had covered the flats between Observation Hill and the ancient lake shore to the south. Today the trees were gone, except for a few moribund specimens in a graveyard of fallen limbs. The scene looked as if Atlas had upended the world, sending the trees crashing against the southern rim of the basin. Scattered pockets of alkaline grassland and thickets of salt bush had replaced the acacia groves.

The mix of animal species mirrored the habitat change. In 1961, primatologists Stuart and Jeanne Altmann had counted 2,500 baboons in the woodlands. Eight years later, fewer than 500 remained. In the eighteen months around my tent, bushbuck and lesser kudu had vanished, and giraffe and rhino had dwindled to near extinction. Every season, zebra and wildebeest pushed deeper into the thinning woodlands, following the invading grasslands. Birds, ever a barometer of habitat shift, told the same story. The Verreaux's eagle owls booping outside my tent had abandoned the dying woodlands, along with the gray hornbill, African hoopoe, and slate-colored boubou. Their successors, the woodpeckers, were having a field day, monotonously tapping away at the dead tree limbs in search of wood-boring grubs and insects.

Much as I relished disproving the theory that overgrazing was making Amboseli a dustbowl, the area was undoubtedly losing its aesthetic appeal along with its diversity. What could explain the impoverishment if not the Maasai? The dying woodlands begged for an explanation. Providing one proved to be a murder mystery abounding in clues—most of them false.

With the Maasai exonerated, the elephant became the prime suspect. The incriminating evidence littered the ground as offensively as a machine-gun massacre. Mature trees showed heavy tusk gouges, some to the point of being ring-barked. Grove upon grove of regenerating trees lay twisted and broken like the aftermath of a cyclone. Saplings lay macerated on the ground, snapped off and chewed up by passing elephants.

I was not altogether convinced by the obvious though, knowing how compelling the evidence of overgrazing had been. What, for example, could explain the death of many trees with no visible sign of elephant damage? Surely this observation exonerated the elephants and pointed to a deeper cause. My suspicions began to center on fluctuations in the water table, which had to be high to support the water-loving fever tree confined to lake and river margins. The tree's very name alludes to the malaria regularly contracted by early explorers in the damp woodland groves. Fluctuating water tables were no more than a hunch at first, one I might not have followed up had not an unexpected event catapulted Amboseli's woodland destruction to the top of my research agenda.

The international symposium on mammalian reproduction and physiology held in Nairobi in 1969 brought a lineup of prominent physiologists, endocrinologists, clinicians, and anatomists. What might otherwise have been a staid scientific meeting became a hotbed of contention when Richard Laws presented his latest findings on Tsavo National Park. Two decades later the repercussions of his talk made themselves felt in an international furor over culling, the ivory trade, and the fate of the African elephant.

Laws, a self-assured Cambridge biologist, came to scientific prominence studying whales and sea lions in the Antarctic. Later he assumed directorship of the Nuffield Unit of Tropical Ecology and turned his prodigious talent to the vexing problem of habitat loss in Uganda's Murchison Falls National Park. Laws attributed the woodland and forest devastation to too many elephants on too little land, an echo of the overgrazing theory of Maasailand, but on a far greater scale. Elephants, in Laws's view, had turned woodlands to grasslands and in the process destroyed the park's biological diversity. Being a cautious scientist, he didn't blame the elephants directly. The ultimate cause, he insisted, lay in the growth of human numbers, settlement and poaching, which forced elephants to retreat to the safety of Murchison Falls National Park. Laws prescribed the same solution the conservationists did for overgrazing in Amboseli—cutting numbers. But whereas the proposal to save Amboseli's woodlands by hoofing out the Maasai evinced no protest from conservationists, Laws raised a furor when he culled 2,000 elephants in Murchison Falls National Park.

Laws's teammate was a wiry Kenya-born Briton, Ian Parker, an ex–Game Department warden who had set up his own consulting agency, Wildlife Services. Parker took great pride in his surgical operation. Entire herds of mothers and calves fell in seconds to the rattle of gunfire. The loss of life apart, the cull contributed meat to the local market and valuable scientific data. Each animal was painstakingly dissected, weighed, and measured. The results, which Laws summarized in scientific journals, became the standard work of reference on elephant reproduction and population dynamics for two decades. His relentless statistical detail and scientific objectivity won high praise and eventually a knighthood.

After briefly describing his new assignment in Tsavo National Park, Laws turned on the projector and showed slide after slide of wrecked trees, barren ground, and dead elephants. The scenes looked reminiscent of Armageddon rather than Kenya's most famous park. The analogy was not lost on Laws; switching off the projector, he hammered his point home to eliminate any vestiges of doubt: "Elephants are destroying Tsavo's woodlands. Unless we take action, Tsavo will become a desert. We have already done a scientific cull of 300 elephants. We must cull a further 3,000 to avert a crisis. Other areas, including Amboseli Game Reserve, are showing signs of elephant invasion and habitat destruction. I advocate early culling to avoid a similar loss of biological diversity."

Visions of acre after acre of dead elephants in Amboseli sent alarm bells clanging in my mind. Fortunately, Amboseli was quickly forgotten. Sitting to my right was Perez Olindo, the first African director of Kenya National Parks. A kindly looking man with a lantern jaw, he sat impassively, giving nothing away. Beside him sat David Sheldrick, who for twenty years had labored at carving Tsavo National Park out of dense bush and cleaning out the Waliangulu elephant hunters.

Sheldrick, a strong personality and fine amateur naturalist in his own right, had proprietary feelings about Tsavo and took a dim view of Laws's proposal. "While I don't disagree with your observations, Dick, I can't agree with your interpretation," he began in a clipped Kenya accent. "The area was under grassland when the Gala grazed cattle in Tsavo last century. Their graves are still visible. The area later turned to bush after they abandoned the area and is in the process of becoming grassland again. What's happening in Tsavo today is part of a natural cycle and there is no need to cull."

The carefully orchestrated lecture broke up into an acrimonious exchange as speaker after speaker took sides in the standoff between Laws and Sheldrick. I questioned Laws's conclusion about Amboseli, citing the many dead trees with no sign of elephant damage. Laws gracefully conceded the need for more research.

"The real issue is whether the cycle is natural or caused by man," one speaker concluded, "and therefore whether we should let nature take its course or cull. What's the national parks policy on culling?"

All eyes turned to Olindo. He stood up and slowly scanned the room, commanding attention and building expectation. Ambassadorial in his bearing, Olindo smiled to ease the tension. The real issue for many preservationists in the room rested less on ecological cycles, meat for protein-starved Africans, and scientific data than on the morality of slaughtering thousands of elephants in cold blood. It was one thing to talk about evicting the Maasai and starving their cattle to death, quite another to talk of killing elephants. Nature was free to take its course and for elephants to die of starvation, but culling them to relieve their suffering and spare the ecosystem was rather like euthanizing your ailing grandmother. It just wasn't discussed, at least not in public. Olindo, a consummate diplomat, sensed the emotional implications of an elephant cull in Kenya.

"We have no policy on culling. We will consider each argument on its own merit and consult widely."

The meeting broke up into small animated groups. Ian Parker, the man called on to do the cull, was in the thick of it. Iain Douglas-Hamilton approached me. He was studying Tanzania's Manyara National Park and gaining worldwide recognition for describing the intricacies and warmth of elephant family life. "What do you make of Laws's arguments, Jonah?" Douglas-Hamilton asked me. "I'm facing a similar problem with elephants killing the acacia tortilis woodlands in Manyara. Laws mentioned Amboseli. What's the story there?"

I shrugged. "I'm not sure. The elephants are certainly a big factor, but there's more to it than that. I can't figure out what's killing some of the trees, and I'm dubious about culling before we know." Douglas-Hamilton seemed decidedly low key and cautious around scientists, in contrast to his charisma in front of the press and derring-do in the bush. Our personalities were as different as chalk and cheese, but I felt sure our paths would cross again on the subject of elephants.

Laws's lecture put the Amboseli woodlands back at the center of conservation debate. Although the Maasai could no longer be blamed for the destruction, it was important to know what was going on now that Laws had raised the specter of culling elephants.

The timing for a study of the woodlands was perfect. I had just met Charles van Praet, a young Belgian forester who felt wasted at a United Nations agency in Nairobi; he eagerly agreed to team up on the study. His expertise on trees would complement my own on animals. I eagerly headed back to Amboseli to prepare for the study.

The moment I stepped into Daniel's office to tell him about the woodland study, it was obvious that something was wrong. He sat slumped at his desk, looking as if the world had collapsed around him. It was September 23, 1969, seven weeks after the meeting of the Maasai elders. After the meeting, his mood had lifted like the dawn mist on Kilimanjaro and he had ribbed me mercilessly about my solitary life. In fact he had been in such an ebullient mood that he'd even joked about Oloitiptip becoming a reformed poacher.

"You're not going to believe this, Jonah. Oloitiptip has thrown out the Amboseli plan."

The room went silent. My throat tightened in panic. "I don't believe it. You're joking again?"

He shook his head in defeat.

"But how could he?" I blurted. "He knows the Maasai will lose Amboseli to the government if they don't do something to conserve it."

"The Maasai are furious over the land grabs by other tribes like the Kikuyus and Wakambas. They are scared of losing their land, and the elders have told Oloitiptip that unless he guarantees title deeds for every inch of Maasailand—including Amboseli—they will vote him out in the coming election."

I waited for Daniel's anger to surface, for some sign of hope, but the life had gone out of him. "You have to understand," he went on, "the Maasai never owned land individually. With the other tribes moving in, they feel trapped. They want protection. The elders know their only hope lies in getting legal title to the land, not in the spear. Oloitiptip is a politician. He needs their votes, and he will get them, even if it means shelving Amboseli. Maybe he thinks he can resurrect the idea of a Maasai park once they've been given title to the land. For now, it's dead. His election slogan is 'Not one more inch of Maasailand.'

"I've done what I can, Jonah. I've written to the permanent secretary in Tourism and Wildlife urging him to have the minister of agriculture suspend any adjudication of the reserve until we can resolve its status. I can't do more. I'm an employee of the council, and Tiptip has them all in his pocket."

Back at my house I slumped in a safari chair on the veranda and stared glumly at the herds of animals grazing around the swamp thickets. What next? If the Maasai won the land and refused to set up a park, shambas would soon destroy Amboseli. If the government took over, the Maasai would block the migrating animals and resume their protest spearing of rhinos. Either way, Amboseli was doomed.

I was desperate to consult Parashino. When I finally located him back at Meshanani, he killed the last glimmer of hope. Preoccupied with the impending drought, he dismissed my fears for Amboseli. "Oloitiptip must support our land claims or lose the election. The plan for a park is finished."

I pressed him harder for some small sign of hope. "What's it to you?" he asked. "It's we who are angry, we who would lose the land to wild animals. Amboseli Park would be no different from Serengeti or Tsavo. We know that, and the warriors are willing to fight for it. The elders tell them not to. So what do they do? They kill the rhinos in anger. You get us title to our lands, then we'll decide about wildlife."

He rushed on, unstoppable and angry. "The British came and saw our herds moving like wildebeest and thought we didn't own the land. So they took it for their farms. Then, because they killed off all their wild animals, they wanted to steal ours, even though the animals were safer with us. When the British left, the Kikuyus took over. Tourists make them greedier than ever for our land."

What Parashino was saying explained Oloitiptip's about-face. Finally, I understood his point. No plan, however economically and socially sound, could erase seventy years of suspicion over land grabs. The elders' approval of a Maasai park had been forced on them by Oloitiptip; they simply didn't believe in it. Wildlife belonged to the government, and a park could mean only one thing: the government would take it over, no matter what Oloitiptip or the government said to the contrary. I'd overlooked the Maasai's deep love of the land and their fear of losing it in the mistaken belief that my rational plan would assuage their worries and fill their wants.

The Maasai advance south from the Nile Basin to East Africa a few hundred years ago had been halted in central Tanzania, not by superior force, but by tsetse fly. The Maasai people believed that all cattle were given to them by God, or Enkai, when the sky and earth split apart. So utterly rooted in cattle had their society become, and cattle on the grass and the grass on the earth, that no Maasai would defile the land by farming, digging wells, or burying their dead.

Parashino, a member of the Laitaiyok clan, spoke proudly of beating the Iloogolala—the people of the hard teeth—at Enkongo Okengeri. He saw land as God-given, and the Maasai as inseparable from it. "How can you own something you are part of?" he asked when I pressed him on land ownership. Ownership became sharply defined only when the British began settling East Africa at the turn of the century. Until then land had been won and held by the sword, not by the pen.

A series of misfortunes—smallpox, the rinderpest pandemic, drought, and internecine wars between the Laikipiak Maasai and southern sections—left the Maasai at low ebb and vulnerable to the colonists. In the words of Genesta Hamilton, a pioneer and inveterate diarist, Lord Delamere, the leader of the settler community, saw this "wild and beautiful, exciting and enticing land" and led the rush to "acquire huge tracts of empty, fertile country where they established houses, cattle and sheep."

The British grabbed the arable land around the Rift Valley lakes and, under an agreement with a half-blind Lenana, the Maasai laiboni, in 1908, split the remaining Maasai into two reserves north and south of the white settlement. Still not satisfied, and using the pretext of disease and cattle raids, the settlers hustled the entire section of northern Maasai into the Southern Reserve. A second agreement, drawn up in 1911, ceded the Southern Reserve to the Maasai "for as long as they shall exist as a people." Much as the Maasai resented the annexation, they accepted it. After all, the British had won by superior force and used the land for farms, homes, and livestock. It was some consolation that the Maasai were left alone, in their own minds separate from other tribes and Kenya.

But by the 1930s the British were at it again. This time the excuse for grabbing more land was wildlife preservation, something the Maasai never understood nor accepted. Land conquered and settled by superior force was one thing, land appropriated for wild animals quite another.

Wildlife had always been free to come and go as far as the Maasai were concerned, and like land, free to use if never to own. As such, wild animals thrived under their protection. The only animals exterminated in Maasai-land were those killed by whites, on the stolen lands of the Laikipia, Uasin Gishu, and the Rift Valley. To rob the Maasai of their remaining lands, guaranteed "for as long as they shall exist as a people," and give those lands to wild animals was not only incomprehensible, it was an insult.

Lynn Temple-Boreham was one of the few British who sympathized with the Maasai and single-handedly fought their cause. He astutely saw the futility of pressing for more parks like Tsavo and Serengeti, especially with independence approaching. He came up with a compromise solution: game reserves vested in the local councils but run by the national parks authority. However farsighted his idea, the omission of the Maasai on the ground merely spelled "national park" by a different name. "The county council is second government," Lochokop told me in disgust. "The council takes our land and money like the government does. Except of course the money goes to Kajiado, not Nairobi. What's the difference?"

Had I taken the time to learn Maasai history and understand their fear of losing land, had I recognized and tried to assuage their fears before Oloitiptip forged ahead with the plan, perhaps its rejection could have been avoided. As it was, the depth of their feeling put an end to the Maasai park.

Just when it seemed things couldn't get worse, Sindiyo resigned. His hopes, like mine, were dead. Once the council gave up in defeat over a Maasai park and slashed the budget for the reserve to rock bottom, he quit. "There's no point in staying," he told me. "The council has virtually surrendered Amboseli to the government by pulling out and spending no money on the reserve. They won't raise my salary either. How can I educate my kids on $1,500 a year? I'm going back to the Game Department in Nairobi."

After Sindiyo left, I visited his house. The spacious rooms once filled with warmth and laughter echoed to my footsteps. I lingered in the dining room, recalling happy meals of goat meat and rice shared under the red-and-gold "God is the Head of this Household" sign. Dust from an afternoon storm peppered the waxed floor. I walked out onto the veranda and looked across the empty swimming pool to a convoy of minibuses moving through the thickets in search of lions.

Sindiyo was gone, and, with him, all hope for Amboseli.

Sindiyo's departure left no one officially trying to solve the Amboseli problem. I could barely muster the will to write the report Royal Little wanted, let alone sort out the problems created by Sindiyo's departure. I had no authority to act as warden, and what was the point if I did? Oloitiptip had scuttled any chance of a Maasai park and played into the hands of the government. Bitter and disillusioned, I gave up, too, and went back to my research.

Charlie van Praet's arrival and the urgency of the woodland study rekindled my enthusiasm for research. Charlie and I worked well together and brought out each other's natural curiosity. Within a couple of days we were batting ideas back and forth like Ping-Pong balls. Our respective skills in forestry and wildlife complemented each other nicely, and we joked a good deal to kill the boredom of collecting data. By the end of the week we had measured hundreds of trees and firmly ruled out Maasai, pests, and disease as a cause of death.

"Charlie, how are we going to explain these dead trees?" I challenged him, pointing to a grove with no visible elephant damage. We were standing at the edge of Ol Tukai Orok, the thickest stand of trees in Amboseli, taking a short break after a grueling session digging holes in the ground on the off chance that the answer lay in the changing composition of the soils. The woodlands thinned to the west below Observation Hill where the remaining live trees grasped at the air like wizened gray hands clutching at life. To the east the woodlands thickened to an impenetrable tangle of thorn and wild dates palms.

"We're missing something. We have to be, Charlie. Why are the trees dying along a gradient from west to east? And why are some trees dead with no sign of elephant damage? If the fever trees do need a water table close to the surface, wouldn't they die if the water table dropped?" I inquired, trying out my water-table hunch. "That could've happened in the '61 drought. Or maybe the floods which followed drowned the trees."

Charlie thrust out his jaw and puckered his mouth. "I agree. We are missing something. Droughts and floods, though? Nah. Something else is going on, something in the soil. We'll know when we get the samples back from the lab. But, Jonah, one thing's sure. These woodlands aren't old. Most stands are even-aged. That means they started growing together and started dying at the same time. What does that tell you? Some big successional change in vegetation, eh?"

A few weeks later Charlie was back with the lab results. We were sitting on my veranda going over the analysis. "What do you think of this?" he asked impassively, handing me a sheaf of tables. I scanned down the thirty-three items on the soil-analysis sheets. Some of the categories were familiar: pH, texture, moisture content, color, exchangeable cations. Other terms, including "ECe" left me blank.

I shrugged. "OK, Charlie, what are you getting at? You're the soil scientist, not me."

He leaned over and jabbed at the ECe figures. "Look! Look! The figures are high in dead stands, low in live stands."

His excitement was beginning to get the better of his carefully composed scientific detachment, and he couldn't repress a grin. "Salinity, Jonah! Salinity! Salt is killing the trees. Here, I've plotted tree condition against salinity in this graph. Look at this. All the dead stands are on saline soils, all the live ones on nonsaline soils. The saline soils have so much salt that only salt-tolerant plants can survive. Fever trees need fresh water and are intolerant of salt."

Charlie's forestry credentials and his graph, which neatly divided the woodland into dead and living trees, won me over. In the dead plots the levels of salt ran so high that the trees could not suck up the water from the salt and were dying of "physiological drought," as he put it. Here was the mystery killer lurking in the soil, the white salt encrustation the explorer Joseph Thomson had noted in 1883. No wonder everyone had missed it. Once discovered, it explained the transition from moisture-loving to arid vegetation, especially the invasion of the salt bush, *Suaeda monoica*. All that remained was to explain how the salt levels rose and killed the trees with the rapidity of a plague.

"The trees need more water as they get older and therefore suck up salt to the surface and eventually die from dehydration," Charlie ventured. "When the trees die off, the more salt-tolerant bushes like *Suaeda* take over."

I didn't care for this explanation, even if Charlie was the forester. It smacked too much of suicide for my liking.

Charlie's departure for Nairobi left me excited and puzzled. It was time for another trip to Observation Hill to look for new clues. The answer had to be there, reflected in the distribution of vegetation, if only I could read the patterns.

Patterns! Suddenly I had it: the water table, my original hunch. The water table must surely rise and fall with rainfall in wet and dry cycles. The rise and fall in the water table would affect salt levels in the soil and mediate the woodland cycle. As the rainfall increased, the water table would rise, bringing salt to the surface and killing the trees. In droughts, the opposite would happen: the water table would fall, salt levels would decline, and the trees would flourish. All I needed was evidence of rainfall cycles coinciding with the growth and die-off of the woodlands.

When I rushed round to Charlie's office on my next trip to Nairobi, he was no more impressed with my rainfall cycles than I had been with his suicide theory. What we needed, he insisted, was hard evidence. Undeterred, I retreated to the University of Nairobi library, knowing that records went back several decades for some East African weather stations. Sure enough, there it was, summarized in the *Geographical Journal* by George Lamb, a British climatologist researching rainfall cycles and lake levels. According to his analysis, lake levels had been high late in the nineteenth century, before falling abruptly during a dry spell in the early twentieth century. After a wet cycle in the 1950s, lake levels rose sharply again. Lake Chala, situated on the eastern slopes of Kilimanjaro forty miles from Amboseli, mirrored the broad climatic oscillations for East Africa. Since

Amboseli's water table depended on the same Kilimanjaro catchment as Lake Chala's, its water table would rise and fall in synchrony.

The clincher was buried in an obscure hydrological report on the cause of flooding in the Sinya meerschaum mine at the south end of Lake Amboseli. According to the consultant, the water table had risen precipitously by more than three meters in the late 1950s, drowning the meerschaum deposits. Flush with excitement, I raced back to Charlie's office. "Got it" I crowed. "Amboseli's woodland cycle neatly fits the rainfall and lake level fluctuations."

This time Charlie was all smiles. Between his salt theory and my water-table cycles, we had finally hit the jackpot.

In due course our results appeared as a lead article in the scientific journal *Nature*, arguing that Amboseli's habitat cycles acted as a sensitive barometer of climatic change for the entire East African region. We proposed that continuous change rather than stability is the norm for savanna ecosystems, with habitats shifting erratically in response to rainfall cycles. The article attracted a good deal of attention from ecologists, anthropologists, and climatologists, establishing my scientific credentials internationally.

But, scientific success offered no more than a transient escape from my real concerns. No amount of counting animals, measuring plants, or digging soil pits could hide my failure to resolve Amboseli's problems. Science was secondary to my love of the African savannas. My true mission, however irrepressibly optimistic, lay in finding a way for people and wildlife to share them amicably in the modern world as they had in the past.

Things went from bad to worse after Sindiyo left. The Kajiado County Council assigned a new warden with a nervous disposition and more interest in the bottle than in the reserve. He was eventually sacked for embezzling funds and gross incompetence, but not before destroying Sindiyo's hard-won gains. Under the new warden, everything centered upon the tourist tip. Minibuses banded together to chase gazelle into waiting cheetah and careened recklessly around the basin ripping up the soils and grasses. One morning I rushed over at the sound of distant shots to find Kibori, my old escort, trying to finish off a gut-shot impala with a decrepit .303. "The warden told me to shoot something for the lions so that he can show the tourists and get a big tip," he explained.

The Maasai, no longer deterred by rangers, herded their cattle onto the front lawn of the lodge. Making matters worse, the warriors, egged on this time by the elders, protested rumors of a government takeover by killing six rhinos from mid-October to mid-November 1969, pushing the population below forty. At that rate, the rhinos' extinction stood barely five years away. Far from winning public sympathy, the warriors' vendetta gave the international media a new and compelling excuse to press for a national park, playing straight into the government's waiting hands.

Weeks dragged into months. When 1970 arrived, there was still no response to my report from either Royal Little or the Ministry of Tourism and Wildlife. Loath as I was to lobby in Nairobi, my funding was running out. Then Parashino said something that galvanized me into action. "When the stomach is empty the mind must think," he told me cryptically, referring to how the Maasai would respond to the coming drought.

On my next trip to Nairobi I took Parashino's maxim to heart and dropped in on the Ministry of Tourism and Wildlife, determined to lobby for the Maasai park. Unless something could be done soon, the government would step in to preserve Amboseli and its lucrative tourist industry. Taking the crowded elevator of New Jogoo House, I was directed to a former colonial civil servant.

"Good, I've been wanting to meet you, Mr. Western. About this report of yours. Makes damn fine sense, I must say. But with the Kajiado County Council buggering up the reserve and the Maasai spearing the hell out of the rhinos, how can you possibly expect the Maasai to manage a park of their own? We have to think about the larger national and international interests at stake, you know."

I protested and began to argue, knowing this was the last chance. "Give us time, at least until the dust has settled after the elections and Oloitiptip doesn't have to worry about votes. I'm sure he can sell the idea of a Maasai park again, knowing the alternatives."

The government adviser looked irritated. "There's too much at stake. Too much publicity and international pressure for the government to sit back and wait, I'm afraid. I'll write up my report bearing your recommendations in mind, but it's up to higher powers from here on." Irked at my persistence, he got up from his desk and ushered me out.

Undeterred, I felt the time had come to push hard. Desperate for funds to continue, I went to the Ford Foundation offices in Silo Park

House. My luck was in. Ecology, once an arcane subdiscipline of biology, was circulating in the foundation world as the solution to every environmental ill from industrial pollution to range degradation. For the first time, the logic of studying human ecology was catching on as dangers of throwaway consumerism and industrial pollution in the West and runaway Malthusian growth in the Third World caught the media's attention. With the rise of environmentalism, the universities that had once shunned research on "unnatural" ecosystems were all too ready to embrace human ecology, particularly if it meant a new source of funds. Attitudes were changing at the Serengeti Research Institute, too. Pressured by the Tanzanian government, the institute had turned to the Ford Foundation for funds to study the threat of poaching, agriculture, and ranching to the national park. Fortunately, I had three years' start when it came to human ecology, and the Ford Foundation gave me a two-year travel and study grant to draw out the broader, global lessons of the Amboseli case study.

In a second stroke of good luck, Frank Mitchell was appointed adviser to the Ministry of Finance and Economic Planning, a position which gave him the ear of powerful decisionmakers in government and, through the national purse strings, an influence on the policies of the Ministry of Tourism and Wildlife. Mitchell was in an ideal position to make Amboseli the golden model he had seen with such prescience during our earlier collaboration.

Both Mitchell and I recognized the dangers of a unilateral government takeover of Amboseli. Driven more by concern than by enthusiasm this time, we spent weeks exchanging ideas and working up economic figures to justify our case. Then, out of the blue, President Kenyatta announced that the government would annex the 200 square miles I had proposed as a Maasai park.

I was stunned. Surely the government knew how the Maasai would react? The warriors would spear the remaining rhinos and start on the lions and elephants too, to say nothing of burning the swamps. Then again, perhaps the government didn't care, given its contempt for the Maasai. The only glimmer of hope in Kenyatta's announcement was that he made no mention of the annexed land becoming a national park, leaving open the prospects of somehow cutting the Maasai in on Amboseli's wildlife.

Oloitiptip had the same thought when he took a large delegation of

Maasai to see Mzee, or the Old Man, as Kenyatta was known. The delegation got the annexation reduced by 50 square miles. This small victory did no more than keep alive Maasai hopes of further compromises and an eventual share in revenues. Without a firm statement of what the government intended to do with the other 150 square miles, Mitchell and I worked on a damage-control plan to ensure Maasai participation. Fortunately, Mitchell's powerful connections gave us two openings.

The first involved a livestock program aimed at developing the rangelands, including wildlife-rich Maasailand, for commercial beef ranching. On hearing of the plan, Mitchell and I hurriedly assembled our economic projections and went along to see the World Bank and government officials involved in appraising the $40 million project. Our message was simple: the value of wildlife in areas like Amboseli is greater than livestock. You stand to write off wildlife in Kenya if the livestock plan goes ahead. Worse, the Maasai will be deprived of an enormous economic asset far more valuable than commercial beef ranching. If wildlife is included in the program, everyone stands to gain and the World Bank and the government of Kenya will be spared the environmentalists' wrath.

Fortunately, the economists saw the logic of our proposal more readily than the wildlife fraternity did. Select three key wildlife areas, pull together policy guidelines, rough out a plan and budget, and the consultants will finagle something into the loan agreement, we were told. In fact the economics of wildlife looked so favorable when compared with the livestock figures the consultants were busily massaging to acceptable levels that the World Bank urged the government to submit a separate proposal for tourism and wildlife based on the Amboseli model. If all this seemed a convoluted way of saving elements of the original plan, I wasn't going to argue. On the contrary, wising up to the ways of policy wonks, we saucily slipped in local participation as a precondition of the livestock loan agreement between the bank and government. This move would commit the Ministry of Tourism and Wildlife to local participation as a precondition of its own funding from the World Bank in the near future.

The second opening came from the New York Zoological Society. The World Bank, though warming to the idea of balancing conservation and development, fretted about the response of conservation groups. The last thing the Bank wanted was a roasting from the environmentalists for letting the Maasai get a foot back in Amboseli after Kenyatta had annexed the land for wildlife. With New York Zoological already committed to the program through Royal Little's money and the foresight of the society's director, Bill Conway, the credibility of a blue-chip conservation organization tipped the World Bank's hand. If the prestigious New York Zoological was for it, there must be something to this newfangled approach, even if it sounded more like economics than preservation.

With a bit of backroom diplomacy and a touch of economic shoe-shine, coexistence was back in the cards for Amboseli.

‹ 8 ›

Drought

NOTHING IN FIVE YEARS of research had prepared me for the signs of drought I saw when I drove across the basin flats of Amboseli in August 1973 after an eighteen-month stint in Nairobi, writing up my thesis and lecturing at the university to make ends meet after my Ford Foundation grant ran out.

Bumping over the washboard road in a brand-new Toyota Land Cruiser donated by the New York Zoological Society, along with a new grant for my research and conservation work over the next three years, I had every reason to feel on top of the world. The time in Nairobi had had another useful outcome: the Ministry of Tourism and Wildlife had asked me to prepare a detailed management plan and investment budget for Amboseli in collaboration with economist Philip Thresher. The plan, spelling out the principles of local participation and the need to involve the Maasai in benefits accruing from Amboseli, provided a blueprint for a $35 million wildlife and tourism loan from the World Bank to the Kenya government. The conservation and development plan would be the largest ever contemplated for Africa.

Although the break and the company of friends in Nairobi had been enjoyable, I had missed the solitude and stark beauty of Amboseli; it was time for another long spell in the bush. But this was not the Amboseli I had known.

Gone was the sea of ruffled yellow grass hiding gazelle fawns from the searching eyes of cheetahs. Grazed-down tufts of grass barely broke through the miniature sand dunes blanketing the plains. Few animals were to be seen, apart from the odd Thomson's gazelle patrolling its barren territory enveloped in a shroud of white dust.

The drought had been a long time coming. It had begun imperceptibly, due more at first to the swollen herds than to lack of rain. Then, from 1969 on, an inexorable decline set in, culminating in severe drought in 1973. Thousands of bones hidden by long grass in wet years now lay exposed and bleaching in the sun. Where were all the animals?

The answer lay behind my house. Tens of thousands of animals clustered back to back on the dwindling greenery of the swamps, ripping at the grass with monotonous intensity. Never had I seen such a spectacular concentration of animals. Elephants had pushed deep into the permanent swamps, their backs barely visible in the tall rushes. Buffalo, still in large herds, grazed the beaten-down margins of the marsh. Zebra and wildebeest nosed through the swamp-edge thickets previously shunned for lack of grass and fear of lions. Thomson's gazelle and warthog nibbled on the heavily grazed outer lawns around the thickets. The browsing animals— Grant's gazelle, rhino, giraffe, bush buck, and lesser kudu—occupied the scrub and thinning fever-tree patches.

How could so many animals survive in such a tiny area? Emaciated as they looked, few had died of starvation. I felt a tingle of excitement as a new and unexpected insight bubbled up. Of course: elephants had thinned out the thickets of Sodom apple and *Pluchea* shrub, allowing a dense sward of cynodon grass to penetrate, providing a new pasture for zebra and wildebeest. The elephants had also trampled and chewed down the ten-foot-tall rushes, enabling prostrate and palatable sedge species to colonize the wetland margins and proliferate. Small knots of zebra and wildebeest had discovered the new lush growth trailing the elephants' steady push into the swamp.

The swamp, acting like a giant sponge, kept replenishing the pastures as the elephants foraged harder in the thickets and swamp. Five years earlier, in a time of plenty, it had been hard to understand how so many species of herbivores could coexist in Amboseli. The drought made it abundantly clear.

The coexistence of so many species comes down to niche specialization, the ecological slot each species occupies. At the extremes, niche separation is easily discerned. A giraffe browsing fifteen feet in the trees cannot exploit the forage eaten by the hare, a foot above the ground, and vice versa. The more similar two species are in size, anatomy, and physiology, the more their feeding niches overlap. Both the wildebeest and buffalo feed on the same waist-high sward in Serengeti: a million and a half wildebeest on the march make serious inroads on buffalo forage and numbers.

Niche separation takes on undue importance in ecology because the degree of overlap should, in principle, determine the degree of competition between species and, ultimately, the number of species that can pack into a single habitat. Niche differentiation, measured by feeding specialization, has long intrigued ecologists, especially in the African savannas, where as many as twenty herbivores share the range. How do species coexist in such arid conditions? Does the wealth of mammalian life imply that savannas are richer in plant species than temperate regions—or that the niches themselves are divided more finely?

The answer has both theoretical and practical implications. Theoretically, narrow niches imply keen competition and specialized feeding adaptations, brought about by a long history of coevolution. In practical terms, coevolved clusters of species such as the East African plains herbivores should be more productive than simpler groupings of recent invaders such as livestock.

Feeding specialization lies at the root of ecologists' claim that wild species are ecologically more efficient and less destructive than livestock. For example, Lee Talbot, who followed up Grzimek's work in Serengeti, claimed that the savanna could support six times as much wildlife (measured in terms of live weight) as livestock. David Hopcraft set out to prove this theory on his father's game ranch on the Athi Plains, thirty miles from Nairobi.

In the 1960s, ecological theory, conservation philosophy, and economic aspirations all hinged on the assumption that narrow niches existed. The only problem with the narrow-niche hypothesis was that it hadn't been proved. Hugh Lamprey, director of the Serengeti Research Institute, touched on the question during research at Tarangire Game Reserve in Tanzania and showed subtle differences in habitat choice and feeding selection among large herbivores. What he did not establish was how closely feeding niches were divided.

Desmond Vesey Fitzgerald, a genial naturalist working in Rukwa

Game Reserve in southern Tanzania, made the startling observation that large herbivores don't actually coexist in one place so much as follow one another in migratory sequence—a grazing succession—with buffalo moving onto the floodplain grasslands ahead of zebra, topi, and gazelle. The grazing succession, he suggested, not only reflects different feeding requirements but actually depends on the larger herbivores "preparing" the pasture for the smaller animals which follow in their wake.

These heady findings implied not only niche separation but also a tightly interdependent herbivore community which, through the grazing succession, boosted range production.

Amboseli is a simpler ecosystem than Serengeti in terms of plant species, despite having as many large herbivores. What explains the richness of herbivores on such poor grasslands? How do they manage to avoid intense competition through grazing succession?

The short-grass plains wither and dry before the migrants return and are unresponsive to grazing animals; they show no regrowth when grazed. Grazing succession must therefore be determined largely by the different energy needs and digestion patterns of the buffalo, zebra, wildebeest, and gazelle. Much as the buffalo would prefer to stay on the short sweet grasses favored by Thomson's gazelle, but their huge energy need compels them to abandon the palatable pastures in search of bulkier forage sooner than smaller animals. The zebra and wildebeest follow in order of body size and energy need. The tiny Thomson's gazelle, needing the least food, manages to stay longest and to get by on the sparsest fresh growth.

The swamp, on the other hand, is highly responsive to grazing. The elephants pushing into the marshes in search of bulk forage inadvertently chew and crush the course sedges, stimulating secondary growth of grasses and sedges. Buffalo, taking advantage of nature's bulldozer, penetrate the swamps to graze the new growth. Zebra, wildebeest, and gazelle follow suit, taking advantage of the greater visibility and lower predation hazard as well as fresh growth. Active interaction between animals is the secret of the swamp's wealth and abundance of species. Were it not for elephants, Longinye would be a drab marsh devoid of plains species.

If it took a drought to explain Amboseli's wealth of wild animals, what of coexistence between the Maasai and wildlife? How did the Maasai and their livestock fit into the picture and survive the struggle for existence?

The wind was blasting across the basin when I headed for camp. Stopping briefly at a small grove of regenerating trees surveyed in 1968, I was dismayed to find hundreds bent and twisted, looking as if they had been caught in the path of a cyclone. No sooner had Charlie and I published our findings than drought and elephants challenged our theory. Our theory predicted water-table and salt levels dropping and trees recovering during droughts. Instead, the acacias were going down like nine pins, destroyed by elephants, not salt. Rather than abandon our carefully researched hypothesis, I surmised that drought was forcing elephants into the basin in unusual numbers, temporarily suppressing tree regeneration. Content with this explanation, I turned my attention to the more important question of how the Maasai were doing. Empaash, a kilometer south of Longinye Swamp, was a good place to start.

The scene where the elders had arbitrated our ilmodiok war five years ago had changed from a verdant woodland into a Sahelian landscape stripped of any plant life except a few wiry clumps of grass and scraggly bushes. Soft, acrid dust swirled up, enveloping my vehicle. Dozens of dead cattle littered the trails to every settlement. The outlying carcasses lay parched and mummified where they had fallen, untouched by herders or predators. Closer in, animals had been skinned but not butchered, despite the famine. Stepping out of the car, I was met by a gust of hot wind and wondered how Amboseli could ever recover.

Kerenkol came out to greet me. I had first met him at a warrior settlement below Kitirua Hill in 1969 when he became spokesman for the warriors. His regal bearing and shy demeanor had impressed me immediately, but we had difficulty communicating because he understood no Swahili and I no Maasai. Since then he had matured and lost most of his reserve. We had become good friends.

"Our herds are dying," he told me in passable Swahili after we exchanged greetings. "We are in big trouble. Our cattle are so thin they are worthless, and we have no money to buy *posho* [maize meal]."

"Why don't you eat the meat of those dead cows?" I asked, pointing at the carcasses scattered along the trails.

"They are thin and have no fat left by the time they die. Sheep and goat still have some meat on them, but mostly we eat posho. We skin the dead cows and sell the hides in Loitokitok at twenty shillings each to buy posho. It's a long way, though, and sometimes our donkeys die of weakness. Can you take me?"

I agreed, but first there was another call to make.

Parashino looked older and thinner when I found him at Risa on the Eremito Ridge. Wrinkles trenched his eyes, and he was uncharacteristically withdrawn and defensive. "Would you like tea?" he asked. "I have only *chai kafu* [dry tea]. Our cows are dying and give no milk. My family eats posho four days out of six to save eating all our sheep and goats." He showed no hint of regret or irony in eating the food of the farmers he had once disparaged.

For the thirty-mile trip to Loitokitok, Parashino and Kerenkol filled the back of the Toyota with crackling, sun-dried skins sharp with the smell of salt. Droning up the lower slopes of the mountain we passed dozens of Maasai plodding behind donkeys piled high with bolts of skin, making for the Saturday market a day-and-a-half walk away.

My first stop was at the crowded market to buy a few vegetables. Kilimanjaro rose sharply behind the barbed-wire fence, towering over the tin-roofed stores strung along the one-street town. Kikuyu women in bright flowered dresses, head scarves, and homespun shawls squatted behind handfuls of potatoes and tomatoes. Maasai women wearing ocher sarongs and aquamarine underskirts sauntered past, giggling and pointing at my mop of hair bleached white as a mane. "Olngatuny," lion, they bubbled through their laughter.

After stocking up on supplies, I drove up the brick-red main street deeply eroded by runoff from the mountain. Far below, the green thread of the Lolterish River and the verdant stab of the Kimana Swamp broke through the dust haze. Half a dozen spiraling dust devils meandered lazily across bleakness. A throng of grimy Maasai were milling about under the corrugated tin roof of the trading store when we drove up. "Ondoka, ondoka," get out, an Indian trader was shouting at an elderly Maasai elbowing his way to the front of the crowd. Parashino pushed his way through, hoping my presence would make a difference. He had no better luck. "Why are you charging more than the government price for posho? You know we are poor and hungry," he carped.

"If you don't like it, go. Go find a better price," the Indian shouted back over the haggling voices and the blare of a transistor radio. He knew, as they did, that the Maasai had no option. Most of them had already walked a day or more to sell their skins and buy posho, and the next trading post was miles off in Tanzania. The traders preyed on the Maasai's vulnerability by halving the price of skins and tripling the price of posho. All the frustrated herders could do was to shout and swear. Twenty shillings a cow skin barely kept a family alive for three days, but three days was better than starvation.

The dust, heat, and haggling got to Parashino. "Let's go," he said, hefting a ninety-pound sack of maize into the Toyota. "This is bad. Bad. How can the Maasai survive if they are cheated like this?"

On the drive back to Amboseli dozens of skinny donkeys staggered under the weight of heaving sacks trailed by leaden-faced herders.

There was no escape from the suffering, not even at my house. Sitting on the veranda at midday, I watched a wildebeest and her calf give up the will to live. Their hides were drawn tight round a barrel of protruding bones. At first they stood head low and aimless. Eventually they sank to the ground and lay on a small mound, struggling pitifully to regain their feet as the herds passed by. Soon they gave up altogether and merely nodded their heads pathetically. They became oblivious to the battering afternoon dust storms, and by the time the calf died on the third day, its eyes had taken on the vacancy of death. Two days later its mother sank into a torpor and died of cold in the early morning.

Even the lodge offered no respite. The tourist talk was as insipid as it was galling. "Say, Joe, did you see the lions? And all those wildebeest? Like something out of a movie, eh? Just wonderful. Hey, look, Maasai." And up would go the long lenses, trained on a group of women plodding along the road, weak and dejected in the sweltering heat.

If my house was no hiding place from drought, at least it offered some consolation. In the first gray light the little plain outside heaved with anticipation. The long lines of zebra and wildebeest filed silently into the swamp thickets, jittery at the slightest rustle. A delicate veil of dust trailed the animals until they reached the densely matted grasses at the edge of the swamp. Occasionally, the drum of hooves and rush of bodies pinpointed lions in a thicket; otherwise the herds spent the day feeding in head-down intensity.

At dusk the herds made for the open plain, the zebra weaving in and out, braying to reassemble their families, the wildebeest calves stotting in head-up anxiety bleating for their mothers—all cascading in a roiling stream of bodies through howling winds and blinding dust to the safety of the open plains. Finally, an hour after dark, the herds hunkered down against the bitter cold night in a raft of bodies.

One night the herds stampeded past me like a cavalry charge, their hurtling stretched-out bodies flashing out of the dust and swerving round my inert form before thundering off into the gloom. When the ranks finally thinned and rumbled off into the distance, a lone Maasai came stumbling like a drunk out of the solanum thicket, groping panic-stricken toward the flicker of lodge lights.

Drought also brought a delightful unexpected intimacy. The zebra and wildebeest eventually became so absorbed in feeding and so lethargic from malnutrition that nothing but the gravest danger spooked them. One or two animals would momentarily lift their heads as I approached to within ten feet and would stare at me with blank, incurious eyes before resuming their feeding. I often sat quietly within a herd absorbing its ethos—the sniffing mouths and shuffling feet, the musty sweat and nutty dung, the agile prehensile lips, the latent tension between adjacent animals—and the constant vigilance.

Approaching to within three feet of a zebra, I watched as its muzzle moved through a tuft of grass. The zebra's extraordinarily long filamentous eyelashes had always puzzled me. Here, close up, their usefulness was obvious. The moment a chewed-off spike jabbed at its face, the zebra's eyelids closed involuntarily at the touch of a guard hair.

My reaction ranged from awe to curiosity and finally despair as the drought hardened. Rationally, this was a unique opportunity to chronicle nature's struggle for survival. But Parashino's maxim about an empty stomach making the mind think didn't help this time. The problem wasn't so much my empty stomach as his—and the wild animals'. The Maasai and wildlife had become such an intimate part of my life that their problems were my problems. I could no more treat them as numbers on a computer coding sheet than I could my own family.

Inexplicably, the serene solitude of the barren lake gave me the resolve I needed to keep going. Quite why desert bleakness brings inner peace and clarity, whether to Mohammed, Christ, or lesser mortals, eludes me. Perhaps the sense of endless space, infinite time, and lifeless earth strips away all but the irreducible and self-evident, leaving us humbled and grateful to be those rarest of all things in the universe, sentient beings.

Whatever the reason, a long, hard walk across the wind-swept flats cured me. Think, plan, act, think, plan, act, I kept repeating in a mindless mantra. My debilitating self-pity seemed so utterly selfish and pointless in the face of all the suffering. Nothing but my own introspection stood in the way of doing something to find a solution to Amboseli acceptable to the government and Maasai alike.

◀ ◀ ◀

BY 1973 I WAS stretched tight as a drum, struggling to coordinate fourteen agencies in Nairobi and consulting with the New York Zoological Society in the United States. At the same time I was continuing my research, writing reports and scientific papers, and trying to maintain my contacts with the Maasai.

Faced with weekly seven-hour round trips to Nairobi, I plucked up the courage to ask New York Zoological to buy me a plane to cut the commuting time to Nairobi and expand my research program. Royal Little, who had become a good ally and generous financial supporter after our bad start, came through once more.

I had barely earned my wings at the time and eagerly checked out on the tail-dragging Cessna with four seats and the registration sign 5Y-TCL, or Five Yankee Tango Charlie Lima, as it was called in radio parlance. "There are only two types of 180 pilots," my instructor told me gleefully, "those who've ground-looped and those who are about to." I was too thrilled at getting into the air and down to Amboseli to heed him. Kerenkol, who often accompanied me on my drives around Amboseli, lost no time asking for a flight in Charlie Lima to check out the new machine. I strapped him in and pulled up sharply into a gusting headwind. The ground fell away abruptly beneath us.

"Sheeye!" he gasped in exhilaration and alarm, peering down at the receding ground. I banked sharply right, his side. He pulled away from the yawning void and caromed off me. "Sheeye!" he gasped again, battling to keep his warrior cool. "We are so high." After recovering his bravado, he pointed out a settlement several miles ahead on Eremito Ridge. "Over there. My boma. I want to look in the thickets. The herd boys tell me a rhino which chases our cows hides out there."

Kerenkol soon became as familiar with Amboseli from the air as he was from the ground. He used the plane to make rapid herding decisions which took warrior scouts days to make on the ground. In verbalizing his observations and decisions as we flew around Amboseli, Kerenkol gave me a deep insight into the pastoral mind and the importance of migration. At the end of one hard dry season, when thousands of cattle were dying and the new calves faced starvation, he directed me east, over the path of light rains which had fleetingly blown off the Chyulus Hills to the east of Amboseli. The thirty-mile trek across barren ground was sure to kill off scores of emaciated animals before they reached the new growth. Should he risk it or not?

Most Maasai had decided to stay put on the basis of fragmentary secondhand information. Kerenkol, who wanted to scout things out for himself, sat twisting this way and that in the plane, plotting the safest route to the grassy ridges. A few small pockets of green grass along the route from Amboseli apparently made all the difference. "I move tomorrow," he yelled excitedly. "I've found a way."

A day later he moved to the Chyulus with a handful of fellow herders. He lost fewer than a quarter of his calves that season. The Maasai who stayed lost most of their immature animals and many adults.

The 1973 drought changed many things, including my ideas about elephants and their future. In 1972 I had invited Harvey Croze, a lecturer at the university, to study the Amboseli population, arguing that it was one of the few herds anywhere still relatively undisturbed and using its age-old migratory pathways. He chose Cynthia Moss, formerly a research assistant to Iain Douglas-Hamilton, to help. Croze was a stocky, sandy-haired American with John Lennon glasses, a bushy mustache, and a fondness for sleeveless safari jackets. He had studied under the Nobel Prize–winning behaviorists Nikko Tinberg and Konrad Lorenz before conducting research on the elephants in Serengeti and moving on to a lectureship at the University of Nairobi. Croze's regular presence in Amboseli and experience in bush piloting gave us an opportunity to collaborate on aerial counts of the Amboseli ecosystem every couple of months.

"Hey, seems a lot of elephant carcasses here," Harvey yelled above the engine roar on our first count. "I can't believe they died of drought." He twisted back to observers in the rear. "Count any carcass you see." Even before we landed we knew that Amboseli's elephants were under assault from the Somali poachers killing animals by the thousands in adjacent Tsavo National Park.

We shot off a letter to Sindiyo the moment we got back to Nairobi. Sindiyo's star had risen since leaving Amboseli; he was now the deputy to the Game Department's chief warden and thus well placed to do something about the poaching. More than 250 elephants have been killed for ivory around Amboseli in the last year, we wrote to Sindiyo, and something has to be done to save the remainder. We got no reply. This was not the Sindiyo I knew. His silence gave substance to rumors of Game Department complicity in an ivory racket reaching into the highest political circles. Nothing less would muzzle Sindiyo.

The poaching scourge, according to Ian Parker, who had become undisputed ivory maven after his elephant-culling days in Murchison Falls National Park, involved top politicians—the ivory czars—who used "ivory collectors" licensed by the Game Department to turn in "found" ivory. Although rewards for found tusks originated as a colonial practice, the newly licensed collectors were hirelings of the Game Department and political godfathers. The collection licenses gave them legal cover to poach elephants with impunity under the pretext of having "found" the ivory on dead animals.

Despite the political patronage, the international storm brewing over the elephant slaughter, captured by news crews from all over the world, forced the chief warden to act. His response—a ban on elephant hunting and a call for a public seminar to discuss the problem—outwardly placated conservationists. But given the fact that sport hunters never killed more than a few dozen elephants a year, the hunters suspected that the ban was simply a ruse to protect poachers and their ivory czars from detection. As for the seminar, it verified the poaching crisis, but that was all.

Held at the University of Nairobi, the meeting drew a crowd of biologists, hunters, and conservationists, all of them white. Peter Jarman, a research biologist in the department, got everyone to contribute data and make an estimate of Kenya's elephant population. The total, 160,000, surprised everyone until Parker cut through the illusion. In a bravura performance he wove a tapestry of innuendo and intrigue, leaving no doubt about the involvement of the Game Department and high-level political backing. Oddly, he explained the poaching losses as the outcome of human population growth, not demand for ivory. No one challenged his assertion at the time, and why should they have? His command of the facts and gutsy forthrightness were nothing less than heroic.

The seminar had only two consequences: Parker received a visit from security personnel, who told him to shut up or face the consequences; and Jarman was forced to leave Kenya. The Game Department, according to one official I spoke to, dismissed the seminar as a racist attack on its exemplary conservation record.

The wholesale elephant slaughter first documented in Kenya would metastasize through Africa in the coming decade, instigated as often as not by government officials. Learning that Amboseli's poaching problems were not exceptional offered little consolation. No sooner had Harvey Croze and Cynthia Moss embarked on a study of an "undisturbed" elephant population than half its numbers were eliminated and the migrations disrupted. The impact would affect the entire ecosystem and severely deplete Amboseli's biological diversity.

Ecological research seemed arcane, almost irreverent, among the stinking cattle carcasses and agonized Maasai faces—so much so that I regularly took to the air to shut out the misery and get a dispassionate view of things. Seen from 15,000 feet, the arid bush extended in all directions, dwarfing the green specks of swamp and dark smudges of acacia woodland. The swamps appeared tiny and fragile, an altogether improbable bulwark against drought for the 50,000 wildlife and livestock crowded into Amboseli. Back on the ground, with a sense of perspective recaptured, I refocused on the big unanswered questions, ready to pry the answer from the dying herds and troubled minds of the Maasai themselves.

Once again Parashino drew me deeper into his world to supply the answers, although he had a motive which was not apparent at the time.

"Yonah," he told me, "We are already supen. It is time for us to become *pakiteng* [cattle partners]. I will give you two cows. Accept them as a gift from me. They will be yours to herd and look after. You must see Amboseli through the eyes of a cow. Only then will you understand its importance to the Maasai. Look, this white cow is Sotwa. And that black one over there is Martingab. They are yours. Come, see them often. Herd them. Watch them. You will learn quickly."

Sotwa and Martingab became my passport into the savanna world I had researched for seven years. How little I actually knew of that world soon became clear.

Until now, my perspective on Amboseli and the Maasai had been chiefly that of a scientist and conservationist; though conceding that people were an integral part of the African savannas, I still reflexively saw human activity as an "impact" on them. My African upbringing and western scientific training were not fully reconciled; consequently, my views on the role of humans in that landscape were somewhat schizophrenic. I could and did act in dichotomous intellectual and emotional worlds, depending on whether I was rationalizing the continued presence of the Maasai in the Amboseli ecosystem or reacting to incursions of their cattle into the wildlife sanctuary.

Becoming a cattle owner brought me face to face with this contradiction. From now on I accepted Maasai livestock as a natural element in the ecological landscape on an emotional as well as intellectual plane. As a cattle owner I took a deep interest in Sotwa and Martingab to the point of becoming loving and protective, just like Parashino. My reaction made sense, for in getting to know and name these animals they become as sentient and sympathetic as the sable antelope and, in their way, just as intriguing.

Soon I could instantly pick out Sotwa and Martingab and trail them through the herd, captivated by what Parashino referred to as a cow's-eye view of Amboseli. The snuffling and wrenching of grass, the waft of fresh dung, and the perpetual motion of cows fanning out in the open and funneling back together in dense bush became my entire world for hours on end. Against all my instincts, I worried about Sotwa's and Martingab's welfare and survival. What had become of me since Meshanani Hill in 1968, when I wished every cow dead?

The life of a Maasai herder, so idle and idyllic to the outsider, calls for skill, endurance, and courage. The skill comes in knowing when to leave the boma, the right pastures to select, how fast to push the animals, how to split the herd, when to let them ruminate, rest, and water, when to return to the settlement, how to diagnose and treat sick cows, how much milk to siphon off, how much to leave the calf, and a hundred other details. All this would be hard enough for any rancher raising a dairy herd in arid land. But in addition, the Maasai herder also needs physical strength and courage.

In the dry season, herders set off before dawn and return at dusk after a twenty-mile round trip to grazing and water, enduring temperatures of 100 degrees Fahrenheit, fierce winds, and blinding dust storms. They survive off the milk, meat, and blood of their herds for weeks on end. They also ensure that their livestock thrive alongside wildlife perfectly adapted by millions of years of evolution to herbivorous perfection. Finally, Maasai herders face the most formidable large mammals on earth—elephants, buffalo, and lions—and defend their herds at the risk of their own lives.

Americans and Europeans raised in a setting of high-tech convenience can have no sense of these hardships. Over the months I picked up some of these abstruse skills which Parashino had tried to convey that first day on Eremito Ridge.

Maasai life centers upon cattle, from the time they first inherit an animal or receive it as a gift to the time they build a herd large enough to pay a bride price and marry. Cattle, and to a lesser extent sheep and goats, not only provide their staple diet but also serve as currency in economic and social transactions. Managing a herd entails a complex level of husbandry, financial, and social skills unimaginable to any western rancher.

Parashino had astutely drawn me into his world and won my understanding and sympathy. He would soon cash in on that investment.

As the drought worsened, Sotwa's and Martingab's ribs and hips protruded more and more until it appeared they would burst through the drum-tight skin. By comparison, the emaciated wildebeest were pictures of health. I took this as confirmation of the ecologists' belief that wild herbivores are evolutionarily better adapted to the savannas than livestock. Parashino shrugged when I suggested using domesticated wildebeest instead of cattle.

"We've tried them, and they're not as good," he told me matter-of-factly.

This seemed unlikely, but I listened all the same. He had taught me so much already that I no longer had any pretensions to superior scientific knowledge.

"Are you saying you have tried to herd wild animals and found cattle better?"

"Yes," he said, troubled by my doubting tone. "Before the white man said wild animals belonged to them, that is. We tried eland. We tried buffalo. I knew of two eland kept in cattle herds when I was young. But they didn't survive. Eland must wander far looking for food. If you tame them and herd them like cattle, they grow thin and die."

"But that doesn't mean wildlife are useless," he added as if to console me. "It was the wazungu who made them so. Before the wazungu came we ate wildlife to survive the big droughts. Wild animals were our second cattle, you know. The laiboni told us not to kill them, except when our own animals died. The ancients still tell how warriors bought bows and arrows from the Sonjo near Magadi and hunted wild animals in times of drought."

Parashino's comments hit me like a hammer blow. "Are you telling me Maasai used wildlife as second cattle?" I asked.

"Yes. Why should I lie?"

"Listen," I told him excitedly, "if that is true, surely you can convince other Maasai to save wildlife? It's your tradition, even though everyone believes the Maasai love their cattle too much to bother about wild animals. I have been trying to tell people in Nairobi that wild animals can be useful to the Maasai—and now you have given me the reason you didn't wipe them out like other people did, a reason for protecting them on your land today."

He smiled patiently. "It's true, but it's not that simple. The ancients who understand these things are few and dying out. The young Maasai? Well, they only know wildlife as *ngombe za serikali* [government cattle]. How can we convince them?"

Despite Parashino's reticence on the matter, his story was a breakthrough. His account neatly explained the tolerance Maasai had for wild competitors. Here was the answer I had been looking for, a strong argument, based on traditional practices, for conserving Amboseli's wildlife.

More important, I came to realize that the boundaries of the park I had delineated were unworkable. If the entire swamp were closed to livestock, the Maasai would be marginalized and starve. During droughts their animals packed the swamp no less than wildlife and survived the harsh times feeding on its greenery. Parashino had already told me this, but I had dismissed his worries because I had no idea how vital the swamps were in droughts; I had insisted that the extra grazing opened up by the outlying water points would make up for the lost swamp pastures.

The swamps had always been at the heart of the Maasai's struggle to hold on to Amboseli against all advances. Nothing else so profoundly tied them to the place or made them so fearful of annexation.

The revelation posed an agonizing conundrum. The Maasai could no more lose the swamps and survive than could the wildlife. And yet, as much as they needed the swamps, population growth and the outer world were transforming their lives to the point where they would be inadequate to sustain the Maasai in the future. Fortunately, new opportunities were opening up, making the younger generation more worldly, educated, and mobile than its parents. For Simon Salash, the Maasai in the black-patent shoes on Kitirua Hill, the swamps were no longer the ecological and spiritual centers they were to Parashino.

While the Maasai could change and move on, wildlife didn't have that option. Robbed of the swamps, the elephant and rhino would die out. Did it make sense to favor animals or the Maasai, to focus on the pastoralists' present-day needs, or take a longer view and ignore their suffering for the sake of future generations and all Kenyans?

Deep down, I knew the answer to that question. If the Maasai lost the swamps, they would destroy Amboseli. The future of wildlife lay in their hands one way or another, as they had proved with their protest spearing of rhinos. More than anything, I wanted to get the government and Maasai together to discuss the options openly, rather than face the torment of such a decision alone. For the moment, though, I continued to play ambassador, hoping to keep alive the prospects of winning a place for the Maasai in Amboseli.

However essential my role as a go-between, my greatest enjoyment and revelations came from being among Amboseli's animals, including my cattle. Sotwa and Martingab offered new insights with every visit and soon revealed how intricately intertwined are the social and ecological realms of the Maasai—that in a cattle society who you know is as important as what you know. Parashino clearly understood the interdependence of knowledge and social skills, for it was he who first raised the subject.

"It isn't good to have big herds in a drought. You have to walk them a long way to find enough food. It is better to split them into small herds. You can only do that if you have many children and friends, especially supen and pakiteng, to help herd them. Having many children and friends here and there also helps you build a herd quickly after drought."

Parashino's predicament slowly dawned on me. Despite being a superb herder, he was something of a loner like me. Having skillfully built up his herd during good years, he failed to invest his hard-won gain in social networking. Consequently, in droughts he had few people to call on. Over half of his herd of 350 cattle died in 1973 and 1974, far above the one-third average of other herders. With every dead cow, his confidence waned. Gradually he lost his old cocksure banter and sounded more like Mashakio and less like Kerenkol.

My earlier surmise that population growth among the Maasai would eventually outpace the productivity of their herds and scuttle their subsistence economy proved correct during the drought. Parashino obviously wasn't going to make it, so how was he going to cope? As in all things, he kept his plans to himself. And, true to form, he acted stoically and decisively when the time came.

Parashino returned unexpectedly after several months, looking distinctly pleased with himself. "Come to Endonet. I have a boma there," he urged. Endonet was a farming area up against the forest, an odd place for him to move. "Fine," I told him, "but what are your cattle doing there? It's not like you to graze them there during the dry season."

"No, you don't understand, Yonah. I have a shamba. I'm a farmer," he added proudly.

I shook my head, thinking he was pulling my leg as he often had before the drought years.

"Yes, yes. A shamba—seven acres," he insisted, grinning mischievously.

Convinced he was taking me to a surprise festivity, I drove him up through the thickening thorn scrub toward the mountain along a dirt track deeply incised by dry gullies. The last few miles took us along converging cattle trails to newly worked fields. "My boma," Parashino pointed, directing me along the edge of a hoed patch.

The incongruity of Parashino's traditional boma plunked in the middle of plowed maize fields jolted me. "Why?" I asked angrily. "Why have you become a farmer. You told me the Maasai never dug the earth. You hated farmers."

He looked hurt. "Why? Because the drought killed my cattle. I can't live off my herd any longer. I need a shamba to grow maize, to avoid being cheated by those Loitokitok traders. If I don't get a shamba now, the Kikuyu and Wakamba will steal our land."

The iced mass of Kilimanjaro, foreshortened from his shamba, jutted cold and clear in an azure sky. From Endonet the jagged ice cliffs of Kibo looked more forbidding than the soft ethereal dome seen through the thin filaments of cloud and haze of Amboseli. Close up, the formless blue of the forest became a riot of alien greens, a profusion of foliage erupting from giant trunks.

Parashino walked along the irrigation ditches between the crops, talking volubly about his maize and bean harvest and the prices he expected to get. I stumped behind him incredulous, notebook in hand at his insistence that I record this new life as I had the old. How could he, the most recondite of herders, give up nomadic life to become a farmer? The evident pride he took in this new and alien life offended me. I barely nodded as he kept turning to me for approval.

Parashino called over two laborers digging in the shamba. Both were Warush, cousins of the Maasai, who more than a century earlier had been forced by drought to take up farming on the slopes of Mount Meru, forty miles south of Kilimanjaro. What a paradox he looked, standing there in a maize field in traditional dress as he thrashed the air with his knobkerrie yelling out orders.

By his own account, Parashino had seen the writing on the wall and bought a shamba before all his animals died. Knowing nothing about farming, he had hired two landless Warush on a crop-sharing basis. They were reliable, spoke the same language, and could teach him farming. Once he learned enough, he told me, he would hire daily laborers and double his income. He hadn't given up herding, he insisted. He still sent his remnant herds down to the lowlands when they weren't grazing maize stubble or the forest glades.

For Parashino to abandon Amboseli because he was starving was one thing. To give up the life of a Maasai for that of a peasant farmer so enthusiastically was another matter altogether. It was hard to hide my disappointment. What would become of the Maasai in their new life when the ancient rhythm of migration was stilled by a lattice of national and administrative boundaries and enforced settlement?

Modern African governments eschew the nomad, seeing him as factious, unproductive, and primitive. They have a point. The Somali warlords defy the unifying efforts of the modern nation state with their endless clan fights over figurative waterholes. The reality is that the nomad owes no allegiance and recognizes no ownership of land, except that used and defended momentarily. Oloitiptip's words to Nyerere at the eunoto ceremony kept coming back. "We will not wear trousers, you tell Nyerere that." His defiance reflected a fear of change.

He need not have worried. When the time came, the Maasai buried their fear and embraced a new life with remarkable alacrity.

The more the Maasai way of life crumbled in the drought, the more prescient Parashino's decision appeared. The entire fabric of Maasai life had been frayed thin by population growth and cultural change even before the drought. Drought merely quickened the transition, the changes that affected every family eventually. Simon Salash had become a farmer a decade earlier than Parashino, and Parashino a few years earlier than Kerenkol and Lochokop. Parashino had astutely made a virtue of necessity and leapt into the future, leaving his age mates and me mired in the past.

With Parashino's departure, Kerenkol took his place as my closest friend. It didn't take a clairvoyant to see that he was a man destined for power. The signs had been there in the tall gaunt warrior spokesman in 1969. By 1974 he had filled out and moved more languorously, in keeping with his rising stature. During the drought he forged his quiet confidence into active leadership by taking charge of famine relief. He occasionally wore a safari suit but never discarded his beaded bracelets and earrings. I went through the same formal exchange of friendship Parashino had insisted on, ending with a meat feast.

A meat feast, or *orpul,* is an excuse for warriors and elders to hole up with their closest friends. I jumped at the opportunity to join Kerenkol and six of his age mates. They planned to consume a few bulls before they became too stricken by drought.

The preparation for the feast began with a drug-collecting expedition up the mountain. "This is *endenayi ilkiliriti*," Kerenkol explained as we dug up the roots of *Acacia nilotica*, "and this bark we call *olalaani ilkiliriti*." We dug up more roots and chopped off bark from trees Kerenkol called *ingitaro, olndemigomi,* and *embenge* and dumped them in a bag. We were all in high spirits by the time we found a secluded palm grove in Ol Tukai Orok and stacked up a thorn boma dense enough to keep out lions. The warriors stripped off their jewelry, wrapped it up in spare shukas, and tucked them away in the back of the thorn corral. A meat feast was a time to shed all the encumbrances of life and enjoy themselves.

My gift, a large black bull, was brought to the grove from a settlement at Eremito. The animal bellowed loudly when one of the warriors forced it onto its brisket. A massive man with blacksmith's hands, he positioned himself behind the bull's neck, held a double-bladed knife against its axial vertebra, and, in a single swift hammer blow with his fist, severed the spinal cord. Showing not a twinge of emotion, the warrior slashed a swatch of green grass and thrust it into the wound to staunch the blood before wrestling the bull onto its side. He then sliced through the jugular and let the blood drain into the skin of the dewlap before slopping it into a gourd.

The other warriors began meticulously dismembering the carcass. Nothing went to waste. Soft viscera likely to rot first were diced, fried, mixed with blood, and boiled in fat to preserve them. The vile-looking mixture, called *ngirdi,* was stored in a pot for later consumption. The yellow-green tripe squeezed from the bull's intestine was boiled and eaten with soup, and the bones were broken open to extract the marrow.

We began the orpul with roast meat cooked over a wood fire, gripping long slabs in our teeth and slicing off bite-sized chunks with a sharp knife. An hour of steady eating later, my gut was filled like a balloon, and I lay back sick at the smell of blood and roasting flesh. Strips of meat, viscera, and entrails hung on racks above my head. Was there not a hint of symbolism in all this, some ceremonial reincarnation as a lion, the animal they most feared and admired?

Kerenkol laughed as if reading my thoughts. "Jonah, you need some ilkiliriti. It will make you eat like a lion. You will see. And ndemigomi. It will ease the pain and stop diarrhea."

He stirred a huge aluminum pot of viscera and bark. The stench was overwhelming. The glutinous mass tasted like suet mixed with bitter herbs but worked wonders. Within an hour the stomach cramps had vanished and my appetite was back. When we stretched out to sleep my body trembled involuntarily with protein toxicity as if convulsed by mild electric shocks. My mind was a flurry of vivid dreams and wild hallucinations. Swarms of minor quakes regularly shuddered through Amboseli that year from an epicenter low on the mountain. "Is that my body or the earthquake I feel trembling?" Kerenkol yelled out, sending us into fits of laughter.

We consumed three bulls and three sheep over the next three weeks, an average of six pounds of meat each a day. Milk is forbidden during an orpul, so we slaked our thirst on the fatty soup, lay around, talked, slept, and ate again. "The *ngitaro* makes warriors brave," Kerenkol told me as he emulsified the fatty soup with a vertebra stuck on the end of a long stick. "*Embenge* protects us against the heat and cold and gives us strength, strength to run far and fight hard. This is how we used to prepare for battle and for cattle raids."

The meat feast made the warriors nostalgic for the days when the Maasai raided as far as the coast 150 miles away. They lay around talking and singing of great raids and heroic deeds for days on end. Raids were a thing of the past, though, and their talk took on a maudlin tone. Their spirits revived when someone spoke of killing lions and rhinos instead, and I am sure they would have done so were it not for me—and the ring of minibuses surrounding every one.

I left Kerenkol and the warriors to their dreams and emerged from our hideaway to face the task of excising a portion of the swamps for the Maasai.

After a brief trip to Nairobi to win the support of Daniel Sindiyo, the permanent secretary from the Ministry of Tourism and Wildlife, John Koitie, and his under secretary, Ezekiel Nyarangi, I flew back to Amboseli to meet them on the ground. Later that morning we joined a group of warriors and elders in the shade of a fever tree behind Ol Tukai to discuss the swamp excisions. Tourist faces gawked out of minibuses at the two contrasting faces of Kenya: the Maasai in their red robes and ochered hair squatting stoically in a huddle, and opposite them a row of government officials in two-piece suits and ties, fingering their sweating collars. The neat row of officials broke up into an untidy zigzag as the chairs sank in the powdery dust and had to be repositioned.

The district commissioner, dressed in safari jacket and pith helmet, addressed the Maasai in Swahili. Sitonik, the assistant warden, translated into Maasai. The elders were visibly nervous. These were the first direct talks with the government about Amboseli and tacitly accepted Kenyatta's decree that the Maasai would give up the 150 square miles annexed for wildlife. Not until the closing moments of the meeting did the permanent secretary mention the swamp exclusions the Maasai had come to hear about.

The mood of sullen dejection was broken by a momentary pause, then an excited murmur as those who understood Swahili waited for the rest to hear the Maasai translation. Spontaneous applause broke out when Sitonik finished announcing that a portion of the swamps would be excluded from the park for Maasai use. I found myself trying to suppress a rush of emotion. The compromise over a tiny area of swamp spelled the difference between hope and despair for the Maasai—and success and failure for Amboseli.

Immediately after the meeting, Parashino came striding up, grinning broadly. He shook my hand and told me how seriously I had taken my lessons from Sotwa and Martingab. I laughed. Parashino might not have been able to save his herd, but he had certainly had me figured out.

Chief Ole Soimwere, the Maasai spokesman, was in an equally expansive mood. "Western, stay behind," he ordered as the government officials made for the lodge. Then, addressing the Maasai, he pointed at me. "I want you to know that this is the man who got you back the swamps. You are one of us," he added.

Reaching out, he took my hand. "Western, it is time for you to take a Maasai wife and settle down."

‹ *9* ›

A Break in the Weather

I T IS DARK. I AM SITTING ON the veranda on a cold morning, listening to the night sounds die down. A hyena whoops out across the plains as it heads for a communal cubbing den beyond the airstrip. Somewhere by the swamp, a jackal yips sharply. Slowly the sky lightens toward the Chyulu Hills, and a dead tree takes form by the house, its broken limbs pointing like signposts to the fading stars. The upper branches are spiked with orange as the gathering light unveils the familiar landscape, suffusing it with warm, deep colors. A crested francolin yammers harshly behind the house; a hoopoe barely visible, pecks in the soil underneath the tree. Every dawn brings the same refreshing peace and renewal to Amboseli. It is a time to enjoy the sights and sounds and take stock.

Amboseli no longer occupies my every moment. The park is too full of tourists and too familiar to satisfy my curiosity for the unexplored and unknown. I have begun to venture into new areas and new research themes these days, even to travel internationally on behalf of the New York Zoological Society, setting up research and conservation projects. My conservation work is no longer done in isolation, but through a network of colleagues and organizations in Kenya and around the world. To sustain these growing outside interests, I have set up a second home on a ranch rich in wildlife thirteen miles outside Nairobi. Despite Mweyendet's advice, I am not yet ready either to settle down or to move on. Amboseli remains the focus of my research and conservation, a place where I can immediately find the pulse of savanna life.

There is still so much research left to do as the ecosystem changes and the Maasai develop. The decision on Amboseli's conservation status has not yet been made; I feel obligated to see it through. Even when it is, the ecosystem and Maasai will continue changing, posing new threats and calling for new solutions. Conservation never provides a final solution, only a temporary reprieve for wildlife. Amboseli, which I know so intimately, is a microcosm of the African savannas as a whole, a sort of crystal ball which I can peer into to anticipate the changes ahead and test new solutions.

The dialogue between the Ministry of Tourism and Wildlife and Maasai elders began in earnest after the swamp concessions of 1973. Despite Kenyatta's annexation of the 150 square miles of Amboseli, no announcement had been made about how the government intended to manage the area. I was still confident that good sense and fair play would prevail, that government would involve the local Maasai some way, even if a Maasai park as I had originally envisaged it was no longer on the cards. The continuing dialogue was, in fact, a search for a middle ground between a national park and a Maasai park.

It therefore came as a bombshell to hear over the radio in 1974 that President Kenyatta had decreed that the 150-square-mile annex would become a national park. The discussions and the promises about reaching a compromise had been a sham. The presidential decree shattered the dialogue and understanding painstakingly built up over the course of a year. What next? Would the national parks service take over immediately and eject the Maasai without further discussion? Whoever had advised the president needed his head examined.

The usual huddle of Maasai elders around the store at Ol Tukai heard out the radio announcement in malevolent silence. A national park could mean only one thing: they would be evicted without concessions or compensation, as they had been in Serengeti and Tsavo. The Kikuyu government had cheated them no less than the British, uhuru or no uhuru. The Maasai would take Kenyatta's decree as an act of war.

Taking out their anger on the animals wouldn't win any friends for the Maasai. In fact, contrary to my suspicions, it transpired that the county council's virtual abandonment of the game reserve following Kenyatta's original annexation of the 150 square miles and the spearing of the rhinos which followed had tipped the president's hand in favor of a national park.

"Amboseli is bigger than the Maasai," the permanent secretary in the Ministry of Tourism and Wildlife told me when I protested the national park declaration. "We owe it to the national economy . . . and to future generations. Who are the Maasai to hold back the nation and poach wildlife?" As an adviser with no formal standing, I was in no position to protest the presidential decree, however much it sacrificed the Maasai on the altar of the national good.

To sound out the Maasai mood, I picked up Parashino and took him to Longinye for a game drive. He flailed his arms angrily. "Does the government think it can protect all these animals without us? We will burn the swamps, spear the rhinos, and poison the lions. There won't be any animals left in the national park by the time we've finished."

Given the mood of the Maasai, this was no time to protest the animal's innocence. "We'll harass tourists and beat up rangers who cross our land," Parashino yelled. "The government started this fight, not us." I could only nod in agreement. We had come so far in building trust and hope, only to have the presidential decree set Amboseli back all over again.

Within days of Parashino's threat, three elephants, two rhinos, several hyenas, and a lion had been speared by warriors and a litter of leopard cubs clubbed to death near Enkongo Narok. The killing had begun.

Without awaiting instructions from government, the trustees of the Kenya National Parks, under whose jurisdiction the agency fell, held a board meeting in Amboseli under the pretext of taking a break from town. No one was fooled. The meeting sent a clear signal that the trustees were down to grab Amboseli even before a formal handover was negotiated by the Ministry of Tourism and Wildlife. In a brief address I told the trustees that a park modeled upon Serengeti would court disaster, using the rash of recent spearings to warn that Amboseli was dead without Maasai backing.

Perez Olindo, the director who had so deftly diffused the row over culling elephants at Dick Laws's lecture on habitat destruction in Tsavo, took me aside. "Don't worry, Jonah," he reassured me avuncularly. "I hear what you say. I know we have to change our approach to parks, and we will. Believe me. We intend to start here in Amboseli. I'll send down a warden who'll listen and work with you and the Maasai. We'll pretend the boundary doesn't exist for now and come up with a plan agreeable to the Maasai and my board."

Olindo is a man of great charm and compassion, and I was in no position to fight the decision. One of the trustees had already taken me aside and hinted darkly that I was stepping on politically sensitive turf in querying a presidential decree and should watch my step. Fortunately, I had enough credibility in government to get away with it this time, but he was right. No one publicly challenged Kenyatta's decrees.

The best hope, in fact the only conceivable hope, of winning some financial concession for the Maasai lay in convincing the government and trustees to reconsider the role of a national park. If they could be convinced of the wisdom of local participation, there was still a slim chance of pulling off a national park tailored to ecological and local interests. I was so demoralized by the latest setback that it was hard to muster the strength for a new round of lobbying and negotiations. I wasn't even sure the Maasai would want to listen to me after my futile efforts with the government.

The warden Olindo sent down was Joe Kioko, a tall reed-thin Mkamba with a quiet unassuming manner. He didn't impress me as the sort of man to handle a tough assignment, but he proved an astute choice. He quickly reestablished Sindiyo's committee of elders and assured them that Amboseli National Park would be no Serengeti or Tsavo. He was in favor of Maasai participation and would take up where earlier discussions on the modalities had left off. In fact, he added, the Maasai would not have to quit Amboseli until alternative water sources were in place and an agreement on revenue sharing had been reached. Kioko's assurances cooled tempers, although the Maasai remained dubious about the promises and fearful of being banished from the park.

Kioko also rebuilt an operational park out of the dross left by a string of lame-duck wardens after Sindiyo's departure. All the same, Kioko was a warden who represented Olindo and the national parks, an agency known for stealing Maasai land. However hard he tried, he could not play the role of mediator. Everything he did was sure to be seen by the elders as a veiled trick to steal more land. Calming tempers and winning a stake for the Maasai in the new park required impartiality and trust. Sindiyo would have been ideal, but he had transferred to the Game Department after quitting Amboseli. The Game Department was responsible for hunting and game-control programs and had no jurisdiction over national parks. That left only me, despite my past failures and shortcomings.

Sindiyo knew my failings, but he also knew there wasn't anyone else who had the vision or enjoyed the trust of both parties. "You have to do it yourself, Jonah—if you want any Amboseli left to enjoy," he told me. So I took on the job of trying to claw back concessions for the Maasai, knowing he was right. What joy would there be studying a dying ecosystem, and what freedom when the wilds vanished?

The frustrations of being an informal negotiator soon took their toll. The mediation, added to all the research, supervision of the NYZS project, writing, and contacts with the Maasai, became sheer drudgery. I sat through interminable meetings at government ministries disdainful of the World Bank–funded plans for livestock watering points, new viewing circuits, and a headquarters complex, knowing full well the multimillion-dollar investment was worthless without Maasai backing. My combined shyness and determination made me hold back too long, then come on too strong when I did interject, giving the appearance of dogmatism and impatience. This was not the African way among civil servants any more than among the Maasai, and it wasn't my way either; I was out of my element, grumpy, resentful, and getting nowhere.

Eventually I realized that the problem lay with me. I willingly put in hours huddled under a meeting tree with Kerenkol and Maasai elders in Amboseli but resented one minute in a civil servant's office. My impatience made it impossible to get things done. I had dutifully watched Sindiyo handle the leopard incident among the elders on Il Marishari Hill and learned the art of negotiating with the Maasai, but I had ignored the time he spent with the councilors, parliamentarians, and civil servants. Things happen in Kenya when people sit down and talk, establish a rapport, explore options, and reach an agreement. The African bureaucrat is still persuaded by this easygoing traditional way of doing business; the New York lawyer's three-minute time slots and embossed letters have no place in this officialdom. Either I curb my impatience or watch the last opportunity to win a place for the Maasai in Amboseli slip away. After a decade of effort, the sacrifice of a few extra days in Nairobi seemed a trivial price to pay.

Notwithstanding my funds and backup from the prestigious New York Zoological Society, I still had no official status, no office or phone, and no title other than ecologist. I was skating on thin ice acting as a go-between, having to avoid inciting the Maasai and obstructing the government.

But although I had no official status, Amboseli had important backers. With Daniel Sindiyo in the Game Department, Perez Olindo in National Parks, Frank Mitchell recently moved to the World Bank in Washington, and Bill Conway at the helm of New York Zoological, there were powerful voices rooting for Maasai participation in Amboseli National Park. Largely through efforts by Mitchell, the World Bank's offer of $37.5 million for tourism and wildlife development had advanced to the negotiation stage. Having been an architect of the project, I was asked by the Ministry of Tourism and Wildlife to help prepare a justification for the loan, expanding on the principles of local participation already sketched out for Amboseli. I accepted the challenge willingly, seeing a new chance to influence the course of events in Amboseli and nationwide.

In 1975 the wildlife policy Mitchell and I initiated sailed through the cabinet. The policy introduced a new conservation philosophy based on local participation rather than exclusion. A year later the national assembly passed the new wildlife bill based on the policies. Among other things, the bill created a single wildlife agency, the Wildlife Conservation and Management Department, amalgamating the former Game Department and Kenya National Parks. The aim was to integrate the conservation of wildlife in and outside national parks.

Only Maasai anger and mistrust now stood in the way of winning major concessions from the government and ensuring Maasai involvement in the national park.

Kerenkol Ole Musa, a custodian of Maasai traditions, emerged as the peace broker. As the warriors' leader and spokesman, he was a skilled arbitrator and knew how to settle the most contentious dispute. He also knew the risks of a confrontation with the government.

Once he agreed to act as peace broker to calm down the Maasai, he commanded the attention and possessed the oratorical skills to persuade his peers. More to the point, he urged the Maasai to speak for themselves, rather than have Oloitiptip speak for them. This was a brave stand on his part, given Oloitiptip's formidable power and intolerance of any opposition. Kerenkol was not a traditional spokesmen for nothing, though, and in his quiet, eloquent way he won over the warriors and elders.

Mitchell also understood the need for a compromise. In 1975 the three of us pulled off an unprecedented meeting between a team from the World Bank and the Maasai elders to discuss the position the bank should adopt in funding the national park and ensuring that benefits flowed back to the Maasai. An oddly assorted group gathered in a corner of the newly constructed Serena Lodge. On one side of the table sat safari-jacketed bank experts scribbling away in notebooks and sipping from plastic coffee cups; on the other side sat Maasai elders in red loincloths, reciting oral history to bolster their case. Everyone knew how much hung on breaking the stalemate, none more than the Maasai elders.

"Yes, the Maasai do intend to accommodate wildlife . . . as we always have," the Maasai spokesman assured the World Bank officials. "We protected wild animals from hunters, and wildlife protected us from drought," he continued. "So we see it as fatal that we should not be allowed to move back into Amboseli. We will leave the park to show our good intentions. We will allow wild animals onto our land, stop our young men from harassing them, and discourage poachers. But we expect that when it is seen that we cannot survive without Amboseli, we too shall be extended the same treatment as the animals and that we will derive benefits from the park. If such reciprocity is not shown, we cannot make assurances for the future of wildlife outside Amboseli National Park. And if wild animals are restricted to the park, their numbers will fall. If we are excluded, our livestock will die. Coexistence is the essence of survival for us both. We will leave it to the government to show us they have our interests in mind in setting up the national park."

The timing could not have been better: most conservation organizations and donor agencies had come to see Africans less as a threat to wildlife than as the ultimate answer to its survival. Despite the philosophical shift, not one of them employed an African in a senior position; neither did the intellectual commitment extend to dialogue on the ground. For this reason alone, getting the two ends of the conservation spectrum together was a breakthrough.

The meeting at Serena Lodge and others reopened the dialogue between the government and the Maasai and led to a tenuous agreement. Under the terms of the agreement the Maasai would move out of Amboseli in exchange for water in the outlying areas. The park headquarters would be situated on the boundary, with a Maasai community center, school, and health clinic adjoining it. Of greater importance, the Maasai would be given an annual wildlife utilization fee in exchange for allowing Amboseli's migratory herds to move onto their land in the wet season. The Maasai would also be given hunting fees for the first time, instead of seeing the money skimmed off in Nairobi. The Kajiado County Council would retain 400 acres incorporating the Ol Tukai lodge and a share of the gate receipts for use by all the Maasai in the district.

The pipeline providing alternative water to the Maasai became operative in August 1976, the last year of drought. Clear cold spring water coursed through fifty-five miles of plastic pipe to six outlying troughs. The Maasai made for the new troughs immediately, taking advantage of the grasses beyond foraging range of the permanent swamps.

"Now we've fixed those damn Maasai," an ex-Indian army officer working under the auspices of the East African Wildlife Society told me with glee after the pipeline began operation. "They have no excuse to come back again."

The end was not yet in sight, however. The agreements had yet to be ratified by the minister for Tourism and Wildlife and the Maasai could hardly be evicted in the middle of a harsh drought. One particular incident among many demonstrated the fragility of the truce.

With negotiations at the last and most delicate stage, a pride of lions began killing livestock. The warriors worked themselves into a fury when Kioko's rangers did nothing. Look, they yelled at a gathering of warriors, it shows the national parks prefer lions to Maasai. So they showed their resentment the way they knew best, by reaching for their spears. Within days they killed eight lions, two rhinos, two elephants, a buffalo, and a hyena. Then, capping it all, a rogue elephant began terrorizing the Maasai. The Maasai elders demanded immediate action to save the talks from collapsing.

Kioko was in Nairobi again when a report came in of a tuskless bull having killed a Maasai warrior up near Lemi Boti, twenty miles northeast of Amboseli. The assistant warden dispatched two rangers to kill it. They returned empty handed with fresh reports of two more attacks, one against a young boy, who narrowly escaped by diving under a thornbush, the other against an elder, who miraculously escaped after being savaged.

With the elephant likely to kill again, the animal had to be destroyed. The rangers, scared of what they had seen at Lemi Boti, begged off tracking down the marauder in thick bush. Knowing my hunting background, they asked me to take charge. My first job was to establish details of the attacks and the animal. Despite its size, it was likely to be a female; Cynthia Moss had never recorded a tuskless bull in Amboseli.

I took a sergeant and small detail of rangers up to Lemi Boti and picked up a couple of warriors present at the attack. They led us through a tangle of wait-a-bit thorn to a shallow swale. "Here," one of the warriors pointed to the ground. "There were five of us. These are our tracks. We came on the elephants over there, under that tree. The bull attacked us without warning. We scattered. The elephant chased our friend through the thicket over there."

I checked the tracks under the tree where the elephants had been shading from the midday sun. There were seven in all. We followed the path of the biggest elephant from the point at which it had begun its charge. From there we picked up a warrior's tracks weaving round a tangle of bush in a shallow swale. Never had I seen an animal so determined; it had ploughed through bushes like a bulldozer, making a beeline for the warrior. Everyone was on edge and began looking nervously around, half expecting the elephant to come crashing out of the bush. Fifteen paces from the point of charge we came on the warrior's remains—a patch of dried blood, ocher, and a wig of long braided hair. A shallow trough showed where the elephant had crushed the body again and again, attempting to bury it. The sergeant, a Maasai warrior himself, walked off a few paces and began sobbing. I struggled hard not so show my own feelings, remembering my father's blood-soaked clothes.

Kenya had imposed a ban on killing elephants in 1973, so I flew up to Nairobi the next day to explain the situation to Sindiyo and seek his permission to shoot the marauder. By the time I got back to Amboseli, he had radioed clearance from the chief game warden. Finding the elephant in heavy cover could take days, so I took to the air with the assistant warden and a couple of rangers to scout the outlying water holes. We eventually found the tuskless cow and her herd at Namelok Swamp, half a mile from Kerenkol's new shamba. With settlement close by, the danger of another attack was imminent.

I flew the assistant warden to headquarters for him to pick up a truck, rangers, and guns and then returned to Namelok to warn the farmers. An hour later a Toyota pickup arrived with a gang of rangers in the back. Jumping in, we bounced into the dried-up swamp toward the elephants.

The attack came before we had driven far. The matriarch bore down on the back of the Toyota with astonishing speed over the broken ground. The rangers, totally unprepared, fiddled with their safety catches and huddled against the cab for safety. The Maasai sergeant, the only one to stand his ground, leveled a double-barreled .458. Kibori, the ranger Sindiyo had assigned to me when I first arrived in Amboseli, thrust his gun into my hand, remembering how I had dispatched a rogue elephant he had wounded a few months earlier. "Here, shoot," he pleaded. Just then, the sergeant let off both barrels. The first missed completely. The second hit the elephant low in the chest. She slowed, then spun round and headed into a thicket close to the shambas.

Pandemonium broke loose as farmers rushed forward expecting a kill. "Get back, get back!" the sergeant was yelling from the back of the truck. With no hope of penetrating the thorn thicket and the elephant likely to attack at any moment, I rushed over to the plane and clambered into the air, hoping to drive the wounded animal into the safety of the park. I zoomed low overhead again and again until finally the herd emerged and began moving. Once in the park, I landed and rejoined the rangers. This time I took no chances and relieved Kibori of his gun, a .375 magnum. The elephants were hurrying ahead of us, drawing water from their stomachs and squirting it over their backs to cool themselves.

The herd was fast approaching the tourist circuits up ahead, posing a new danger. We sped ahead then cut the engine and waited. Again without warning, the female peeled off for a charge. I took rapid aim and brought her down with a single brain shot. She crumpled in a heap, her fury gone.

In every elephant's death I relive the anguished eyes of the dead tusker following my every move under the Kigelia tree at Mikumi. Their size endows them with such abundance of life that you sense a disproportionate loss when the vitality goes out of them. In this case there was no option. Maasai lives were at stake. Acting decisively showed caring and kept the negotiations on track.

"The benefits the Maasai are to get from the park haven't been final-
ized," I told Yuda Komora, the new permanent secretary in the Ministry
of Tourism and Wildlife. "Unless they receive assurances before they move
out, the distrust and killing will begin all over again."

Fortunately in Komora—a member of the Pokomo tribe who had
grown up among wildlife and pastoralists—I found a kindred soul. He
readily agreed to delay the Maasai exodus until a negotiated settlement was
reached and the drought broke.

Late in November 1976—following five years of drought—the rains
finally arrived. The first storm clouds gathering over Kilimanjaro rumbled
ominously and dropped a gray curtain of rain over the forested slopes.
Slowly the clouds unfurled and rolled east across the savanna toward the
Chylulu Hills, filling the parched water holes. Three days later the Maasai
herded their cattle stiff-legged with emaciation through fierce gusting
winds, the smell of fresh rain in their nostrils. I sat watching the last Maasai exodus from my Toyota discreetly parked at a distance, knowing the
abandoned settlements would soon decay and disintegrate, leaving no
more than small aberrant patches of vegetation to show where they had
camped. Zebra and wildebeest, almost as emaciated as the cattle, moved
slowly north in small hesitant clusters, reluctant to make the arduous trek
until sure of the rain's intent. Finally the last herds dragged themselves off,
leaving nothing but twisted bolts of desiccated hide and scattered bones.
The drought was over.

I should have been euphoric and run wild through the mud and rain,
but the departure of the Maasai weighed heavily on my conscience. Amboseli would arguably remain as crucial to the Maasai in the future as it
had been in the past, but never again would it be their spiritual and ecological center. The intimate bonds between ecology, culture, and spirit had
loosened with the Maasai's exodus. Watching the barriers of Maasai culture
and Amboseli's ecosystem penetrated by the homogenizing forces of the
outside world brought on a wave of nostalgia and guilt. To be sure, the disintegration of Maasai culture had begun imperceptibly decades ago with
the advent of colonialism, accelerated by a drought which saw Parashino
abandon Amboseli. But the exodus taking place before my eyes was not
the outcome of these insensible economic and social forces or the Maasai's
own volition. It was undeniably my own doing as much as anyone else's.

In my defense I could claim that the Maasai were headed for worse disaster the way things were going and could justify the changes as the price they had to pay to hold on to what they had. I could even uphold the Maasai's own adaptability and eagerness for change in contrast to my own nostalgic yearnings. But, stripped of all the rationalization and excuses, I was still the eight-year-old sentimentalist touched by the soul of a sable antelope beside the hunting trail and would always regret the Maasai exodus from Amboseli.

Amboseli's recovery after the rains happened with such rapidity that it dispelled the notion widely held by ecologists at the time, myself included, that savanna ecosystems are intrinsically fragile and easily disrupted. Having gone from floods to drought and back again in a decade and a half, Amboseli undeniably oscillated between extremes and seldom fell into a groove of regularity. Wildlife and the Maasai had adapted to the constant flux over the millennia, moving opportunistically with the shifting pasture conditions. The shifting pastures and resulting migrations called for space, lots of it. If that space were carved up by fences, the migratory system, the abundance of wildlife, and its very diversity would collapse. Boiled down to fundamentals, the conservation of Amboseli's biological diversity came down to keeping the ecosystem open and the migrations alive.

In June 1977 the government was ready to conclude the drawn-out negotiations with the Maasai. The venue this time was a tortilis tree near the source of Enkongo Narok spring. On one side, several hundred Maasai squatted in the dirt. On the other, government officials, press, and visitors sat uncomfortably in hardback chairs. I made a conscious choice and squatted next to Kerenkol. This is where the future of Amboseli and my conscience lay, and I intended to show my colors and gauge Maasai reaction. Would the concessions please the Maasai or not? Most important of all, would the terms of the agreement mean a better future for Amboseli and its wildlife?

Oloitiptip was first to speak. Now Minister for Natural Resources after siding with a small group to ensure that Vice President Daniel succeeded Kenyatta on his death in 1977, he was arguably the third most powerful man in Kenya. Despite his past vacillations, Oloitiptip came out staunchly in support of my recommendations and the compromise plan. He closed by saying the Maasai would vacate the park in return for benefits. "We will make Amboseli more famous than ever—it will be to our benefit now," he concluded in a booming voice. The crowd around me looked unhappy. Oloitiptip had confirmed their fears of having to abandon the park but had said nothing about what the benefits would be. Everything now hung on the minister of Tourism and Wildlife.

The minister had a reputation for bawling out his political enemies in front of the press rather than sticking to the matter at hand. I tensed involuntarily, expecting him to launch into one of his famous diatribes. Oloitiptip's presence kept him on track, however. The minister began by reminding the Maasai of Kenyatta's decree and their agreement to move out once the alternative pipeline was complete. "As of today you will not be allowed back in," he went on. "The park is in the best interests of Kenya as a whole."

"Come on, come on," I muttered nervously, conscious of the grim faces all around me. "Say what's in it for the Maasai."

"However, to show the government's concern for the special role played by the Maasai, we are today launching a new policy to ensure that you benefit directly from Amboseli." Then he listed the benefits the Maasai would earn from wildlife.

The crowd began to move excitedly before the minister ended his speech. Murmurs of surprise punctuated by spontaneous applause greeted every announcement. Knowing the years of conflict and drought were over, I felt a rush of excitement and relief. The zebra, wildebeest, and elephants were free to roam the ecosystem as they always had, rather than face confinement in a megazoo.

"Why didn't you tell me all of this before the meeting?" Kerenkol ribbed me.

"I told you it would happen, but you didn't believe me, did you?" I laughed, knowing full well that our long talks had paid off more than either of us had dared imagine. Sindiyo and Kioko were equally ebullient, for this was their moment as much as anyone else's.

The one person who had been there at the beginning of it all was nowhere to be seen; Parashino had long ago abandoned Amboseli for another life.

A year later, in 1978, the first money flowed to the Maasai, fulfilling the government's pledge of making wildlife a financial asset. Ole Mwenyendet, the aging chief, held up the check for everyone to see and summed up their feelings amid renewed applause:

"Today you have proved that wildlife has a place in our land and in our lives. Today you have shown us that wildlife can again become our second cattle as they were in days long ago. We know that in the droughts when our cows run dry, we can depend on the milk of our second cattle. Wildlife is now our property as much as it is yours. Today you have acquired 2,000 extra pairs of eyes to watch against poachers. The money we get from wildlife will build our schools and hospitals. The park will provide the jobs our children need."

Mwenyendet had read the future and echoed Parashino's forlorn hope of renewing his people's ancient tradition of coexistence. Oloitiptip, the inveterate politician, also read the future when he opened the Maarba School, the first community project funded by wildlife revenues.

"Amboseli, your park, built this school," he bellowed at a huge crowd of Maasai. "You are now the wealthiest group ranch in Maasailand because of Amboseli. But that is not enough. We need schools. We need Maarba School. Look at what is happening all over Kenya. The Kikuyu, the Kamba, the Luo—all of them are getting educated, getting jobs, getting rich. The Maasai must not be left behind as watchmen and herders. You need this school to progress. Who will send their children here to Maarba School?"

Elders in shukas, younger men in shirts and slacks, and one or two in rumpled cotton suits looked around uncertainly. A small group of warriors squatting under a tortilis tree feigned lack of interest. They had appearances to uphold. A group of women clustered in front of Oloitiptip ululated their approval, and a few raised their hands hesitantly.

"Not good enough," Oloitiptip roared back. "Only the educated tribes like the Kikuyus will rule from now on. I am the last Maasai who will make it to the top without education. I did it by cunning," he added to an eruption of laughter. "But you—you can't do that any longer. You will leave your children behind in shukas when others are wearing suits and driving around in Mercedes unless you educate them."

Could this be the same Oloitiptip who had bared the warrior's buttocks at the eunoto ceremony in 1968 to taunt President Nyerere's ruling on Maasai nudity? Like Sindiyo, Oloitiptip had become an advocate of the pen rather than the spear. He was working the crowd now, his huge neck flared like that of a cobra about to strike as he flayed the air with his fly whisk and hurled out intoxicating phrases with the mesmerizing power of Lenin during his revolutionary days. "Who will send children to this school now?" he thundered again. Never did I think the day would come when I forgave the politician who nixed the plan for a Maasai park, but here I was, cheering him on along with the rest of the crowd.

I looked out across acacia scrub, up the long shallow slope of Kilimanjaro to Parashino's farm. The scattered shambas had coalesced into a continuous belt with a few tassels running down the valleys toward the plains. In the foreground stood Maarba School, freshly painted red and white and marked off from the surrounding bush by a picket fence.

A loud satisfied growl from Oloitiptip and half-screamed ululations drew my attention back to the crowd. All hands were raised at last. Oloitiptip knew a winning cause when he saw one and had become a forceful ally for conserving Amboseli. Some change for the poacher who dared Sindiyo, I had to admit as I let out another whoop of approval.

"Amboseli National Park is the reason for this school," he concluded. "Guard wildlife well. Tourists will bring you money and progress."

« 10 »

Changing Worlds

SEPTEMBER 1981. THE PLANE lifted cleanly off the airstrip into a gusting wind as a herd of wildebeest pounded off in a swirl of dust beneath the cowling. Leveling off, I banked toward Longinye Swamp in high spirits. Taking stock from the air was delightful and reassuring these days: after years of confrontation and drought, the Amboseli ecosystem was finally on the mend.

I throttled back over Longinye Swamp and scanned the remnant thickets expectantly. A rhino briefly raised its head at the sound of the aircraft before sinking back to its siesta. Another rhino ambled into the open up ahead, stopped briefly, ears erect, then moved on as a tiny calf huddled at its flank trotted to catch up. By 1977 only eight black rhinos had survived the spearing by Maasai protesting the government's attempted takeovers of Amboseli. Since then, numbers had risen to thirteen even as losses continued elsewhere throughout Kenya.

A herd of elephants came into view below the left wing. How delightful to watch two infants nonchalantly clambering over a recumbent adolescent as the herd idly foraged all around, flanked by an escort of white cattle egrets. Like rhinos, the elephants had flourished since 1977, climbing to over 600 from the 480 surviving when poachers had shot half the population. Making up for the last year of drought when a mere twelve calves were born, more than 100 tumbled to earth once the rains resumed. Fittingly, given that one in 100 births are twins, the last of this number were the Gemini Twins as Cynthia Moss proudly named them. Her research flowered with the soaring birth rate and drew international attention when the *New York Times* profiled her work in a front page article titled "Family Circles."

Here was proof, if any was needed, that Ole Mwenyendet had delivered on his promise of 2,000 extra pairs of eyes to guard wildlife. In the couple of rare spearing incidents since 1977, the elders had turned the culprits over to the warden for killing "our" animals, as they referred to them.

The recovery of elephants and rhinos dates precisely to the day in June 1977 when the government and the Maasai struck an agreement under the tortilis tree. Until then, Somali poachers had hit Amboseli's herds with impunity. The first test of Ole Mweyendet's promise to stop poachers came three months later when a gang of five heavily armed Somalis walked into Amboseli in search of elephants.

The Maasai immediately picked up the telltale sandal tracks and made straight for the park headquarters. "Stop the *shifta* [bandits] shooting our elephants and scaring off our tourists," they told the rangers. The warden was in Nairobi, and the rangers called on me to help. Their ill-equipped .303 bolt-action rifles were no match for the shifta automatics, so I posted a ranger on Observation Hill to monitor their movements while I dispatched a vehicle to Loitokitok for reinforcements. Seventeen armed police arrived by Land Rover late in the afternoon. I circled overhead as they took up position, knowing the shifta would try to slink off the moment they realized the odds against them: they were unlikely to fire on the plane for fear of giving away their position. All the same, I felt like a solitary duck circling a hide of hunters as I scanned the thickets ready to peel away at the first puff of smoke or drum of bullets on the fuselage.

After half an hour of fruitless circling, I landed in a clearing and joined the police and rangers combing the area. There was no sign of the Somalis, except for a dagger dropped in a thicket. How they evaded the dragnet no one knew, but then they had a reputation for melting into the bush. Perhaps their escape was fortunate, anyway, for the gang apparently spread word of the Maasai's vigilance; after that there were no more poachers.

So much for the elephants and rhinos, but what about the rest of Amboseli?

I had reached Namelok Swamp a couple of miles short of Amboseli's eastern boundary. Below, a sprawl of Maasai huts and thatch-roofed houses bordered a green swatch of squared-off maize fields. The irrigation channels watering the shambas had shrunk the swamp by half since 1975. Wildlife had dwindled to a solitary herd of buffalo skulking in the acacia thickets. Amboseli would have become another Kimana and Namelok too, had it not been for the protection of a park.

Swinging south, the stark block of the new park headquarters buildings rose at the southeastern boundary. A stone's throw away, on the other side of the boundary, stood a community hall and health clinic built for the Maasai as part of the 1977 agreement. Stretching out from the headquarters were newly graveled game-viewing circuits that had cut off-road driving to a tenth, giving the lions and cheetah respite from tourist harassment. With the Amboseli herds safe, tourism under control, and the Maasai benefiting financially from the park, there was no denying the improvement on all fronts.

To assure myself that Amboseli's turnaround resulted from Maasai protection rather than a general improvement in the status of wildlife in Kenya, I decided on a whim to fly over to the Tsavo West National Park, twenty minutes away.

No trace of elephants survived in the bush between the two parks, except for dozens of white skulls left over from days when the herds seasonally migrated out of Tsavo and got gunned down by poachers. Crossing into the park over the black cinder cones south of the Chyulu Hills, I picked out a half-dozen rhino skulls scattered in the bush, the remains of the 8,000 rhinos biologists counted in Tsavo in the late 1960s. Between 1970 and 1981, black rhino numbers slumped from 20,000 to 380 in Kenya, and from 70,000 to 14,000 for the continent at large. The species would be all but extinct in ten years if the killing continued.

Flying deeper into Tsavo I came across a huddle of freshly killed elephants, their faces hacked to pieces, their bodies spattered with white vulture droppings: Somali poachers.

The bad years for Kenya's pachyderms began with the latest scramble for the horn of Africa as first the Soviet Union, then the United States plowed so much military hardware into Somalia that the cash-strapped militia took to poaching and banditry in gangs fifty strong, armed with Kalishnikovs. The West called it the Cold War, a euphemism absolving it of any responsibility for the dozens of real wars spawned in its tussle with the USSR over political hegemony in the region. The poaching wars that killed thousands of people, tens of thousands of rhinos, and hundreds of thousands of elephants throughout Africa were anything but cold.

All there was to see in Tsavo West National Park that day were scattered bones and a solitary herd of 100 elephants clustered nervously around the safety of Ngulia Lodge in the center of the park. What was the point of setting aside such a huge park unless its elephants and rhinos could be protected?

The antipoaching campaign of the 1950s, soon after the park was established, was waged against far lighter odds. A few traditional Waliangulu hunters shafting a poisoned arrow into an elephant sent the herd hightailing for cover. The hunters spent hours, sometimes days, on the track of a wounded animal, waiting for it to die. The ill-equipped poachers were no match for the warden's disciplined and well-armed rangers and barely put a dent in the herds. With the influx of Somali bandits, the odds changed dramatically. Driven by poverty and dispatched by their despotic president, Siad Barre, the shifta were out to destabilize northern Kenya and incorporate it into greater Somalia. Knocking off elephants and rhinos hit at the heart of Kenya's thriving tourist industry and pumped money back into cash-strapped Somalia.

The Cold War and the influx of shifta had a profound impact on Amboseli. In 1967, before the Somali poaching began, elephants migrated back and forth over some 4,000 square miles of country around Amboseli. In response to heavy poaching in the early 1970s, the elephants abandoned the outlying areas for the safety of the Amboseli basin, an area one-tenth of their former range. Within five years, elephant densities tripled, confronting the park with the problem Dick Laws had documented in Murchison and Tsavo—too many elephants on too little land.

With so many elephants holed up in Amboseli, something had to give. In the drought the elephants had played a vital role by opening up the thickets and trampling down the tall reed beds, giving access to smaller species. Within three years the dense thickets flanking the swamp gave way to a mat of cynodon grass. Wildebeest and zebra, no longer deterred by predators on the close-cropped grasses, doubled in number. Though a boon to the grazing animals, the transformation trashed Amboseli's biological diversity by driving out giraffe, lesser kudu, bushbuck, primates, small carnivores, and numerous bird species dependent on the woodlands and thickets. Even the black rhino, few as they were, all but abandoned Longinye Swamp, their favorite haunt in earlier days.

The predators, if nothing else, thrived in the drought, so much so that potbellied hyenas turned up their noses at the two wildebeest which lay down to die outside my house and mummified in the salty dust. When the rains resumed, fresh grass sprang up and knotted itself through the twisted bolts of skin and bone. Slowly a host of small scavengers devoured the brittle leather and zebra ripped away the knots of grass, breaking up the skeleton. Five years later only a few bones survived, weathered and splintered by sun, rain, and hooves and ignored by the daily procession of animals filing in and out of the swamps. With the swamp accessible from all directions, the daily procession petered out, giving the lions no cover to attack.

Life around my house changed with the demise of the woodlands and procession of animals. The tangled thickets of bushes and trees so full of bird and animal life before the drought gave way to the lifeless monotony of flat grassland. I missed the welter of animal activity and lost the pulse of Amboseli once the screening vegetation disappeared, leaving my house visible to the lodge and every passing minibus. To recapture the intimacy and demonstrate the role of elephants in the habitat transformation, I set up an experimental enclosure around my house in 1981. The experiment was simple enough—a four-foot-wide moat around a plot twenty by twenty yards, just enough to keep the elephants out. Within months, acacia saplings sprang up tall and healthy after twenty years of failure. The experiment confirmed once and for all that Charlie and I had been wrong in blaming the death of the woodlands on salt and fluctuating water levels. In a way, that was a relief. At least in proving that elephants were to blame there was a chance of restoring Amboseli's lost diversity—if only elephants could be encouraged to resume their migrations.

During the 1970s scientific views of nature were changing no less than my own ideas on Amboseli. George Perkins Marsh's nineteenth-century picture of nature as harmonious and immutable unless disturbed by geologic upheavals and human beings seemed quaintly out of date in the emerging world of chaos, complexity, and change. Eugene Odum's view of nature as a steady-state self-regulating engine, though still holding sway, was gradually yielding to a more complicated world of flux and unpredictability. Stability in tropical ecosystems, once an ecological axiom, could no longer stand up to the emerging evidence of large-scale climatic oscillations and the disruptive forces of fire, drought, floods, and disease, all of which threw disorder into biologists' world at equilibrium. And even if few ecologists yet accepted human activity as a natural force in nature, the new view posed fewer problems in accommodating such a heretical possibility.

Inevitably, the sea change in the scientific view of nature had a profound impact on conservation. Until the 1970s, top-flight biologists dismissed conservationists as wildlife managers. Hard-core scientists had bigger problems to attend to, such as unraveling life's mysteries. Disdain turned to concern as biologists saw their study animals fall victim to poachers, habitat destruction, and pollution. Jane Goodall working on chimps, Dian Fossey on gorillas, Birute Galdikas on orangutans, Roger Payne on whales, Iain Douglas-Hamilton on elephants, and George Schaller on jaguars were among the renowned field scientists whose animals came under threat. Identifying as closely with their study animals as they did, they could no more ignore the dangers to Flo, Digit, and Boadacea than a threat to their own families. One by one, conscientious scientists developed a conscience and took up the cause of conservation.

The emergence of this new breed of biological conservationists closely paralleled the transformation from hunter to conservation manager seen in Rushby, Ionides, Rufiji, and my father as they took up the defense of their favorite animals. Concern among biologists went far beyond the big and charismatic species, however. By the 1970s, habitat destruction was so rampant and invidious that Jared Diamond working on New Guinea birds, Ed Wilson on tropical ants, Michael Soulé on Californian lizards, John Terborgh on Amazonian monkeys, Peter Raven on tropical trees, and Peter Vitousek on freshwater fishes were among the growing ranks of biologists taking up the call of conservation.

No one interested in nature could turn a blind eye to the rising tide of extinction. In 1978, an assortment of top zoo managers, lab and field scientists, conservationists, wildlife managers, and fish and forestry biologists met in San Diego to discuss the crisis. Speaker after speaker detailed the threat to biological diversity posed by the Evil Quartet: habitat fragmentation, overutilization, ecological disruption, and the introduction of exotic species. Greatly alarmed, the biologists predicted an "extinction spasm" as catastrophic as the asteroid which snuffed out the dinosaurs at the end of the Cretaceous. A quarter of all species could disappear by the end of the century, warned biologists in *The Global 2000 Report to the President.*

The upshot of the academic soul-searching in San Diego was conservation biology, a crisis science dedicated to saving biodiversity in all its forms. The new science legitimized conservation as a noble, even moral academic pursuit, drawing in the best minds and new research funds. The academic spotlight turned on extinction and the foundation theory for predicting the mass extinctions to come.

Known as the theory of island biogeography, the idea first formulated by Robert MacArthur and Ed Wilson in 1963 rested on a century of observations by natural historians and biogeographers. Charles Darwin and Alfred Russell Wallace, cofounders of the theory of evolution by natural selection, painstakingly documented the importance of ecological isolation in the creation of new species. Wallace also astutely observed that smaller, remoter islands tend to have fewer species. It took the combined mathematical and taxonomic skills of MacArthur and Wilson, however, to draw a deeper conclusion: small and remote islands support fewer species because of their higher rates of extinction and slower recolonization. Islands also tend to support a constant number of species, with the number of extinctions balancing new arrivals. With these neat deductions, MacArthur and Wilson telescoped the whole science of extinction into a simple equation predicting the number of species from the area of an island.

The elegant simplicity and profound implications of island biogeography spawned a growth industry in conservation biology, with study after study substantiating MacArthur and Wilson's theory. Of momentous significance to conservation, it also transpired that the theory applied equally to habitat islands on the mainland, though the number of species at equilibrium tended to be greater. In other words, a chunk of forest surrounded by plowed fields is as isolated ecologically as a real island. This implied that national parks, far from saving species, could become an extinction trap if ecologically isolated by human activity. The smaller and more isolated a park, the more species it stood to lose. Michael Soulé and Bruce Willcox of the University of California, San Diego, predicted that 10 to 50 percent of all species in East Africa's parks would go extinct over two to three centuries, depending on their size and isolation.

Imagine the jolt to conservationists who had spent a lifetime carving out a park, only to learn it would become an extinction trap as a result of a hitherto unknown biological force—lack of space. No park, no matter how big, could ever be a self-sufficient ecosystem.

Island biogeography shook up the preservationists complacent about the effectiveness of national parks. It also added the voices of respected scientists and testable theory to the case for keeping the migrations alive and the national parks open.

Turning island biogeography to the service of conservation should have been a straightforward matter, but in practice it raised a divisive debate in the fledging science of conservation biology. It stood to reason that bigger was better when it came to national parks, right? No, insisted a faction of biologists. If you put all your eggs in one basket, you could end up losing species to a single catastrophe such as fire or disease. Better to allocate several smaller parks adding up to the same size to avoid such risks. So began a heated debate that lasted for a decade. Adding to the confusion, the shape of a reserve and the corridors between isolated parks became further points of contention. Was the best shape round, oval, or square, and would skittish species use narrow habitat corridors anyway? What should have been a valuable tool for conservation managers became mired in a sterile debate over geometry. Scientists got carried away in the intricacies of configuration and overlooked the obvious: few existing parks could be magically transformed into some idealized shape, and the determining optimal boundaries of those yet to be commissioned was best done the old fashioned way—by an ecological study on the ground.

Scientists thrive on controversy and dare each other to disprove their pet theories. If they are proved wrong, as Charlie von Praet and I were with our theory of woodland loss, they discard the theory and move on to another. For the scientist, theories are cheap, so long as they aren't defended beyond their durability. The conservation manager is a different breed altogether. The manager wants solutions, not theories, and is slow to adopt untried ideas, however intellectually appealing. The reason is not hard to fathom: adopt the latest theory and find it's wrong, and in the meantime an endangered species may go extinct. Arcane and untested ideas carry a high risk, and in the final analysis, the conservator, not the scientists, must take the blame. Consequently, managers tend to stick to theories in which they were schooled, and for most that means "Mother Nature knows best": leave things alone, and perfect harmony and order will be restored.

It is easy to criticize a long-standing theory when a new paradigm is in ascendancy, but, I, too, had set out to document Amboseli as an ecosystem in equilibrium, governed by homeostatic forces. Even after the evidence proved me wrong, huge anomalies cropped up to challenge another view of equilibrium—that with few exception mammals maintain a stable metabolism under extremes of heat and cold. This mistaken assumption and my ignorance of Maasai knowledge led me to overlook the resilience of the Maasai and the savanna ecosystem under stress.

I had used standard biological methods and analytical techniques to predict the survival of wildlife and livestock during the drought. This entailed measuring the available forage and the number of mouths to feed, multiplied by their energy requirements. Looking at the neat, predictable graph of dwindling food supplies, I might have felt as omnipotent as a space scientist watching Neil Armstrong touch down on the moon, had the prediction not been mass starvation. Instead I agonized over what would become of Parashino, Sotwa, and Martingab once the grass ran out. Inexplicably fewer than a quarter of the cattle and a tenth of the zebra and wildebeest died that first year of drought in 1973. The death toll didn't begin to climb until three years later, in the latter half of 1976. Where had the predictions gone wrong?

The change in swamp vegetation gave a partial answer. That in itself was an eye-opener and my first taste of humble pie. Who but a Maasai with generations of accumulated knowledge would have guessed that during long droughts elephants could transform the swamps and ward off starvation? Even this intriguing twist turned out to be too simple an explanation, however. The herds would have perished long before the elephants transformed the swamps had it not been for another and more bizarre phenomenon. Inexplicably, the animals hung on, even if they did look like walking skeletons. Somehow they managed to stretch the depleted pastures like the parable of loaves and fishes, until the elephants had transformed the swamps and thickets to palatable grasslands.

East Africa's wildlife is supremely adapted to the savannas, according to ecologists. One could therefore expect wild herbivores to have an adaptive trick or two up their sleeves. But what of Maasai livestock? By all accounts, they were ill-adapted and inefficient exotics recently introduced into Africa. If the ecologists and cattle experts were right, how was it that Maasai cattle not only survived such formidable odds but also contributed over half the liveweight of all large mammals in the savannas? The answer, as so often happens in science, came about serendipitously.

Virginia Finch, a bob-haired American colleague at the University of Nairobi, became as intrigued as I was with the hardiness of Maasai cattle and wildlife. There had to be a common answer to their walking hibernated state. To figure out the answer, we devised a series of experiments to simulate Maasai herding practices by subjecting cattle to long daily treks, infrequent watering, and starvation diets—all the cardinal sins revealing the depths of Maasai stupidity, according to livestock experts. The results were stunning.

Under food and water deprivation, cattle not only lost weight—which of course saves energy—but at the same time dropped their metabolic rate by almost half. Put another way, Maasai cattle got by on half as much food and water in bad times. In one completely counterintuitive experiment, half the cattle were herded ten miles a day and watered once every two days while the other half were walked half the distance and watered twice as often. Despite the difference in deprivation and stress, both herds lost identical weight during the experiment.

How could cattle under the stress of a two-day watering system lose no more weight than cattle walking half the distance? When Virginia put the experimental animals on a treadmill and measured their energy consumption, she found that stressed animals compensated by lowering their metabolism faster and further to offset the greater energy cost.

Though unable to explain this physiological quirk to the satisfaction of a scientist, the Maasai evidently understood it intuitively and gainfully employed that knowledge in their husbandry practices.

Greater mobility, less food, less water: these adaptive traits, together with the greater efficiency with which the hardy Maasai cattle digest food when their metabolism slows, explain their incredible resilience to drought. The energy-sparing tricks the Maasai employ are no different, it turns out, from those used by any mammal faced with starvation. The same physiological traits are common to starving Sudanese and dieting Americans who find their weight loss stalled as their metabolism adjusts to the lowered calorie intake.

The Maasai discovered generations ago what scientists are only just beginning to appreciate: physiology is adaptive too, and mammals can turn down the fire of life and behave like reptiles if they have to. Maasai knowledge of such scientific matters can be read in their herding strategies rather than in technical treatises, but they posses it all the same. Studying their actions unearths generations of knowledge acquired through trial and error, a method far more rigorous and insightful than a year or two in the lab. For the Maasai, the success and failure of the cattle is measured in terms of milk yields, rates of growth, and number of births, the ultimate arbiters of natural selection in the wilds. Small wonder that the East African pastoralists have developed migratory and herding patterns similar to those established over eons by wildlife.

The more I learned of Maasai ecology, the more it made sense and refuted western prejudices about the ignorance of preliterate societies. It took firsthand experience—a close tracking of Sotwa and Martingab—to understand Maasai herding practices. Parashino had known that when he gave them to me. Such insights, tested and handed on generation after generation, explain the Maasai's survival and how they attain levels of production as high as the best-run Australian cattle ranch.

‹ ‹ ‹

CHANGE AFFECTED the Maasai as it did everything else in Amboseli in the 1970s, finally breaking their dependence upon livestock. Up against starvation and cultural disintegration, the Maasai proved socially adept and adaptable, dispelling the myth of their brittle tradition and doubts about their survival.

As it turned out, the impacts of population growth and drought were not entirely negative. On the contrary, the collapse of traditional cattle practices forced even the dyed-in-the wool conservatives to look for other ways of making a living. Wildlife, the traditional buffer against drought, offered a viable alternative once again. In their new life, the proceeds from wildlife filled the Maasai needs of cash for blankets, torches, drugs, school fees, and just about everything else.

Ironically, it was Kerenkol, the traditional warrior leader, who was among the first to grasp the potential for jobs and social services offered by wildlife. True, he had the advantage of becoming a councilor during the transitional period and, like Simon Salash, of seeing the world beyond Amboseli during his travels. But by any measure, Kerenkol was a leader and innovator in his own right. Like Oloitiptip, he grasped the essence of how money translated into power and influence far beyond the domain of the traditional *laigwenani* (spokesman). His metamorphosis from traditional warrior to politically savvy councilor occurred with unnerving speed.

Kerenkol, like other Maasai, began to look after his own interests as the drought hardened: family came first and community second. One day he surreptitiously slipped me money to buy tins of edible oil in Nairobi so that he could secretly share it out among his family. On another occasion he asked me to drive him out to a distant balanites tree to retrieve a tin of dried meat he wanted to share with his brother, Tia, when no one else was around.

Kerenkol was not one to sit around watching his cattle starve and his family go hungry. He began to explore new avenues and his first venture was an instant success, drawing as it did on his biggest asset, a large social network. His movement into the cash economy began when he gave Tia 6,200 Kenya shillings to buy stock in Tanzania. Initially he intended to wait until the animals fattened up with the rains then sell them at a profit. Instead Kerenkol found it more lucrative to buy cattle from his fellow Maasai in Tanzania, run them 150 miles north to the black-market butchers supplying the agrarian and urban populations, and recycle the proceeds in fresh cattle purchases. The real payoff came in playing the currency black market, where he traded in his Kenya money for twice the legal value of the Tanzanian shilling.

There were risks, of course, both in cattle trading and in black-marketing. Legally all meat had to pass veterinary inspection and be sold at government auctions. Then there were the police checks along the way. But for Maasai raised to cattle raiding, the risks added spice to their lives.

For a while Kerenkol kept his money stashed away in a cupboard in my house; when the value of the wads accumulated to thousands of dollars, I pointed him toward a bank vault. Unfazed, he opened an account and used his assets to run for area councilor. Once elected he donned a safari jacket and slacks to attend council meetings in Kajiado, always reverting to traditional dress the moment he got back to Amboseli. In contrast to Parashino, he was refreshingly candid about his new aspirations. "I want only one wife and a few children so that I can educate them all, build a house at Risa, and buy a taxi to make more money.

"So, Jonah, you must teach me to drive," he added disarmingly.

Not everyone possessed Kerenkol's extraordinary adaptability or fared as well. I hadn't seen Lochokop for a couple of years when he reappeared one day. "I need a job," he pleaded, "any job." He had run afoul of the law for doing what any self-respecting warrior should do but seldom did these days. His first stint in jail was for spearing a lion, the second for running cattle across the border for Kerenkol.

Lion hunts and cattle raids ran in Lochokop's blood. His exploits still brought him kudos from his warrior friends but the chastisement of his family. A Kenya jail was no longer the Hoteli ya King Georgi it had jocularly been known as in colonial days. Poor food and forced labor sapped the last of his youth, and he faced elderhood with nothing to show for his warrior exploits. The hardship and anguish of the last few years were etched in his face.

"I don't have a job," I told him.

Lochokop shook his head and clicked in desperation. "I don't want to return to my father's settlement without pride or money. They're relying on me." He turned away, embarrassed to look me in the eye. Dressed in grubby slacks and a patched shirt he looked like the hundreds of indigent farmers driven to the shantytowns around Nairobi, not at all like the dandified warrior I had met in 1968.

Lochokop's plea for help hurt me deeply. I had helped Parashino and taken on Kerenkol's relative David Maitumo as a field assistant. There was only so much I could do to help close friends, let alone the thousands of desperate Maasai.

All of a sudden Lochokop brightened and gave me his old cocksure grin. "Perhaps I can make money selling gemstones. There are plenty in Tanzania and many dealers in Nairobi," he tailed off, lost in another fantasy. Some herders did make a few shillings picking up gemstones from the Tanzanian Maasai and selling them to the curio sharks who hawked poached ivory, leopard skins, and tribal artifacts in Nairobi. Most got ripped off or landed in jail.

I had seen too little of Parashino to know how he was faring, so I was surprised and flattered when he solicited my support in the upcoming county council elections. However, he was no match for his wealthier rival, Kerenkol, in the campaign. He hadn't seemed to have the makings of a politician in him, but then he didn't seem to have the makings of a farmer, either.

Drought had pushed the Maasai over the threshold of social change where everyone had gathered, nervous and hesitant like penguins at the edge of an ice floe, waiting for the first one to plunge in. The tension, frustration, and confusion of their new world had yet to catch up with them in their sense of heady escape from drought. Their cultural leap into the future depended on their self-worth, and in turn on finding a secure living. Their confidence would ebb in the twinkle of an eye if they lost their identity and pride in the cultural miasma of modern Kenya.

The future of wildlife was predicated on social change. The aspirations of the younger Maasai were emerging and crystallizing fast. Unless wildlife featured in their vision of the future, the youth would see wildlife as an embarrassing symbol of a primitive past, just as the Tanzanians had in the days before independence.

Amboseli epitomized the changes under way among the Maasai, in Africa, and in ecology, conservation, and society. Nothing stood still anymore, if it ever did. The question uppermost in my mind was how much change nature, the Maasai, and society at large could absorb without flying apart.

Change was afoot in my own world, too. The days were gone when I thought of nothing but the peace and seclusion of Amboseli. In confronting the conflict between people and wildlife, I had been forced to show commitment. That meant taking on new roles alien to my former persona and adapting to new circumstances, as the Maasai had done so ably. I had also taken on new assignments elsewhere, setting up research and conservation projects throughout East Africa for the New York Zoological Society. With the society's programs expanding worldwide, I was also called on to do international work, most recently in Latin America. The travel to new places was refreshing and offered valuable insight into the global threats to nature and how they were being tackled. Despite the expanding scope of my work, Amboseli remained central. I had also gotten better at balancing freedom and responsibility to the point of contemplating the biggest commitment of all.

Time to settle down, Chief Soimoire had told me at the Ol Tukai meeting between the Maasai and the government in 1973. A decade later, at age thirty-nine, I was well past warrior age and still not married, though I did have someone in mind.

I first met Shirley Strum at a Zoology Department seminar in 1973. The magnetism had been there from the first eye contact, but mutual awe and radically different lifestyles kept us apart. Voted "the most physical anthropologist of the year" by a group of field scientists who admired her lithe figure in *Natural History* magazine, Shirley had a reputation for breaking hearts and moving on. A free-spirited Berkeley radical didn't seem the sort of match made for a retiring bush type, so we made do with allusion and innuendo for six years.

It wasn't Shirley's looks alone which attracted me. She had made a reputation for herself studying baboons near Gilgil in the Rift Valley and was already shaking up the male-dominated view of primates and human evolution. In her version of baboon society, males, far from dominating females by brute force, as depicted in Robert Ardrey's *The Territorial Imperative*, were most successful reproductively if they formed friendships with females and coalitions with males. In other words, social skills and a network of friends and alliances rather than a dominance hierarchy alone were the foundations of success for a male in baboon society. This put an entirely different spin on human evolution. If baboons were anything to go by, finesse and social skills counted as much as, if not more than, the clubs and aggression used by our ancestors in getting women.

Despite our different backgrounds, Shirley and I shared a love of animals, intellectual curiosity about the natural world, and a strong sense of social equity and justice. Endowed with independence and confidence in the worth of her own work, she was deeply committed to the baboons she studied, just as I was to Amboseli. Naturally, she loved long walks across the savannas every evening.

So I flew down to her Rift Valley research site often under the pretext of learning more about baboons, and, as Shirley wrote in her book, *Almost Human*, we were soon in consort. As far as the Maasai were concerned, that was as it should be. My warrior days had stretched on too long, and it was about time I became an elder, settled down, and had a family.

Part Four

Architect of the Forest

‹ 11 ›

Forest Interlude

JANUARY 3, 1986, FOUND us high over Lake Kyoga in Uganda. A thick haze from countless bush fires had cut visibility to a few kilometers. I had reluctantly sold the Cessna 180 and bought a larger six-seater 206 for the trip, banking on the extra payload to give us sufficient fuel reserves to make it across Africa in a pinch.

Peter Matthiessen sat in the copilot's seat. His long ascetic face was knotted in concentration as he caught up on his notes. We first got to know each other in 1970 when he was writing *The Tree Where Man Was Born*. Since then our paths had crossed often. A writer, traveler, and naturalist with an eye for the elusive and a penchant for adventure, Peter had done it all, from searching for the great white shark with Peter Gimble to tracking down the snow leopard with George Schaller in the Himalayas. His latest venture, to help me check on the conservation status of the forest elephant and search for the mythical pygmy elephant, was right up his street.

Some estimate of the number of forest elephants was needed to resolve an acrimonious debate which had drawn me into the conservation of the African elephant—and no one knew anything about the pygmy elephant, not even whether it really existed. The pygmies of central Africa swore that two distinct species of elephants lived side by side in the forest, and references to the enigmatic dwarf form made it into the guidebooks on Africa's mammals, always with the qualifier that its existence was unproven. The continuing mystery over the pygmy elephant testified to the size and ignorance of Africa's vast central African forest, where we were now headed on a six-week expedition.

I had been all set to make the trip alone when Peter had asked to join me. Shirley, who would remain at home in Kenya with our eight-month-old daughter, Carissa, urged me to take along a companion. Although she had brought me out of my shell since our marriage in 1983, she hadn't yet gotten used to my disappearing into the middle of nowhere and felt it would be safer if someone were with me. The chances of surviving a crash in the central African forest were no greater for two people than for one, but if the company reassured Shirley, then I was happy to oblige. When Peter asked if he could join me to write about the forest elephant, I agreed. I greatly admired his work and felt that with his expeditionary experience he would be an ideal companion.

We cleared Lake Kyoga and droned on northwest toward the Zaire border in thickening haze. I checked my watch again, 4:30 P.M. A late start and strong headwinds had slowed our progress and scrambled our already tight flight schedule. We had left Shirley looking pensive as we struggled into the air, wallowing with fuel and headed for tracts of Africa with no landing site or village for hundreds of miles. Try as I might, I couldn't shake off the drowsiness of a missed night's sleep and the monotony of mile after mile of charred grassland relieved only by the occasional abandoned village which rose and sank in gloom.

We had made up lost time on reaching Murchison Falls National Park in western Uganda, so when Peter shouted above the engine suggesting we detour to look at the headwaters to the Nile, I was all for it. The southward diversion took us across a fire-blackened park devastated first by Idi Amin's bloody regime and then by Tanzania's liberation forces. Peter looked out glumly, recalling the great herds of elephant, buffalo, and Uganda kob in the years before Amin took control and renamed Murchison Kabalega National Park to erase the colonial stigma. The unfamiliar name survived no longer than Idi Amin's intolerable regime.

"I don't believe it. Not a single damn animal anywhere. They've even killed off all the Uganda kob."

By the time researchers returned to Murchison after Amin's ouster, only 400 of 12,500 elephants survived, most in a single herd that stampeded across the open grasslands at the first sound of an engine. Amin's troops had reportedly machine-gunned the herds for target practice, leaving hundreds of animals maimed and wounded. Dick Laws's controversial cull of 3,000 elephants looked like a minor footnote in the slaughter of Uganda's elephants under Amin's regime.

We banked south over the falls. A turbulent jet of white water spewed the booming Victoria Nile river through a narrow defile. "Well, at least the falls are the same," Peter observed wryly.

My mistake in making the diversion became evident the moment we resumed our flight northwest to Garamba National Park, our overnight stop on the Zaire-Sudan border. The smoke haze had thickened to a fog, and the sun, still well above the horizon, had dimmed and reddened to a large orb the moment it plunged into the gray pall. Our chances of making Garamba National Park by nightfall were slim. I opened the engine full bore, intent on making up time by intercepting our course over the Albert Nile.

Somehow or other we missed our checkpoint in the haze and unfamiliar terrain. I switched from Peter's Carte D'Afrique to an out-dated map of Haute Zaire Province as we crossed into Zaire and followed what I presumed to be the Arua Road running due west. The road petered out unexpectedly, and the terrain buckled into a jumble of low hills. I checked the map in disbelief. No sign of hills. So where were we? My stomach tightened as I looked around frantically for a landmark.

"We're never going to make Garamba before dark," I yelled across at Peter, making no attempt to soften the bad news. "No place to land here. We've got to get out of these hills and put down before it's too late." I could see the disbelief and fear register in his eyes, wondering how in hell we had got ourselves into such a fix the first day out.

I peered out of the darkening cockpit, frantic for open country. Nothing, only more hills and valleys. Finally, just as the light failed, we broke out of the steep hills into undulating country. All the same, the thick bush and heavily wooded valleys below offered no place to land. Just then a small clearing opened up below us in the murk. I banked hard and circled several times. God, we'd never get off the ground again. With luck we might just get the plane down safely, and that's all that mattered now. It was either that or crash in the dark. So I made a final pass, lining up a precarious path between the aardvark holes, termite mounds, and trees.

The flaps whined full down, and the plane wallowed heavily as we slowed to stalling speed on the final run. I dropped the nose sharply as we cleared the tree line, then jammed hard on the brakes as we hit the ground with a thud and bounced wildly over the rutted ground. Trees and termite mounds shot out of the gloom; a heavy branch walloped the tail-plane; saplings whacked away at the fuselage.

Then it was over. Peter began laughing and pumping my hand in relief. I leaned back exhausted, feeling as if I had finally broken the surface with my lungs on fire after a long dive. Suddenly out of the dark dozens of black figures converged on the plane. Moments later we were enveloped in a jostling crowd, shouting and banging on the plane. We stepped out in an effort to wave back the surging tide of bodies. Our emergence only excited them more, and we soon had an angrily shouting mob on our hands. Peter found two French-speaking youths and began explaining our forced land-ing with a lot of hand gesturing. The youths looked skeptical and backed away. Evidently President Mobutu's ploy to raise U.S. military support by playing on the fears of a Libyan invasion had raised suspicions to the point of paranoia in the remotest Zairean villages. The suspicions turned sinister when we failed to produce an official document for the village headman, who introduced himself as Opiti.

Drunken elders shoved their glistening faces into the dim circle of torchlight and accused us of sneaking in under cover of darkness. Opiti, losing control of the crowd, led us off to the safety of the nearby village of Dibwa. Our interrogation continued before a noisy mob around a roaring fire, telling and retelling the story of today's "apparition." All done in, I asked if we could sleep.

Opiti bundled us into a dingy hut. Peter, still wound up, launched into a detailed reconstruction of our harrowing flight and hostile reception with a writer's zest for drama and detail. I was too tired to care and too upset at having botched our trip before we made the forest. I was also wor-ried sick about Shirley, knowing she might learn from our friends in Garamba that we were missing. What had possessed me to take off on this junket, anyway?

MY DECISION to establish the status of the forest elephant grew out of my disillusionment with Amboseli and a craving for new frontiers. The 1977 accord had gone so extraordinarily well that no one could imagine that the Ministry of Tourism and Wildlife would renege on its commitment. But four years later the government stopped its annual payment to the Maasai, quit pumping water for the livestock, and imposed a hunting ban, which cut off their last source of wildlife income. By 1983 the Maasai had no choice but to drive their stock back into the park for water. Some warriors began venting their fury at the Wildlife Department by spearing animals again. Long-suffering as ever, most Maasai still believed the government would live up to its side of the bargain once the newly appointed minister moved on in the next cabinet reshuffle.

In 1981 I reminded the minister of his obligations under the terms of the agreement struck by his predecessor. He looked into the matter and promised to restore the wildlife utilization fee and to cover the operating costs of the water scheme. Two years later, nothing had happened. By then serious financial problems had engulfed the entire nation. The 1970s oil crisis provoked years of steep inflation that virtually scuttled Kenya's fragile economy and government budgets. The Wildlife Department, which fell under the Ministry of Tourism and Wildlife, was not a high priority anyway, given the government's preoccupation with education, health care, social services, and agriculture. The other problem lay with the Wildlife Department itself.

Contrary to all expectations, Perez Olindo, the successful director of Kenya's prestigious national parks, was passed over as head of the Wildlife Conservation and Management Departments when the former National Parks and Game Department were combined in 1977. The man selected as director, John Mutinda, had earlier been linked to high-level poaching syndicates, according to the international press. Although he was eventually forced out by pressure from the World Bank, loath to start its tourism and wildlife loan under Mutinda's directorship, the damage was done. The Wildlife Department's image was badly tarnished and never recovered. Why the new department wasn't run as a quasi-government body under a board of trustees with control over its own budget and staffing—as the national parks under Olindo had been—was a matter of intensive speculation. Instead the newly amalgamated service became a government department, dependent on the national treasury for its operating budget. The budget plummeted, and morale among the former national parks staff like Kioko eroded as corruption, nepotism, and poaching became rampant. By the time Daniel Sindiyo took over from John Mutinda, the Wildlife Department had acquired the moniker Wildlife Poaching Department.

Having neither the international clout nor the political access to do anything about the Wildlife Department, I sat by helpless and despondent as the situation in Amboseli and throughout Kenya worsened. Never had I felt so angry and frustrated, especially after the heartening turnaround in Amboseli. I felt sick at my own impotence, wondering whether all those years in Amboseli might have been better spent trying to place wildlife higher on the list of national priorities.

At that point, Lee Talbot appeared.

As director-general of the International Union for the Conservation of Nature and Natural Resources (IUCN), Talbot ran the world's largest consortium of government and nongovernment conservation agencies. The union was charged with defining threats to wildlife and habitats around the world and strategies for saving them. The Species Survival Commission, one of its expert bodies, was concerned with threatened and endangered species. When it came to African elephants and rhinos, Talbot had a problem of his own he wanted to share.

"The African Elephant Specialist Group has come to a standstill over the status of the elephant," he confided. "I also want to get things moving on the rhino. It seems sensible to put both groups together because elephants and rhinos face the same problem—poaching. We need someone impartial with first-rate scientific credentials to do that and sort things out. You've done good scientific work on elephants and rhinos and have established a good reputation for the way you handled Amboseli. Would you be prepared to take on chairmanship of the joint African Elephant and Rhino Specialist Group?"

"Sure, why not?" I found myself agreeing all too quickly, ready for something big and challenging to take my mind off Amboseli. I had been deeply interested in both species and worried about their fate for years, having seen them killed off by poachers in Amboseli. Together with Sindiyo I had published one of the earliest accounts drawing attention to the precarious state of rhinos, studied the ecological role of elephants, and got Cynthia's study of elephant behavior going. I felt up to the task, and the time had come to get involved in conservation programs outside Amboseli. Nothing could be more pressing and important for Africa than the fate of its elephants and rhinos. After all the long wrangles in Amboseli, resolving the status of elephants and rhinos and coming up with plans for conserving them would be a pleasant change. No one at the time anticipated how bitter and drawn out the Ivory Wars would prove to be.

The origins of the Ivory Wars, as the fracas over the elephant was known, lay in Douglas-Hamilton's Pan African Survey and Ian Parker's response. The survey, done under the auspices of IUCN's African Elephant Specialist Group, chaired by Douglas-Hamilton, relied on questionnaires circulated to wardens, conservationists, and scientists throughout Africa. The responses included counts, estimates, and guesses of population trends and the threats posed to the elephant.

On the basis of the survey results, Douglas-Hamilton provisionally put the African elephant at around 1.3 million when he compiled his report in 1979. That sounded a safe enough number, were it not for the trend lines. Respondent after respondent reported a sharp drop in elephant numbers, and sometimes wholesale population crashes as in Tsavo National Park. Thoroughly alarmed, Douglas-Hamilton saw a poaching crisis in the making, triggered by a tenfold jump in ivory prices around 1970. Something must be done and done fast, he concluded.

Switching from scientist to advocate, Douglas-Hamilton slapped together a report of his findings and a proposed a million-dollar Elephant Action Plan to save the species. In disregard of accepted scientific norms, neither the report nor the action plan was peer reviewed. Douglas-Hamilton and his mediagenic wife, Oria, then launched a highly publicized campaign to save the elephant. Stardom came easily to the Douglas-Hamiltons after the runaway success of their best-selling book, *Among the Elephants.* Whether the scientific evidence merited the crisis or merely gave the Douglas-Hamiltons an excuse to promote themselves was a question on the minds of conservation experts.

Whatever the answer, the Douglas-Hamiltons carefully orchestrated campaign made Iain Mr. Elephant in the western media. He had just the right combination of charisma, dash, and dedication to capture the limelight. A series of high-profile films and magazine articles turned his save-the-elephant campaign into a cause célèbre in Britain and the United States.

To bolster his case, Douglas-Hamilton commissioned Ian Parker to investigate the ivory trade, fully expecting confirmation of his Pan African Survey. Parker, the undisputed maven of the ivory trade, did nothing of the kind. He was determined to unmask Douglas-Hamilton and scuttle his save-the-elephant campaign. In a statistics-laden two-volume report, Parker insisted that global ivory sales fell well within sustainable limits of Africa's million-plus elephants.

Ian Parker is a small, wiry man with disarmingly boyish looks. The ex–game warden and don of wildlife utilization had made a career of game cropping, elephant culling, and ivory trading. He is a man of singular intelligence and proprietary feelings about Africa and the way its wildlife should be managed. At the time he was indisputably the most respected practitioner in his field of wildlife utilization. I have heard him boast of having shot more elephants than any other man alive—probably more than any poacher alive. That claim alone was enough to enrage the Douglas-Hamiltons.

The two adversaries, one for, the other against the ivory trade, were mirror opposites in style and substance. About all they had in common was a flair for publicity and an unbudgeable insistence on being right. The proverbial phrase "like oil and water" could have been invented for Douglas-Hamilton and Parker. Parker thought of himself as the undisputed and indisputable elephant expert and took exception to Douglas-Hamilton's incursion onto his turf. Parker also despised expatriate conservationists like Douglas-Hamilton, although he was one himself. In short, Douglas-Hamilton was a lightning rod for Parker's pet dislikes.

In his own book, *Ivory Crisis*, published in 1983, Parker bitingly debunked the elephant crisis as a publicity stunt and accused conservationists—read Douglas-Hamilton—of sleight of hand with elephant statistics. He concluded by excoriating IUCN for technical incompetence and the World Wildlife Fund (WWF) for fraudulently relieving the public of one million dollars to save the elephant.

Despite his claim to scientific objectivity, Parker's language was no less histrionic than Douglas-Hamilton's. In a thinly veiled chapter titled "Films and Pharisees" he wrote: "Conservationists are aware of public predilections. Assuming a St. George's mantle they tell the world that they are about to slay the dragon which if it doesn't exist it can always be created.

. . . It is with your money St. George will triumph: he must have your money. . . . Be dramatic. Cause or create a sensation. Elect a champion with whom the public can identify and choose an opponent who is easy to vilify: bring in blood and violence (or sex) in Technicolor."

Parker reserved his most scathing comments for Douglas-Hamilton's multimillion-dollar Elephant Action Plan, claiming that over 90 percent of the populations were either safe or of unknown status. To Parker, the entire crisis was a fraud trumped up by charlatans and cynically exploited by conservation organizations bent on garnering publicity and giving jobs to their cronies.

The climax in the clash of personalities came at Wankie National Park in 1981 at the first All-Africa meeting of the Elephant Specialist Group. Douglas-Hamilton's figures were rejected as sheer guesses; Parker's views carried the day. Confusion reigned in the conservation world. Was the elephant in trouble or not? To hear it from the experts at Wankie, the evidence gave no cause for alarm.

Douglas-Hamilton lost his chairmanship and limped off in disgust. Anyone with eyes to see could tell there was a crisis, he fumed, data or no data. IUCN and WWF blinked in confusion. What next?

With Douglas-Hamilton's departure, Talbot put me in the hot seat between the two archrivals. The new and expanded group I assembled insisted on putting the black and northern white rhinos at the top of the pachyderm agenda. That didn't please everyone. Our first meeting in 1982 looked as though it would be a second-round slugfest between the two elephant adversaries. Douglas-Hamilton was still fuming over the rejection of his Elephant Action Plan and insisted that the new group endorse his report. "We're wasting time talking," he told me after the meeting. "You're making this a technical group when we should be lobbying to save the elephant." He was too bitter and angry to see the danger of leaving himself scientifically wide open a second time, or the risk to the technical group's credibility if it engaged in media lobbying instead of advising IUCN, as it was supposed to do.

"This is a technical group," I told him firmly. "We're not advocates. If you want to advocate, you're free to do so, but don't use the specialist group's name. If you want reliable figures to make your case, then you are going to have to work with the group. And you're going to have to trust me to do an impartial job."

Douglas-Hamilton clearly took my impartiality to be collusion with the devil himself. Even though I invited him to conduct new and expanded elephant surveys, concentrating on areas with repeat counts to give irrefutable evidence of population trends, he was not mollified. He had taken a bad drubbing at Wankie and desperately wanted scientific endorsement to bolster his flagging confidence. He did finally accept my offer, but he never lost an opportunity to tell me that he was right, Parker was wrong, and I was responsible for the elephants dying every day because I was in with his enemy.

Ian Parker didn't exactly help either. Still gloating over his victory at Wankie, he never passed up a chance to attack Douglas-Hamilton and attempt to vindicate the ivory trade. Parker, a merciless debater with a sardonic wit, had no trouble scoring points against his angry and less facile opponent.

"Most of Douglas-Hamilton's figures are sheer guesses," Parker repeatedly asserted. "We can only tell what's happening to the elephant from trade statistics. And the figures are irrefutable. The volume of ivory is steady at around 600 tons a year, well within sustainable limits. The elephant is not threatened by the ivory trade. If anything, the species is threatened by population growth and habitat loss."

I was sick of the infighting by the end of the first meeting, but if there was one thing Amboseli had taught me, it was the rewards of persistence and sticking to the issues. Despite my quiet demeanor, the two adversaries found that they couldn't bludgeon or sweet-talk me into their position and eventually got down to the job ahead. I was intent on getting some definitive answers and forging a consensus on the status of Africa's elephants.

Cynthia Moss, whom I had brought in to give more attention to the social aspects of elephants, voiced her own refrain. "Why all this talk about ivory?" she burst out angrily to everyone's astonishment. "All I've heard is the ivory trade. What about the elephants? I haven't heard a single word about elephants in two days." She was right. But as much as Cynthia and the western world loved elephants, caring alone wouldn't persuade the politicians to stop the killing when they were behind the ivory racket and when African farmers were screaming about the death and damage caused by elephants.

"We have to have a watertight scientific case," I concluded at the end of the meeting. "And even that's no assurance. The rhino horn trade has been banned since 1977, and poaching has increased sharply every year since, despite the best efforts of wardens like David Sheldrick in Tsavo."

The fractious group did finally agree on the need to collaborate on resolving the elephant controversy, but only after two days of incessant wrangling. Anyone who believes that science is dispassionate and objective has never worked with scientists.

Shortly after the first meeting, Tom Pilgram, a young bearded Berkeley graduate with a bent for computers and an interest in conservation, dropped in looking for a job. I lost no time getting him started on a computer model to test how various levels and patterns of hunting—a euphemism for poaching—affected elephant populations. His sincerity, impartiality, and skills were exactly the combination to ensure that the warring factions contributed their ideas and data.

Pilgram's models quickly dispelled the fallacy of Ian Parker's position on the ivory trade. When we tested the impact of poaching on elephant populations, the herds kept crashing to extinction. Even light poaching sent the herds into a nosedive. The reasons for the alarming results, we soon realized, lay in the oddity of tusk growth and in ivory preferences among carvers.

Elephants, especially the males, put on progressively more ivory with each year of life. By their late forties and early fifties, big males add on more ivory than ever as they rise up the dominance hierarchy. Ivory carvers in Japan and Hong Kong prefer big tusks and pay up to twice as much per kilo as they pay for small tusks.

Thus, unlike meat yields from animals killed for market—cattle and pigs, for example—the greatest yield of ivory comes late in an elephant's life. In fact, our computer model showed that poachers would get most ivory by collecting tusks from elephants dying of natural causes. But in reality no poacher, least of all the rural peasants and armed militia doing the killing, was going to wait for an elephant to die of old age. Any elephant with tusks is fair game, and every poacher has reason to kill it before the next poacher does. It paid poachers to hunt big bulls. But once the big bulls were killed off, poachers shot an increasing number of small bulls— and eventually females and calves. The outcome, as predicted by our computer model, was the slaughter of ever smaller elephants until the population collapsed, a result Iain Douglas-Hamilton was beginning to verify with data collected from his repeat aerial counts across Africa.

A check of Parker's trade statistics matched our predictions: although the total weight shipped remained the same, the average weight of individual tusks bought in the Far East had fallen by half in less than a decade—a point Parker had overlooked, or conveniently ignored. These figures meant that twice as many elephants were being killed as ten years before, ever more of them females and young. Parker's own statistics had proved him utterly wrong about the sustainability of the ivory trade. Instead of conceding that the ivory trade was a threat to the elephant, he fell back on a second and less assailable line of defense, resting not on trade statistics but on his claim that most tusks entering the trade carried the distinctive thin, straight, yellowish ivory of the forest elephant preferred by carvers. The high volume and large size of forest elephant tusks entering the world market attested to a huge population, Parker claimed, so large in fact that the species as a whole was safe despite the decline in savanna elephants. Privately, Parker put the forest elephant population at 2 to 3 million, but having vilified Douglas-Hamilton for making such wild guesses, he wouldn't say so publicly.

The models Tom and I put together verified Parker's scenario—up to a point. If the total African population stood at well over 1 million, the African elephant could sustain the existing ivory trade, despite the localized overhunting in East Africa. If, however, the overall population fell much below 1 million, the ivory trade was indisputably driving the elephant to extinction, as Douglas-Hamilton claimed. The swing factor was the little-known forest elephant, hidden beneath the vast canopy of the central African forest.

Counting the forest elephant posed enormous, perhaps insurmountable challenges. The central African forest covers an area the size of Alaska and Texas combined—a million square miles of some of the most inaccessible country on Earth. Few roads penetrated the region, and counting elephants beneath dense canopy was almost as hopeless as looking for fish in

FOREST INTERLUDE ➤ 199

a muddy river. Futile or not, a count had to be done. The next meeting of our group was a little over a year away. If we could only come up with scientifically credible numbers by then, we could influence the all-important 1987 meeting of the Convention on International Trade in Endangered Species.

I decided to ask British biologist Richard Barnes to take on the forest elephant census. Barnes was a quiet, bush-skilled elephant researcher with impeccable scientific credentials and a reputation for tenacity. He would need both to deliver the count on time and to convince the skeptics. The New York Zoological Society agreed to fund his work.

I would pick Barnes up in the Central African Republic to get a feel for the size of the forest elephant population and consider the best way for him to conduct the first reliable count of the Congo Basin.

With the resolution to the debate within reach, I handed over the chairmanship of the African Elephant and Rhino Specialists Group to David Cummings, a highly respected Zimbabwean conservationist, and stepped back to the vice chairmanship. After three years of scientific wrangling I was ready for a break and couldn't think of anything more adventurous and timely than a trip to central Africa to get the forest elephant survey under way and look for the elusive pygmy elephant.

❮ ❮ ❮

THE FIRST DAY'S adventure had not been quite what I had in mind; nor was it over. Soon after I had dropped off to sleep on the hard earth floor, we were dragged out for a succession of interrogations by a newly arrived apparatchik. These episodes continued until 1:30 A.M., when the rusty galvanized door creaked open a final time. A skinny gendarme, reeking of local beer and drunker yet with authority, threatened us with a fanbelt and grabbed me by the arm. I flung him off in disgust.

Outside, an interrogation committee flanked by soldiers toting carbines and snub-nosed automatics grilled me in Swahili. After an hour we were marched off under armed escort through total darkness. Peter missed his footing and stumbled into a ditch, wrenching his ankle. A column of safari ants chose that moment to attack and send us slapping and cursing toward a waiting vehicle. Finally, shortly before dawn, we were thrown into a United Nations resthouse in Aru, the district center.

By the next day we had become lepers rather than apparitions in the eyes of the local administration. No one could get rid of us fast enough. We were driven several times round the dusty, potholed town between the offices of the district commissioner, chief of police, and head óf immigration, before being discharged without explanation. Later we learned that our drop from the sky came on the eve of public holidays that no one intended to miss. No one was prepared to drive me back to the plane, either, until I explained the delicate predicament of getting airborne. Once the prospect of a crash sank in, my takeoff became the great holiday spectacle, and I was eagerly bundled into a crowded Land Rover and rushed to the plane. It was like being part of a taxiload of enthusiastic peons heading for a bullfight. To lighten the plane and improve the chances of getting off the strip, Peter stayed behind.

A milling throng of more than a thousand had gathered around the plane by the time we arrived and the sinister mood of the previous night had given way to a carnival atmosphere. The abandoned shamba was far shorter and rougher than I had realized from the air. The only hope of getting airborne lay in hacking a strip down the hillside into a shallow valley. By standing on the brakes for maximum takeoff power and putting on full flaps, it might just be possible to get off the ground with enough room to bank into the valley and clear the hills on the opposite side.

The moment I explained the plan, hundreds of singing farmers began happily slashing down the bush, demolishing termite mounds, and filling in ruts to prepare a makeshift runway. Things were shaping up nicely for a grand public spectacle, and everyone and his dog was going to watch. The strip ready, I drained the plane's fuel tanks as safely as possible, loaded our baggage into the Land Rover, and turned into the strip for takeoff. It appeared impossibly short. "Yea, though I walk through the valley of the shadow death" came to mind as the engine raced to full revs. Dust billowed out behind the plane, and the crowd danced wildly to the throb of the engine.

I roared down the strip, the plane bouncing like a softball over flagstones. Then it was airborne. My momentary flutter of relief turned to disbelief as a tall stand of trees loomed ahead. The takeoff had put me deeper into the valley than I'd anticipated, leaving little room to maneuver before I plowed into the trees. Fighting all my instincts to pull back on the stick, I held level to gain maximum speed first. Even then, the plane barely cleared the trees with enough speed to bank into the valley. By the time I'd climbed above the hills with a few feet to spare, my entire my body ached with the tension. Down below a sea of tiny figures danced and waved in a frenzy of delight. The tale would be told in Dibwa village for years to come: the apparition disappeared back into the sky. Giddy with relief, I made a low pass and waggled my wings in appreciation before bearing east to pick up Peter and our baggage.

From Aru I dispatched a message to Shirley assuring her we were safe. It never arrived, and neither did the few others I sent during the remainder of the trip. The first she would hear of us was our low pass over the house on returning to Nairobi.

After our delayed overnight stop at Garamba, the flight west to the Central African Republic was delightfully uneventful. Long green tendrils of forest clutched at the fire-mottled savanna beneath us. The further west we flew, the thicker the tendrils grew, engulfing the savanna like some giant amoeba until only a few small glades remained. This engulfment of the savanna is an illusion, of course, easily dispelled by flying in the opposite direction. Then, the white savanna amoeba devours the green forest.

The boundary between Africa's tropical forest and savanna is a vast chaotic interface the size of the central African forest itself. Botanists, unsure of how to classify the jumbled-up habitats, ignore it altogether. In reality the forest-savanna mosaic is rather like the shifting boundary between fresh and saline water in an estuary. The same tidal forces prevail, though in this case driven by solar cycles and the gravitational tug of planets rather than the moon. These Milanovic cycles, as they are called, drive global heating and cooling patterns, the advance and retreat of glaciers and the shifting shores of forest and savanna.

The earth is far richer in species than we ever imagined. Taxonomists have classified around 1.8 million so far. Terry Erwin of the Smithsonian Institution puts the real figure at closer to 30 million. Other estimates range from as high as 100 million to as low as 8 million. Whatever the true figure, the difference between the known and true total is a measure of our ignorance. The uncertainty hinges on how many invertebrates—especially beetles—are housed in the tropical forest. Ecologist Norman Myers believes that over half of all the species on Earth inhabit the tropical forest. What accounts for the extraordinary diversity of a habitat which covers barely 10 percent of the world's land surface?

The answer eludes evolutionary biologists today no less than it did Charles Darwin more than a century ago, but there is no shortage of theories.

The stability-diversity hypothesis of species richness held sway until the last decade on the mistaken assumption that tropical forests were unaffected by climatic events causing the advance and retreat of the ice ages. Under conditions of stable food supply, the theory assumed that competition between species would intensify, causing interspecies competition and the development of ever-narrower niches as animals and plants became progressively more specialized over tens of millions of years. Competition and natural selection is the engine of specialization, producing a bewildering array of adaptations. The passion flowers alone include over 500 species in tropical America. Biologists looking into the war between animal and plant kingdoms, between predator and prey, are discovering a staggering number of toxic compounds which deter all but the most specialized herbivorous animals. Specialized feeders keep up with continually evolving strategic defenses through their own counteradaptations. The resulting biological arms race doesn't come any cheaper for plants and animals than it does for the superpowers, leading to a continual divergence of highly specialized species and coevolved adaptations of plants and animals. And, the most bizarre life forms and fantastic adaptations occur in tropical forests.

Recent evidence has overthrown the stability-diversity theory of tropical forest richness. It transpires that the tropical forests, no less than the savannas, expanded and contracted with the same alternating cycles of global warming and cooling that drove the glacial cycles. During the last Pleistocene glaciation 15,000 to 20,000 years ago, the Amazon forest contracted to fifteen or so isolated remnants, or refugia. The central African rain forest shrank to a tenth of its present size in two isolated blocks east and west of the Congo basin.

If the forest is indeed unstable, what accounts for the richness of species? One view is that its very instability, linked to the persistence of many isolated forest fragments, is the answer to forest diversity. Perhaps fragmentation followed by periods of stability and niche competition is a better answer, but isolation in some form is essential.

In each isolated fragment, species of plants and animals diverged, much as they do on adjacent islands. Charles Darwin's observation of the rich speciation and morphological adaptation of finches on adjacent Galá-pagos islands was the foundation of modern evolutionary theory, with isolation, mutation, and natural selection providing the fundamental forces of speciation.

The richness of the forest is explained by a simple analogy. Thrust the Galápagos Islands together after prolonged isolation, and the resultant mega-island would contain many coexisting species of finch. Repeated often enough, isolation and recoalescence increase the richness of species. Species may go extinct with each cycle—through competition perhaps, or isolation on islands too small and remote for survival—but the net effect is species enrichment.

The forest-savanna mosaic is a microcosm of the fragmented Pleistocene forests. Each patch is a potential crucible of evolution, but one too tiny and ephemeral to spin off new species.

Despite my fascination with the forest-savanna mosaic, the flight proved a letdown. We saw few elephants and hardly any tracks across the burnt savanna woodlands or the long grass of the open savannas. Scattered bones were all that remained of the richest elephant habitat in Africa.

On January 8, after stopping at Bangui, the capital of the Central African Republic, to pick up Richard Barnes, we headed for a sliver of forested country knifing into the Congo Republic and Cameroon. Landing at Bayanga, a lumber town run by a Yugoslavian company, Slavonia Bois, Richard, and I set off for the forest in search of elephants, accompanied by three Pygmy guides of the Baka tribe and Gustave Dungoube, a wildlife official from Bangui.

We spent a couple of hours searching fruitlessly before heading for the Dzanga salt pan where, our guides assured us, elephants would turn up in the late afternoon. Arriving early, we relaxed against the sculptured buttresses of a fig tree and waited in the stultifying heat listening to the monotonous screech of cicadas. I sat swatting the sweat bees crowding my eyes, wondering about the pygmy elephant as the sun sank and warmed up the washed-out forest across the glade, lighting up the ironwood trees in the rich copper and gold reminiscent of a New England autumn.

No one had ever solved the mystery of the pygmy elephant. The German naturalist Noack first described the diminutive creature in 1906. Eighty years later scientists still debated its existence. The few supposed pygmy species raised in zoos all grew to respectable-sized forest elephants. All the same, the evidence pointed to its existence, and Theodor Haltenorth and Helmut Diller's authoritative *Guide to the African Mammals* describes and illustrates the pygmy elephant in detail. According to them, the pygmy elephant stands five to six feet tall, has a flattened forehead, small rounded ears which stand out from its body, and tusks like toothpicks. The tusks stick straight down from the upper jaw, rather than forward like the savanna elephant's or diagonally like the forest elephant's. Despite its diminutive size, the pygmy elephant is said to be far more aggressive than the forest elephant.

I had no opinion about the existence of the pygmy elephant. All the same, like Peter, I was romantic enough to fantasize about discovering the pygmy elephant on our expedition. After all, there were Pygmy people, pygmy hippos, pygmy buffalo, and many other dwarf mammals in the central African forest, so why not pygmy elephants?

"No elephants. Time to go," Gustave announced. "Maybe tomorrow we have better luck." We set off for camp across the pan as the sun slipped below the ironwoods. Oblivious to our presence a solitary bull elephant entered the far end of the clearing. We hurriedly sank back into the cover of the fig tree and watched excitedly as the animal splashed around in the mud. There could be no question about this one. The animal fit the description of a forest elephant: shoulder height around nine feet, back straight, forehead flattish, tusks thin and downward sloping, ears small and rounded. Suddenly another bull entered the glade and joined the first bull at the mud hollow. I did a momentary double take. The new bull was unquestionably a savanna animal. What was it doing here in the middle of the forest?

"Le gros," the big one, a Baka guide whispered to Richard.

Totally mystified, I pointed my camera and clicked away. Then, seemingly out of nowhere, two dwarf bulls trundled across the glade. Richard looked at me in disbelief and turned to our guides. "Qui est la?"

"Assala, assala," one of the Pygmies whispered, using the name for the pygmy elephant given in Haltenorth and Diller.

I hurriedly switched to a long lens and held down the motor-drive button, half expecting the phantom creatures to vanish into the forest. When I was sure of enough film to silence the skeptics, I began to take stock.

The dwarf elephants stood no more than five and a half feet tall and matched Haltenorth and Diller's description of a pygmy elephant to a tee. Long slender tusks reached toward the ground like the overgrown fangs of a saber-tooth tiger. But if the pygmy elephant was so elusive, how come we had discovered it on our first day out in the forest? And what were we to make of three different elephants in the forest—the savanna, forest, and pygmy forms? Surely if there really were three forms the Pygmies would have given them three separate names, not two?

I watched, thoroughly baffled and totally enthralled as the two pygmy elephants trundled up to the big savanna bull and prankishly threatened the huge creature with a mock charge. How odd! Their small, ballooned-out ears looked more like a juvenile's rather than the scalloped ears of an adult. In fact, the more I observed them the more the pygmy elephants appeared to be juveniles, but there was no mistaking the adult size of their tusks.

As if reading my mind, one pygmy bull shuffled off with tail erect and ears flapping like loose sails to a newly arrived herd of cow elephants, where it tried to suckle a female. So there it was, the great mystery solved: the pygmy elephant was nothing more than a juvenile forest elephant after all.

The Baka Pygmies were puzzled by our confusion and treated us with paternal patience. "Yes, those small ones there are the infants of the assala adults they are with. And yes, that big bull at the mud hole is different. That's the one we call le gros."

Finally, satisfied that we had got it right, our guides led off. Of course, it all made sense now that the Pygmies had pointed it out. The confusion all along lay with the scientists and naturalists. Had they watched elephants or listened closely to the Pygmies, the confusion would never have arisen.

Scientists are often portrayed as skeptical killjoys bent on debunking the Yeti, Loch Ness monster, and other mysterious creatures. Perhaps some are, but I would dearly have loved to have found the pygmy elephant. In a way our discovery was no less exciting, for in solving one mystery we unearthed two more: why are juvenile forest elephants so astonishingly precocious? and what was the savanna elephant doing in the forest? I was so intrigued by these biological mysteries that two days later I returned to Dzanga with Peter to see what else we could learn.

That afternoon we watched twenty-eight elephants enter the pan, some of them forest animals, some savanna, most showing varying degrees of hybridization. The widespread hybridization ruled out one obvious explanation—that the savanna elephant had recently retreated to the forest to escape heavy poaching. Hybridization had evidently been going on for decades, given the mixed traits among animals forty years and older. Would all traces of savanna elephant disappear as we traveled deeper into the forest? The answer would tell us whether we were looking at a narrow hybrid zone, or whether two subspecies genuinely coexisted in the forest.

The afternoon's elephant watch at Dzanga gave us no definitive answer to the precocity of juvenile forest elephants, but it did offer a plausible explanation. Perhaps the sparseness of the forest understory forced the juveniles to leave their mothers at an early age in search of forage. Certainly the small, widely dispersed herds of less than a dozen reported for the forest elephant hinted at food competition. A seasonal parallel among savanna elephants added weight to that deduction.

Savanna elephants gather in megaherds of several hundred when food is abundant during the rains. During the dry season the aggregations break up into dispersed groups as the forage gives out, until the herds are as small as the forest elephant's. In extreme droughts in Amboseli, mothers and infants become separated too. Lacking the precocious tusks of the forest elephant, most of the infants die of starvation or are killed by predators. Even if predators aren't a great threat to forest elephants, natural selection might favor juveniles with long straight tusks that enable them to root up food in the understory. But what about the danger of getting lost? How could wandering juveniles relocate their mothers? A recent and enchanting discovery about the elephant offered a plausible explanation.

Katy Payne, who with her husband, Roger, recorded the haunting infrasonic melodies of the humpback whale, is a person alert to the deep, drumlike vibrations the species uses to communicate in low frequencies inaudible to the human ear. Sitting in an elephant barn in Portland's Washington Park Zoo late one evening in 1985, she noticed the rumpled nasal skin of an Asian elephant resonating gently and sensed a deep, almost imperceptible throbbing motion. Later playback recordings confirmed her suspicions: elephants, like whales, do much of their communicating below our own auditory range.

Payne later linked up with Joyce Poole in Amboseli to study the low-frequency communications in elephants using specialized tape recorders. Sure enough, playbacks showed a number of sounds, including musth rumbles, distress calls, and contact calls, in the low-frequency range. The great advantage of the low rumbles, according to Payne and Poole, lies in long-range communication. The lower the frequency of transmission, the greater the range over which the signals can be picked up. In the sea, humpback whales can communicate with one another halfway round the world. On land, where the denser earth attenuates sound waves, elephants may well be able to communicate up to six miles. The strange throbbing pulses Payne heard in the barn that evening in the Portland Zoo may be the forest elephant's secret of staying in touch, and the explanation for the pygmy elephant.

The day after our second Dzanga visit, Richard and I drove north with Gustave and picked up a heavy-jowled Baka Pygmy with filed teeth and tattooed face. We needed to do a survey of the forest to test Richard's method of counting elephants. A direct count of elephants themselves was out of the question. Richard had seen only a handful in Gabon after several months. "Besides," he told Peter with refreshing honesty for a field biologist, "the last thing I want to see close up in the forest is an elephant."

The alternatives were few. Tracks were one, but individual prints were difficult to pick out on the hard-packed forest soils, where elephants follow each other in single file. That left droppings.

Richard, a lean, angular scientist with a serious demeanor, had in recent months studied elephant dung about as closely as anyone would want to. "We have three variables to worry about," he told me with a look of exasperation through heavy horn-rimmed glasses. "The rate of defecation, the rate of dung decay, and of course the accuracy of my counting. I am assuming Buss's constant of seventeen droppings a day for savanna elephants, until we have a better figure for the forest elephant. Dung decay rates vary with habitat and season, but I can apply the negative exponential curve I've established in Gabon. The only thing that buggers up my calculations are bush-pigs. They scuffle around in elephant dung for undigested nuts and scatter the shit all over the place."

Counting elephant dung to estimate elephant numbers is about as intractable as figuring out the population of New York by counting cigarette butts in trash cans, I decided as he explained his problem. But Richard was determined to pin an exact multiplier on a pile of elephant shit and bring precise science to bear on the matter. I listened in growing admiration for the grave man with a tinder-dry wit, knowing there was no better person to stand up to the pummeling he was sure to get from a skeptical Ian Parker.

We followed our Baka guide for two hours that morning through the cool open understory of primary and secondary forest and counted a solitary pile of elephant dung. I was beginning to have second doubts about Richard's methodology when we entered an abandoned garden heavily overgrown with a tangle of broad-leaved plants. Five dung piles in five minutes. At another overgrown field we counted thirteen in ten minutes.

"I've found the same in Gabon," Richard told me. "Low densities, except in secondary growth, especially old shambas."

The pattern we observed that day held up the next, when Peter and I took a trip across the Sanga River in a narrow pirogue. Signs of both elephant and gorilla were everywhere as we ducked, wove, and hacked through dense undergrowth for an hour and a half. We found no sign of old cultivation. Once again, elephant dung was most abundant in the denser understory. More intriguing was the evidence that elephants themselves had expanded the natural light gaps and promoted the thick understory growth they preferred by destroying regenerating trees. Their continual pruning of emergent trees amounted to a sort of shifting cultivation of the forest. To add to the intrigue, the elephant-pruned patches attracted all manner of other large herbivores, including gorillas, bongo, sitatunga, and bush-pig.

I felt a glow of satisfaction at the observation. The large herbivores seemingly gravitated to the most savannalike patches of the forest—some created by natural tree fall and the occasional hurricane, the larger ones by shifting cultivators and elephants. Elephants were evidently a keystone species diversifying the forests just as they did Amboseli's swamps during a drought. What then would happen if poachers exterminated the elephant? Would the forest canopy close up and the panoply of life in the understory vanish? The thought reverberated as we rowed back across the Sanga River in the rickety pirogue.

After leaving Bayanga, we flew across the remotest stretch of African rain forest, a wild and forbidding region along the northern borders of Congo and Gabon. Following a stopover to discuss Richard's project with officials in Libreville, the capital of Gabon, we headed back inland. To reach Richard's research camp, we had to fly over an "inhospitable zone," a region off-limits to single-engine aircraft. Fortunately, we were given special dispensation on the condition that we follow the roads and rivers in case of mishap. Looking down on the endless series of white-water chutes and rapids of the Ogooue River cascading wildly down the Mount de Cristal Hills below us, I felt sure the Gabonese civil aviation's condition had more to do with the ease of finding our remains than with our safety.

Banking northwest at Booue, we tracked the Ivinda River through unbroken forest until a picturesque cluster of houses rose up on the left bank. A lone figure came outdoors to wave at us. "The Makoukou Research Station," Richard signaled. Like the Serengeti Research Institute, Makoukou had been built with donor funds and was used almost exclusively by expatriate researchers. It began falling apart following a tiff between the French and Gabonese government and the ensuing pullout of foreign researchers. Richard and his girlfriend, Karen, waving up at us, were the station's only resident biologists.

"There used to be many elephants close to the research station," Richard told us apologetically as we hiked along an elaborate grid of numbered trails in the forest behind the research station the next day. We checked off a number of birds I had never seen—the yellow-billed coucal, black dwarf hornbill, red-vented malimbe, blue-cheeked malimbe, and yellow-cheeked trogons—but the large mammals, even the ubiquitous duikers, were gone.

"I have to travel miles from villages to find any signs," Richard added, stooping to pick up a spent cartridge. "Poachers are killing anything within a day's walk of settlements, roads, and rivers. They, more than any other factor, determine elephant densities in the forest. I measure poaching activity by the number of these cartridges along the trails. Sometimes it's four or five a day—right in the scientific reserve. The researchers did the poachers a favor in building the trail system."

That night I lay awake listening to the tree hyrax screaming—like someone getting his balls squeezed, as Richard graphically put it—the screech of the crickets, and the rush of the rapids, wondering about elephants and poachers. If poachers had penetrated the deepest forest, what hope was there for the elephant? And what of all the other creatures which depended on the elephant's activities?

A couple of days later we left the silent decrepitude of the research station to check out a report of crop-raiding elephants shot near Etakanyabe village. Forest Department scouts had apparently trumped up an excuse to shoot two bulls for meat and were holding off butchering the animal until we arrived. Both Richard and I were anxious to see the elephant, which we were assured, was a genuine assala. It was not at all what we had expected, though. "Ears small and round, skin virtually black and very hairy," I wrote in my notebook. Neither Richard nor I had never seen anything quite like it and hesitated to make a judgment.

Richard interrogated the grizzled hunter who had led us to the elephant. "You call this an assala?"

He wavered. "Yes. No. Well, maybe a small le gros. It was in a herd of five, two of them bulls."

I jotted down measurements of its feet, ears, and teeth. According to taxonomists, the anatomical distinction between forest and savanna elephants lies in the chin. The forest elephant, unlike the savanna race, has a Tutenkhamen-like protrusion on the end of its chin. This was clearly a forest elephant by that definition, yet the tusks were savannoid.

Much as the Pygmies know their elephants, our guide's confusion over assala and le gros clearly reflected a complicated pattern of hybridization between the two races. It seems the savanna and forest elephant coexist throughout the forest, not only at its outskirts. Yet the puzzle remained stubbornly incomplete as we moved deeper into the forest, even as the keystone role of elephants became a good deal more coherent and the impact of poaching more alarming.

Ard Louis, a Dutch botanist who had worked in Gabon since 1970, was voluble on the ecological role of elephants, claiming they shaped the forest by holding the chablis, or tree-fall gaps, in check. His associate, Jan Reitsma, a tall, blond botanist employed by the New York Botanical Gardens, was even more emphatic. "Large mammals explain the peculiarities of the African forest—why they are so patchy," he told me. "I can't understand why zoologists haven't studied the interaction. It's impossible to find a virgin forest in Gabon." He underscored the point by asking me to fly him over an island off Libreville in his search for a forest untouched by humans and elephants.

Nina Pradel, who looked after camp at Wonga Wongue, where we touched down a few days later, was decidedly agitated. She had not been informed that we had special dispensation to visit President Bongo's jealously guarded hunting reserve, where the genuine pygmy elephant was said to occur. She soon loosened up over a lunch of chicken and forest-buffalo steak and held forth at length on the three races of elephants at Wonga Wongue. Her teenage son, Norbert, launched into the subject of pygmy elephants with a passion.

"The young are knee height and the adults only chest height," he insisted, pulling out a photo of himself catching a sick adult. "At least sixty years old, this one. Look at the worn tusks." I did. It was a juvenile with a telltale short trunk, small head, and hairy body.

That afternoon we set off to locate a herd of elephants in the open grassland. Norbert, out to prove his manhood, thrust a pistol into his waistband with a flourish and drove the bucking opened-topped Toyota at high speed over the grassland. At the first sight of elephants he rushed them full speed, bent on preventing the terrified herd from reaching the safety of the forest. Richard leaned forward and diffidently asked if we could stop and observe them. "Ce n'est pas possible," he yelled. "These are not Kenya elephants. They are very dangerous."

Whatever else Norbert thought about these harrowed animals, they certainly weren't pygmies. Here, as deep into the forest as one could get, the elephants were decidedly smaller than the Bayanga races and almost purely forest form. All the same, an "echo" of savanna traits was discernible in a few animals.

Peter and I left Richard in Libreville on February 24 and flew on to Kinshasa, Zaire. After an overnight stop we made for the Njili International Airport and filed our flight plan to fly across the central Congo basin. "Non, non. Il est terrain terrible," I was told by the tower. "It can't be done in a single-engine plane. Too dangerous." That was all we needed. Peter was already on edge after the warning by our host the previous night of the countless planes lost in "Africa's Bermuda Triangle," as the forest we were about to cross was known.

Back in the air after using a ministerial contact to get clearance, I followed Africa's widest river northward. Ten minutes into the flight, the control tower came through with a storm alert. I veered slightly west as instructed and flew on, expecting to outflank the storm. Instead the clouds grew thicker and blacker. I veered farther west until we located a small gap in the storm front with clear skies beyond.

I headed for the gap. Suddenly all hell broke loose. Luggage and charts slammed against the ceiling as a wind thrust us toward the ground. For twenty seconds I clung to the stick with all my strength, helplessly watching the ground rush toward us. Then, just as it seemed the plane would break up, the gale eased, and we made our escape.

The gale pounded us twice more as we groped for a way through. By now our only chance of making Basankusu, our overnight stop, lay in outflanking the howling wind and driving rain. I roared north full bore at the sight of clear skies in the distance, but each time we made ground a fresh storm wave broke ahead of us like a rolling black surf. Two hundred miles later we were running short of fuel with no end in sight.

"We're not going to make it," I yelled at Peter. "And I can't figure out from the map exactly where we are." He looked resigned, remembering our previous forced landing. That was just as well. The storm had driven us miles west of the Zaire River, perhaps into the Congo Republic.

Racing the storm and battling high winds and driving rain for the next hour and a half was sheer hell. Luckily, with the wind behind us we made Brazzaville, across the river from Kinshasa, just as the storm enveloped the city. Heading into howling winds and pelting rain we dipped under the clouds and found ourselves sandwiched between the blackness of the storm overhead and the huge standing waves of the Zaire River a hundred feet below.

I gave my full attention to keeping the plane in the narrow envelope. By the time we made the opposite shore, the tops of Kinshasa's skyscrapers were blanketed in cloud. "I want Ndola Airport for an emergency landing," I radioed ahead to Njili tower. "We can't make Njili through the storm."

"Negative Ndola," came back the response. "You are an international flight and must land at Njili." The man must be crazy if he thought we were going to risk Njili. "Negative," I shot back. "I am landing at Ndola." Ignoring a peppering of inane bureaucratic questions, I insisted again on emergency clearance for Ndola. The operator began yelling incoherently, then put on a woman who tried to coax me into Njiri—to follow immigration procedures, she kept repeating. "I'm landing at Ndola using my pilot's prerogative," I said a final time and turned down the radio in exasperation.

We were over the city now, with the wind buffeting us down toward the skyscrapers one moment and up into the clouds the next. I looked over at Peter. He was white and rigid but valiantly searching for the airstrip. Then, there it was beneath us. I banked hard left, negotiating our way between the high-rises, temporarily losing sight of the airstrip. Judging its alignment, I came in slow and steep, peering through the pounding rain. A faint radio transmission crackled through the static, giving us belated clearance to land—with the wind at our tail. Ignoring the suicidal instructions, I flared out hard into the wind as the asphalt shot up to greet us. Tires screeched on the wet runway. Never had the ground felt so good.

Totally wrung out, we sat for a moment in silence. Peter looked over at me. "Thank you, Doctor Western. You were incredibly calm under pressure."

"Never again," I grinned back.

The next day was unexpectedly balmy, but we were stuck on the ground for hours hassled by immigration and health officials. One surly medical orderly insisted on a cholera injection before giving us takeoff clearance and pulled a used syringe out of a filthy drawer. With AIDS rampant in Zaire, there was no way we were going near that syringe. Peter began fretting that we would be arrested if the immigration officials discovered that he had written scathing articles about President Mobutu's corrupt dictatorship, so we paid a bribe for the cholera stamp and made our escape.

Thousands of islands, some forested, others covered with a patchwork of shambas studded the sluggish, muddy waters of the Zaire River. We checked off the quaint red-roofed town of Mdambaka on the map and bore east along the tea-colored Lulanga River, hoping to shave a couple of hours off the flight by short-circuiting the giant northward coil of the Zaire River. Hundreds of rippled sandbanks broke the surface of the Lulanga, heralding a brief two-month dry season. Droning on eastward, we followed every nuance of a river until it broke up into myriad headwaters swallowed up by the great heartland of the Congo Basin. From here on there would be no place to land in the event of further problems.

Seen from high overhead, the sky and forest meld into a formless blue unbroken tranquility. The vastness of the forest gives the same reassuring feeling of the Sahara—that it has always been there, and always will be. I knew better than to trust the illusion of permanence and passed away the dead hours over the forest conjuring up the changing landscape below the canopy, imagining the habitats jostling one against the other for control of the Congo Basin as the climate changed.

The enormity of the Mediterranean seen from 35,000 feet up in a jumbo jet beguiles us into believing that it, too, is as permanent as the forest and desert. Deep-sea cores tell a different story. At one stage the Straits of Gibraltar closed in one great tectonic bite and created a huge inland sea. Over several millennia, the sea evaporated, leaving a salt-encrusted desert.

A similar story is emerging for the Congo Forest. Not once, but several times in the last 100,000 years, the climate dried and the Kalahari sands took over. Distinctive wind-blown deposits lie beneath the thin humus layer of the forest to prove it. If climate oscillates from wet to dry and habitats change from forest to savanna, could the flux explain the baffling pattern of hybridization between forest and savanna races?

Surely the forest-savanna mosaic we had traced on our outward journey from Nairobi would expand and contract to the tempo of climate? Forest elephants spread into the savannas along the green tentacles of gallery forest, no doubt their genetic signature diminishing as the forest thinned. The reverse is true of the bush elephant. The bush elephant haunts the savanna traces in the swamps and open glades of the forest and fades to a genetic murmur deep in the interior.

Allow for a moment the paleoclimatologists to reconstruct the recent past. Forests would ebb and flow across the Congo Basin, giving the savanna its chance when the climatic tide runs out. The last low tide occurred 18,000 years ago when the savannas, and even a tongue of the Kalahari, spread across the central Congo. Surely savanna elephants would follow the invading savannas and forest elephants the retreating forests to the river margins and two highland massifs located at the eastern and western extremities of the Congo Basin?

Some 12,000 years ago the climatic tide turned again, and the remnant forests expanded until they lapped into East Africa. This time forest elephants would advance and savanna elephants retreat. Five thousand years ago the tide ran out a final time, creating the present-day forest and savanna. Such short cycles, the ragged edge of the forest-savanna mosaic, and the long life span of elephants could easily blur the geographical division between the two races and explain their complicated overlap and hybridization.

Descending low, I checked the density of elephant tracks across the open glades and sand banks. We flew on without reward. Signs of elephants were few in central Zaire. Evidently not even the largest and most inaccessible forest in Africa offered elephants refuge from the poacher. I doubted that the entire forest held 300,000 animals, say 400,000 at the outside, far fewer than even Iain Douglas-Hamilton had imagined.

On January 30 we were awakened by the loud prolonged shout of a Pygmy hunter. Dozens of voices responded in a cacophony of duiker calls and monkey whoops, speculating on what the day's hunt would bring. Peter and I struggled out of the tiny beehive hut built by the Bambuti Pygmies of the Ituri Forest.

We had reached the outlying Pygmy hunting camp of Akare after a five-hour walk from Epulu, the base camp of John and Terese Hart, two New York Zoological Society researchers studying the Ituri Forest and the Bambuti. Peter had accompanied a hunting band the previous day and returned with five blue duikers, among the smallest of antelopes. That evening we gathered round the fire and listened to the hunters sing and dance to the accompaniment of hide drums and stick bundles. Their leaping shadows reached across the forest clearing and flickered high in the trees. I fell asleep remembering similar hunting rituals at Mbwamaji, knowing this was how it must have been at the dawn of humanity.

After a breakfast of blue duiker, manioc, and plantain, John and Terese, led by a gnarled older hunter named Kenga and his tiny associate Imudi, set out to explore the remote area north of the Idoro River. John was eager to find a site for studying the elusive okapi, a close relative of the giraffe. Imudi led off in short mincing strides, a two-foot-long bow slung from his shoulder. We picked up only three elephant dung piles in the two-mile stretch before fording the Idoro across a fallen tree. Over the river we picked up more dung piles—nine in a mile and a half—mostly in thicket smothering a garden abandoned thirty years before. Close by, a couple of elephants went crashing off through the wall of greenery.

"I think the more open canopy and thicker understory this side of the Idoro is due to elephant activity in earlier years," John told me when I pumped him for an explanation.

We followed a series of crisscrossing elephant trails still used occasionally, but they were already narrowing as fringing vegetation encroached. At one point, far beyond the Pygmy's net-hunting range, Kenga stopped and pointed at some tracks. "Hunters. Ivory hunters," he told us.

John, a sandy-haired American who has adopted the lighthearted nature of the Mabuti he has lived among for years, was uncharacteristically somber. "There used to be many more elephants here," he insisted. "But the poachers, using Pygmy guides, are penetrating the deepest forests in search of ivory. They sell it to district chiefs and the military—Mobutu's perks to his army. One game guard who was unusually enthusiastic recently made a forty-day patrol of the forest south of here. He found few elephants and those he did were being tailed by poachers."

The next day I joined the hunters on a *milka*—a net hunt. Gabi, a short muscular Bambuti hurried ahead in jerky strides. The mesh net bundled over his back made him look like a scurrying Ninja Turtle. There were few signs of elephants anywhere, despite the abundance of their aging trails. Here, within easy reach of Epulu town and the Trans-African Highway, the trails had already been choked by invading understory.

I squatted behind the three-foot-high net made of forest vines and listened to the dogs yelping and the women and children whooping as they drove their quarry toward the nets. How long would the Pygmies and the forest survive the consumer world, I wondered. I had seen the old Swahili hunters carrying muzzle-loaders driven out by poaching gangs heavily armed with modern assault weapons; the Bushmen in the Kalahari give up their hunter-gatherer existence to become settled ranchers and farmers; the Maasai abandon their nomadic traditions to fence and ranch the savannas. And now, deep in the Ituri, the Pygmies' ancient lifestyle was dying out as they became hired hunters for the agriculturists pushing deeper into the forest every year. How long before the Ituri Forest is hacked down by the

advancing fields and villages? For a moment I was lost in troubling memories and dark thoughts about the future.

When the hunt was over, the Bambuti would return to Epulu and live
on the fringes of village life as "primitifs," in the words of a gendarme who
arrested one of John's drink-happy assistants the night we made town.
Lumber concessions and commercial ventures were already planned for
the Ituri. If they were lucky, John and Terese would convince the Zaire
government to set aside a sizable national park where the Bambuti could
stay on in some role, perhaps as guards and trackers.

The park will still be Stanley's Darkest Africa to a New Yorker who has
never seen anything wilder than a tiger at the Bronx Zoo, or an echo of an
ancestral life acted out at a festival of traditional dancing among Kenga's
great-grandchildren. A facet of the wild will survive, if John and Terese see
their plans fulfilled. But for me the empty spaces of a national park are an
artifact in Africa. A national park speaks of people no longer able to coexist with animals—of reservations for Native Americans in the United
States and Bantustans in South Africa. What is truly at stake is the loss of
our ability to coexist among ourselves, much less with other species. With
the disappearance of the Maasai, the Bushmen, and the Pygmies, we have
made space for nature but lost the intimacy of living with it. When you
have lived among people who live with nature, it is hard to accept that
coexistence is dead.

My thoughts were interrupted by a blue duiker breaking through the
thicket, pursued by whooping beaters and yelping dogs. Moments later it
crashed into the net and thrashed around helplessly. Gabi jumped forward
and dispatched it with a single blow to the head. His wife hurried out of
the thicket to load the animal into the woven basket slung over her back
and tell us of a large *sindula*—a yellow-backed duiker—speared farther
down the line of nets. Following her directions we came on a huddle of
hunters excitedly gathered around the 120-pound animal. The sindula,
killed by a spear through the heart as it broke back through the beaters,
was cause for celebration: small duikers are the property of the net owners;
large prey like the sindula are divided among the entire camp.

The Bambuti hunters danced and sang late into the night, mimicking
the yellow-backed duiker's last moments. I sat watching, alternately
enchanted and melancholic, knowing I was watching the last moments of

the Pygmy peoples. Someday soon they would give up this life and become villagers. Most already had. Only the dancing shadows of their ghosts would remain, leaping across the forest glades and flickering silently high up in the trees.

◀ ◀ ◀

THE IMPACT of the trip didn't fully sink in until we were over the last of the forest six weeks after the trip began, flying across a front of advancing settlement. If the forest elephant population didn't exceed 400,000, the continental total must be around 800,000, far below Parker's figure of 1.5 to 3 million.

Iain Douglas-Hamilton was right about the ivory trade, however crude his original estimates. Here in the central African forest, as far from human settlement as one could get, elephants were being exterminated not by habitat loss or settlement, but for their ivory. The computer projections Tom and I had made were close to the mark; at the current rate of loss, elephant numbers would halve again in less than a decade. Few populations would survive for twenty years unless the ivory trade was drastically slashed.

The trip also alerted me to a more devastating and previously overlooked aspect of the ivory trade. If elephants were exterminated, many other species would slip over the brink of extinction, and ecosystems across Africa would suffer a loss of biological diversity.

The metaphor that sprang to mind about the keystone role of the elephant was Architect of the Forest. The metaphor was oversimplified perhaps, but its meaning was not. Saving a species is not enough. Saving the whale, the tiger, and the elephant is only a start. We must look beyond mere survival of a species to the conservation of intricately bound and infinitely complex ecological webs. No species shows the threats to biodiversity as forcefully as the elephant, the Architect of the Forest.

South African ecologist Norman Owen-Smith would soon put forward a similar idea with a dramatic twist. He suggested that the Pleistocene overkill, the mass extinction of the large mammals in the Americas and Europe 12,000 to 15,000 years ago, could not be attributed wholly to early hunters alone. Hunters may have killed off the mammoths, mastodons, woolly rhinos, and the giant sloths in South America, but what of the dozens of species of smaller, fleeter-footed horses, deer, and antelope? Citing evidence from southern African reserves, where the extermination of the elephant late in the last century led to bush encroachment and the loss of many grazing species, Owen-Smith proposed his megaherbivore extinction hypothesis. The extermination of a few big mammals like the elephant may have been all it took to trigger large-scale habitat simplification and an avalanche of extinction.

Looking down on the new shambas, the clutter of thatch huts, and the wisps of smoke drifting up from heaped charcoal mounds among the gray shadows of felled trees, there seemed no hope for the elephant, however long it took for the advancing settlements to reach the Congo forest. Settlement and habitat loss were not the immediate threats. By the time the first shambas inched into the Ituri, the elephant would have already vanished, victims of the Japanese love of hankas and Americans' penchant for jewelry. What could the industrial world's consumers know of their deadly impact on Africa's elephants and the rain forest?

Peter leaned back and stretched his lanky frame in the close confines of the cockpit as we flew over Lake Victoria. "So, what did you think of the trip, Jonah?"

I hesitated, torn by two conflicting impressions, "Tough but fantastic, Peter. And you?"

"In short, agreed!"

Soon we were over the western boundary of Serengeti. I dropped low over the scattered woodlands and passed above galloping herds of wildebeest, low hills, and scattered rocky kopjes to the great open plains. I had never felt headier with the beauty and freedom of the savannas.

‹ 12 ›

Keystone Species

On returning from the forest trip I was all fired up about studying the ecological role of elephants in the savanna and settling the issue of their conservation status in Africa. I was barely back in Amboseli ready to begin on the ecological study when a Land Rover listing with Maasai pulled up outside the house. Elephants would have to wait.

"We need you to get things going again," Jonathan Leboo, the young treasurer of Ogulului Group Ranch pleaded after the ten-man committee spread itself around the Spartan sitting room decorated with Maasai beadwork and spears. Leboo, slender and handsome, with the long narrow face of a classical Maasai, sat next to the secretary, John Marinka. Both Leboo and Marinka had attended school and worked at one of the lodges in the park until elected to the group ranch committee on a pro-development ticket. Though Maasai and proud of it, they lacked the deep insights and strict adherence to traditions of Parashino's generation.

"We haven't held a meeting with the new warden in a year," Leboo complained bitterly. So write the minister, I told him, not wanting to get sucked into endless negotiations again. "That won't work, *daktari* [doctor]. You know that. The minister won't do anything and our complaints will only make things worse between us and the Wildlife Department. We need your help."

I was torn between letting the Maasai fight their own battles and supporting their case. Once they learned to mobilize themselves and lobby the authorities and press in Nairobi, they would be a formidable voice. But they weren't quite there yet, and the warriors' hotheaded spearing of animals wasn't the voice they needed. After mulling it over for a day, I drove to Namelok to hear them out.

I pulled up at a rectangular bungalow built of black lava boulders to pick up my field assistant, David Maitumo. Tiny faces peered out of the glassed windows and a shiny galvanized tin roof shimmered in the sun. David had done well in ten years on the project, and his modern house, set among the Maasai bomas, made a statement about his intention to continue living among his people while moving on in life. The only hint of his pastoral origins was the traditional hut out back, where his wife, Joyce, prepared meals of vegetables and posho on a three-stone hearth. Shirley, with her radical Berkeley proclivities, pressed David to modernize the women's kitchen quarters, too. Joyce, torn between two worlds, smiled politely. Fewer than one in five Maasai women received any schooling at the time, yet Joyce had a good education despite her staunchly traditional family. Traditional and western culture had blended at her wedding up at the Protestant church in Loitokitok—her tall, regal father standing straight as a ramrod in a red blanket flanked by an assortment of Maasai in traditional attire; Joyce dressed in white lace and veil attended by pretty bridesmaids and David, smiling nervously, flanked by four groomsmen in pinstripes with pink carnations pinned to their lapels.

David's mother, heavily wrinkled and shaven-headed, came out and offered her hand. Joyce followed, smiling warmly, then Suzuki, her third child, who hugged my leg affectionately. Suzuki got his nickname when Joyce gave birth in the project vehicle on the way to Loitokitok Hospital. That at least was an improvement on her previous delivery in a public bus.

I followed David into the backyard past the kitchen and hopped over a narrow irrigation ditch into his eight-acre shamba. He briefed a gang of Tanzanian laborers in ragged clothes squatting in a vegetable bed planting tiny onion seedlings by hand. Close by, two Maasai women in red shawls sat picking tomatoes and dropping them into a brightly woven bag ready for market. A thicket of fever trees stretched beyond the field to Namelok Swamp, elegantly making the same point as the ditch behind my house, though on a far grander scale: keep out elephants, and trees will grow. Back in 1969, in disproving Maasai overgrazing as a cause of woodland destruction, for fear of being seen as perverse by conservationists, I had hesitated to say that the Maasai might even be protecting the trees. Namelok was proof of that perverse speculation. Acacias grew so plentifully that farmers regularly hacked and burned whole groves to enlarge their shambas and discourage wildlife; recently warriors had driven off the last of Namelok's buffaloes after a small boy on his way to school was gored to death.

When David was ready we clambered back into the vehicle and drove a quarter-mile to Kerenkol's compound hidden behind a dense hedge of croton bushes. Chickens pecked in the dirt as we greeted a smiling Kerenkol, habitually dressed in a brown safari suit these days. Snickering at my joke about his warrior garb and favorite steer—a spanking new Land Rover—he led me through the door of his clapboard house to the Ogulului committee seated on bright-red plastic sofas in the sitting room, admiring the framed prints and photos nailed to the wall.

The chairman rose to greet me, followed by John Marinka, Jonathan Leboo, and the rest of the committee, some dressed in trousers and shirts, a few in ill-fitting crumpled jackets. Maasai leaders seldom wore traditional shukas anymore. Our jovial greetings brought out an angry swarm of bees nesting in the wooden planking. We hurried out laughing into the yard, where we sat on rough-hewn benches spread out under a shady tree dotted with yellow flowers.

Kerenkol, like David, had switched from the intensely public life of a Maasai boma to the privacy of a bungalow. Not that he hadn't done things privately as a villager; after all, he and his brother Tia had stashed away a tin of meat in the balanites tree during the drought. The point is that they did it surreptitiously to avoid a ring of outstretched hands. His traditional wealth, measured by livestock, was a matter of daily scrutiny, exposing him to constant solicitations from relatives and friends. In the privacy of his new bungalow's back room he counted thick wads of money accruing from his market-gardening ventures, livestock sales, retail stores, and trucking businesses without announcing his wealth to all and sundry.

A private house and a cash economy had subdivided the intermeshed world of Kerenkol's past into discrete economic and social realms. Whereas the old order had relied on extended family, clan, and tribe in an outward ripple of reciprocal interests revolving around the pastures and waters of

Amboseli, the new order relied on commercial expediency. Economic interest rather than social obligation dominated Kerenkol's new life, and you could already sense his preoccupation with nuclear family and urban connections. His kids would soon attend a progressive boarding school in Gilgil two hundred miles away and grow up familiar with the outer world of Kenya rather than the world of Amboseli.

"Mama, bring tea," Kerenkol ordered, as we got down to business. "The Amboseli *bunge* [parliament] is now in session," he chuckled, alluding to the committee he consulted on serious matters. After Stanley Oloitiptip, the undisputed leader of Maasailand, died in 1984, Kerenkol had risen to assistant chief and become the acknowledged leader of Ogulului ranch. Though still illiterate, he was widely seen as progressive and sagacious.

A recent incident provided a colorful example of Kerenkol's ability to blend the roles of traditional laigwenani and modern civil servant.

A band of warriors from his Ilkisongo section had chased off herders from the Kaputei section after finding them illegally grazing their cattle south of the Ol Kajiado River. The two forces clashed briefly with swords and spears along the Selengei River, leaving two Ilkisongo warriors dead. After a lull to gather reinforcements, the warriors were girding themselves for another assault. Meanwhile, the government got wind of the battle and sent in the crack General Service Unit to break up the warring factions.

Kerenkol, fearing the frenzied warriors would ignore the guns, was desperate to avert a bloodbath. "Quickly, fly me in your plane," he pleaded. "I must call off the warriors before the GSU starts shooting." After a long search we found the war party, fifty strong, gathered under a cluster of tortilis trees. The warriors looked magnificent, all ochered up, bright red shukas flapping in the wind, squatting behind huge brightly painted buffalo-hide shields in a thicket of glistening spears. They looked as the warring parties would have to the explorer Joseph Thomson, who first traversed Maasailand in the 1880s and described the fearsome warriors.

"Down, down!" Kerenkol screamed at me over the roar of the engine. Swooping to head height, I cut the engine as Kerenkol leaned out of the window to identify himself to the startled warriors. The war party came to its feet in a spontaneous roar as they watched us circle a second time. Yelling at the top of his lungs, Kerenkol warned them of the GSU and ordered his warriors home. On the final pass they raised their spears and screamed back in acknowledgment.

Kerenkol was unusually quiet on the flight home. Suddenly he burst into one of his girlish giggles. "I must be the first Maasai to command his warriors from a plane. What are things coming to!"

The subject he addressed outside his house wasn't so easily resolved.

"It's bad," he started, clucking in frustration. "We get no response from the Wildlife Department these days. First they stopped the grazing fee, then water for our stock. Now they don't even talk to us. What's wrong with Sindiyo? How can he desert us, his own people? You know him well. Why don't you tell him how we feel?

"We have a new problem, too, this one far worse—as bad as it was before the agreement with the government. We did what we said we would and saved the elephants from the Somalis. And what happens? The elephants lose their fear of people and come out of the park to raid our shambas. We've given up planting maize after two farmers were killed protecting their crop. And the Wildlife Department does nothing. We hate elephants these days."

When Kerenkol had finished speaking, everyone chimed in, working themselves into a lather of frustration, anger, and threats—all to no avail. Sindiyo was not the force he once was. I had called on him already in his office, urging him to do something about Amboseli. He looked tired. "I'm fed up, Jonah. This is too much. The poaching, the corruption. It's everywhere. You know as well as I do who's involved. What can I do? I want to get out and write a book about my people. Can you find me a grant?"

After twenty years working together, he was calling it quits. Rumors circulated around town that he was being blackmailed and intimidated, others that he was corrupt. What had become of the former Amboseli warden so dedicated to improving the lot of wildlife and his people? The political godfathers behind the ivory racket who had reportedly told Sindiyo to keep his mouth shut had to be formidable to cow a man like him.

Sindiyo's defeat came as a blow. I could barely speak when he asked for help with his book, and left him moping at his desk ready to quit myself. If he as director of wildlife had lost hope, what hope could there be?

The time had come to level with the Ogulului committee about the

Wildlife Department. Looking around at the expectant faces, I wondered how they would respond to my admission of defeat. Then I hesitated. How could I give up on them? Hadn't I got them into this, earned their trust, and built up expectations? Hadn't we fought and won together time and again over the years against far greater odds?

"Jonah, what do you think?" Kerenkol was waiting. I needed time to think.

"You never give up do you, Jonah," friends often told me. The eternal optimist. Always convinced things will turn out all right despite all the greed and corruption. Had they only known my darkest fears and the strain of putting on a show of optimism in the face of the skepticism and opposition to changing Kenya's wildlife policies. Optimism is kept alive by reward, however tiny, and Amboseli had nothing left to offer me. With the Wildlife Department's financial support withering, the park faced a dim future.

A familiar, seemingly disembodied voice spoke up unexpectedly, whipping up self-confidence and enthusiasm.

"Listen, who has helped you here at Namelok? You. And look at what you've achieved with your shambas and schools. Did you rely on the government? Did they help you? No. These shambas you did yourselves. The tourist campsite, too. Forget the Wildlife Department. They've forgotten you. It's time to do things on your own, like your shambas, like the campsite."

I snapped out of my trance to find a circle of familiar faces leaning forward, eagerly listening to my plea. Instinctively I had jumped back into the fray.

"Let's talk about the shambas and elephants. Yes, let's talk about that," I continued. "Don't let elephants ruin your shambas. Block them. David knows all about electric fences. He built that one round my house, the one that keeps elephants off my trees. And look how he succeeded. You can do the same for your shambas—fence them in with an electric wire. If all you farmers got together you could build a communal fence. If you collect half the money, I will raise the other half."

"Sawa, sawa—okay—let's do it. We'll select a fencing committee right now." It was the chairman, animated and rallying his committee. "Yes, yes," Kerenkol pitched in, "we can do it ourselves. Why not? We don't need the Wildlife Department." Then it was Marinka, followed by Leboo. Half an hour later the meeting broke up. The Maasai were resolved, the elephant fence would go ahead with movers like Kerenkol behind it. And when it did, the conflict between elephants and Maasai would ease. The solution seemed so trivial in comparison with the magnitude of Amboseli's other problems, but if the electric fence did the trick and got the Maasai to take the initiative, it was a step in the right direction. If nothing else, it bought precious time for Amboseli, time in which to try other avenues, whatever they might be.

Buying time and exploring new options is a stratagem that often pays off in African conservation. Too many conservationists take the opposite tack, forcing a crisis in the belief that demanding a here-and-now last-chance crisis is the only solution. Sometimes it works, though seldom for long. Creating a crisis draws attention and raises money, but the ecowarrior is a misplaced force in Africa, where people must first be convinced then involved, rather than coerced and excluded.

After the hot, dusty drive from Namelok, the shady grove round my house offered a welcome retreat. The regrowth inside an electric fence all around was coming on fast.

Having hit on the cause of tree loss, I found it easier and cheaper to re-create the woodlands of twenty years ago with an electric fence rather than a ditch. Elephants and electric fences are made for each other. With its soft wet trunk and great fat feet, an elephant is the ideal conductor for 5,000 volts pulsing through a strand of wire and learns to avoid it like a gunshot. The amperage in the fence protecting the five acres of woodland regeneration round the house was far too low to do any damage, but one zap posted an indelible warning in the elephant's memory. Within months the acacia seedlings nibbled back repeatedly over the years sprang up to bush height.

The one person unhappy to see the recuperation of acacias was Cynthia Moss. In her mind, evidence of elephants destroying trees raised the specter of culling squads killing "her" animals, as she called them. Having so painstakingly identified and named every one and treated them as part of her extended family, her devotion was understandable. But in categorically rejecting the evidence before her eyes in the hope that the trees would curl up and die of salt poisoning, she was letting sentiment get the better of good judgment.

Sentimentalizing elephants is easy to do, and I am as guilty as anyone. But one must also acknowledge the other face of elephants—the fear, hatred, and suffering they inspire in Africa. Elephants are so tame in Amboseli National Park that they will sidle up to the car and run a trunk all over it, and your arm, if you're trusting enough. Try keeping them out of your vegetable garden at night, and their mild nature turns dangerous. Dozens of farmers lose their lives in Kenya every year protecting their crops from enraged elephants. This is the side of them most Africans see and researchers and conservationists disavow.

Cynthia was quick to berate the Maasai for destroying the park and the peace of her campsite, forgetting it was they who had saved Amboseli's elephants from poachers. She argued that Amboseli should become an elephant park and her animals left alone, shutting her eyes to the outcome: elephants would eventually destroy their own habitat and die of starvation if the population continued to grow unchecked. Fewer than a couple of hundred elephants could be sustained within the park indefinitely. What would happen to the hundreds of surplus animals?

The only solution lay in winning back space outside the park—if the area could be made safe from ivory poachers.

Cynthia choked up with rage whenever I raised these questions and I reacted just as badly to her denial of the problems elephants posed. She had once told me that the Amboseli elephants were her life and that she had no other reason to live. There was no doubting her feelings, but what about the love of the Maasai defending their families and property from elephants? The problems of elephants and Maasai living together had to be dealt with compassionately and fairly, personalizing the victims on both sides of the conflict.

So, after being friends and research colleagues for ten years, we ended up barely talking—Cynthia getting on with her behavioral studies and publicity campaigns to endear Africa's last natural elephant population to the western public, I with ways to resolve the problems that aberrant elephant ecology posed for Amboseli and the Maasai. The standoff was utterly senseless, but at the time there seemed no grounds for compromise.

Laws was right about elephants destroying Amboseli's woodlands and its diversity. Nearly half the plant species had disappeared in the central park since 1967. The trees, bushes, and shrubs screening my fading yellow tent at Kampi ya Western, as well as the bushbuck, lesser kudu, giraffe, eagle owl, African hoopoo, superb starling, crested francolin, and striped skinks filling up my guest book, had all vanished. You couldn't hide a matchbox in the windswept grasslands these days. Like the forests of central Africa, my old campsite had fallen into an ecological silence.

As I mulled over these changes, an intriguing little subplot surfaced. Shrubs and herbs not seen in years quickly colonized the newly completed elephant ditch, heralding the return of Amboseli's lost diversity. Then, in a surprising twist, the understory plants thinned and died for lack of light under the closing acacias. Five years later, the understory lay in deep shade, devoid of life except for fallen acacia thorns and a bed of decomposed leaves. Diversity had plunged even more than it does under a closing forest.

The elephant ditch neatly demonstrated that light gaps in savanna woodland play the same role as in forests. Safe from elephants, the diversity of plants in the elephant moat had initially soared, then crashed. Too few or too many elephants. Both spell biological impoverishment for Africa's savannas and forests. Too few elephants around David's house spelled a uniform thicket of acacias; too many around mine spelled a uniform sward of grass. Either way, the outcome was low plant diversity. Did such an outcome imply that intermediate elephant numbers produced high plant diversity?

In my mind's eye I traced a line between the extremes, from my house to David's. At Olodare, in the center of the park, the trees lay dead and buried beneath *Suaeda* bushes. Beyond the park boundary, where elephants wandered back and forth and seldom settled for fear of people, diversity reached its peak.

Ecologists call this the intermediate disturbance hypothesis, first suggested by Robert Paine of the University of Washington in 1966. Many communities have since been found to be biologically richer at some intermediate density of a keystone species like the elephants than at either extreme.

Amboseli's rich patchwork of habitat arose from elephants roaming far and wide on their migrations, never settling in the park because of the presence of Maasai, never settling outside because of lack of permanent water.

I was in my element sizing up the implications of the experimental plot around the house, loving the ideas, the observations, the weird and wonderful connections, and the far-reaching implications—all coming together in a headlong rush. These deductions led to a new round of ecological surveys and experiments, designed to tease out the factors creating and maintaining Amboseli's biological diversity. The studies culminated in a provocative idea—to marry the adverse impact of too many elephants and too many livestock to mutual advantage, and in the process re-create Amboseli's lost diversity.

The idea goes something like this. When cattle are fenced in, they overgraze, destroying the grasslands and creating bushland. When elephants are fenced in, they overbrowse, thinning the bush and creating grasslands. It takes no leap of imagination to deduce that such habitat simplification is happening in ecosystems all across Africa, wherever elephants flee poachers to the safety of a park and livestock are forced out by rangers. The ecological dislocation can be seen strikingly in Tsavo, where the Mombasa highway divides the open grass of the park from bush-encroached cattle ranches.

If elephants and cattle had their way, they would trade places. In Amboseli they do. Sit atop Meshanani Hill overlooking Lake Amboseli today and you see herds of cattle filing into the park to graze, passing elephants headed out to browse. With elephants and cattle transforming the habitat in ways inimical to their own survival but beneficial to each other, they create an unstable interplay, advancing and retreating around each other like phantom dancers in a languid ecological minuet playing continuously over decades and centuries. Habitats oscillate in space like a humming top, driving and being driven by climate, animals, and people.

The Maasai, with their cogent ecological wisdom, make the same point: "Cows grow trees, elephants grow grasslands." They watch elephants open up thickets and create the grasslands their cattle prefer. They watch grasslands chewed to a nub by cattle revert to the trees and bushes elephants prefer. Like elephants, the Maasai live long enough to figure out the value of trading places in the savannas.

The interactions between plants and animals, as well as unpredictable events such as the rinderpest plague of the 1890s and tribal warfare, joined geology, soils, rainfall, and hydrology in the list of forces explaining Amboseli's hyperdiversity. The list, which began with Kilimanjaro, lengthened over the years as my familiarity with the ecosystem grew. Amboseli could no longer be described as a simple deterministic system running with clockwork precision. Such was its complexity that it was unimaginable to think of the ecosystem looking the same from one period to another.

Twenty years ago, such an admission of complexity and unpredictability went against the grain with ecologists. Today, few claim that ecosystems are constant and predictable. Predictability is also out of vogue for single-species populations as chaos theory, with its strange attractors and butterfly effects made famous by Michael Crichton's *Jurassic Park*, takes hold in biology. Bob May, an Australian-born physicist turned biologist showed mathematically that no two populations, given identical starting conditions, follow the same growth trajectory; such is the role of chance events and complexity. United Nations demographers wallowing in data have been forecasting human populations for decades, seldom with any reliability. This is no reflection on their competence, but on the inability of surprise-free computer models to capture unexpected and abrupt events in the real world. The Cold War of the 1960s, the oil crises of the 1970s, the democratic tide of the 1980s, and the AIDS crisis of the 1990s are some of the surprises computer models missed.

If we can't predict our own population growth, what of lesser-known species, let alone ecosystems made up of tens of thousands of unknown species, all marching to a different drummer? Nonlinear dynamics is the term scientists use for such complex unpredictable systems as national economies, weather, and ecosystems.

This is not to say that prediction is futile. The precise sequence of plant colonization after the abandonment of Maasai settlements differs, depending on the underlying soil, the prevailing rainfall, the length of time it was occupied, the surrounding vegetation, and a dozen other factors. Aggregate thirty or forty sites, however, and a pattern does emerge, with a half decade of bare earth followed by a half-century of dense grass giving way to a couple of centuries of bush and tree cover. The dung heaps of cattle bomas will influence Amboseli's ecology for generations to come, long after the Maasai have settled in concrete houses. That much is predictable, more or less.

Whatever the array of forces shaping Africa's savanna ecosystems in the past, humanity is the dominant force today. Rain and drought no longer dictate where the Maasai herder moves or how he behaves. The Cold War and its aftermath, commodity prices, medical and veterinary services, changing land-use patterns, and a battery of other factors shaping human attitudes and behavior are the new forces driving the ecosystem. When the German explorer Oscar Baumann reached Ngorongoro Crater at the turn of the nineteenth century, he described mass starvation and death among the Maasai, such was the impact of drought and rinderpest. A century later the population is fivefold greater, but few die of drought, thanks to corn from the United States and rice from Asia. The urban convenience of grocery stores has penetrated Amboseli, overriding the constraint of local resources.

Having identified the adverse ecological effects of a breakdown in the creative tension between Maasai and elephants, what next? The only prospect of striking up the ecological minuet and re-creating Amboseli's lost diversity lay in winning back space for the elephants. Winning back space came down to eliminating the threats of the ivory trade, which forced elephants into the safety of the park.

Our forest trip had erased any doubts about the status of the elephant and the impact of the ivory trade. The next step was to reach a scientific consensus. Scientific consensus is elusive at the best of times, and, befitting the size of the beast and the personalities involved, territorial claims are unusually large and hotly contested among elephant biologists. Add to that the public kudos of saving the elephant, and you have the makings of an almighty battle.

It was thus no small achievement for a meeting of the African Elephant and Rhino Specialist Group to reach consensus at its Nyeri meeting in 1987, when the group assembled in the elegant Outspan Hotel looking across from the Abedares Range to the snowclad peaks of Mount Kenya. The stage was set for a rematch of the Wankie meeting, with the scientific evidence going Douglas-Hamilton's way this time. He reveled in the prospects of being proved right after years of dirty, humorless wrangling with archrival Ian Parker. Parker was also in an upbeat mood for someone facing defeat, but then, no one knew how adeptly he would change the goalposts when the time came.

If lack of evidence had been Douglas-Hamilton's undoing at Wankie,

the deluge of data at Nyeri restored his credibility. The plummeting populations graphed from aerial counts across Africa, the population crashes
predicted by Pilgram's computer models, the halving of tusk weights, the
exponential increase in ivory prices, the paucity of elephants, the spent cartridges, the grown-over trails in central Africa's rainforest—the evidence
was all there.

"So can we agree that the evidence points to a rapid decline in elephant numbers due to an excessive offtake of ivory?" David Cummings
asked at the end of the session. A tall angular man with a quiet, firm
demeanor, Cummings brought the right touch of science, common sense,
and compassion to the Nyeri meeting and steered the factious groups
toward a resolution. Only Parker seemed to disagree with the outcome, if
less vociferously than before.

The sixth conference of parties to the Convention on International
Trade in Endangered Species (CITES), held in Ottawa in August 1987, did
adopt the specialist group's findings on the status of the elephant, thus
conceding the ivory trade as the primary threat to its survival a full decade
after Douglas-Hamilton launched his Pan African Survey. The conservation community could breathe a sigh of relief and finally turn its full attention to curbing the ivory trade. Over half a million animals had died since
the Wankie standoff, a high price to pay for scientific exactitude. The battle was not yet over, though, not by a long shot.

Despite adopting the conclusions of the specialist group, CITES did
nothing about the ivory trade.

‹ 13 ›

Ivory Wars

MUCH HAD BEEN MADE of the stunning success of the worldwide ivory ban imposed by CITES in 1989. Science, the media, and animal-rights lobbyists have all been cited as decisive factors. Without the slightest hint of humility, individual conservation groups credit themselves with bringing about the ban by raising public antipathy to ivory through their publicity campaigns.

In reality the ivory ban came about only through the combined effort of many individuals and organizations. It was the culmination of twelve years of scientific investigation, public awareness, publicity, and lobbying, starting with Iain Douglas-Hamilton's Pan African Survey in 1977. Painstaking research and a scientific consensus in May 1987 proved him correct. From then on, no one seriously doubted the threat ivory trading posed to the African elephant. The only question remained what to do about it. The answer was not as obvious at it may seem in retrospect: CITES bans in the 1970s had saved the leopard and cheetah but done nothing for rhinos. Parker got nods all round whenever he warned that once it was banned, the ivory trade would go underground just like the trade in rhino horn. He also pointed out that African governments wouldn't go along with a ban, and at that time he was right. The nations of Africa had been the decisive voices resisting restrictions on the ivory trade at the 1987 CITES meeting.

Three complex and interlacing threads—science, the media, and African opinion—ran through the elephant campaign leading up to the next meeting of CITES in October of 1989. The success of the ivory ban cannot be understood without grasping the role of all three and some of the personalities and organizations involved. The elephant became a symbol of the shifting tides and opposing forces putting conservation high on the global agenda as the Cold War petered out. Everyone involved acquired, if they did not already hold, strong opinions for or against the ivory trade and used science, the media, and politics interchangeably, whenever it suited the occasion.

Being a player makes it all the harder to describe fully what happened; there was so much going on in Africa, Asia, Europe, and North America simultaneously that it was impossible to follow all the threads or anticipate the outcome. The millions of dollars swapping hands among ivory traders and the fury mass poaching triggered in animal lovers gave no grounds for compromise. Yet, for all the vying over money, publicity, and victory, in the final analysis the outcome was a triumph of good judgment, compassion, and unprecedented cooperation among conservationists. The ivory ban brought a reprieve for the elephant and stemmed the trade which, even the advocates of trade admitted, was deeply corrupted and utterly unsustainable. The frenzy of killing and greed over the dwindling herds put the future of ivory traders and elephant alike in jeopardy.

Science undoubtedly played a decisive role and spurred the media and political debates, as Ray Bonner noted in his critique of conservation in Africa.

"The Ivory Trade Review Group, or ITRG, and the study it produced acquired an almost mythical significance in the ivory ban war," he wrote in his book *At the Hand of Man*. "Over and over again, when I asked conservationists who had been opposed to the ban why they had come to endorse it, they answered simply, 'the Ivory Trade Review Group.' WWF-US said it was changing its mind on the ivory ban based on new scientific findings released today," Bonner added skeptically, referring to the trade study's press release in May 1989. Why did the Ivory Trade Review Group wield so much influence in the final debate on ivory?

The failure of the 1987 CITES meeting to act on the ivory trade so incensed me, given the accord reached at Nyeri a few months earlier, that when David Cummings stepped down as chairman, I stepped back in. The only way to sway the crucial African vote lay in reaching a second scientific consensus—this time on how to deal with the trade. Feelings ran too deep for the specialist group itself to take on the job, and it didn't have the time or expertise anyhow. With the next CITES meeting barely eighteen months away, something had to be done fast. The delegates would expect hard facts before making a decision. Only a large group of specialists working flat out could pull off such a feat and command credibility.

Fashion designer Liz Claiborne and her husband, Art Ortenberg, were ready to help with a $100,000 grant to launch the study. They had first come to Kenya on a safari organized by the New York Zoological Society. Intensely passionate about wildlife and human suffering, they were retiring from their enormously successful business and setting up a charitable foundation, devoting themselves to a second career supporting conservation. Their pledge made it possible for me to invite several organizations, including World Wildlife Fund, Wildlife Conservation International, the International Union for the Conservation of Nature, the African Wildlife Foundation, the World Conservation Monitoring Unit, the European Union, and CITES, to coordinate the ivory study and give it blue-chip credibility. Steve Cobb, an environmental consultant, agreed to coordinate the thirty-five separate studies. If this was overkill, then so be it; the ivory traders were sure to commission their own study.

The preparatory meeting took place in the paneled boardroom of the London Zoological Society on May 8, 1988. The prompt response of conservation organizations, better known for squabbling and competing than for collaborating, was reassuring. The Claiborne Ortenberg Foundation money certainly helped to cut through the usual bickering, but genuine concern for the elephant itself unquestionably set the mood of cooperation and unanimity. By the close of the meeting over $250,000 had been pledged for the study.

The next step was to win African support for the ivory study. The first opportunity came up at the inaugural meeting of the African Elephant Working Group held in Nairobi in October 1988. The working group, established by CITES to forge an African consensus on the ivory trade, ran headlong into a tussle over science and freedom of information. Ian Parker was at the center of the conflict.

Parker called an informal meeting the evening before to discuss tactics. Predictably, his position came down to blaming the elephant's woes on human population growth. I was angry at his latest attempt to sabotage the consensus reached at Nyeri and insisted that the African delegates hear the ivory trade proposal and make up their own minds. Astonishingly, Jacques Bernais, the secretary to CITES, sided with Parker.

In the coming months, the CITES secretariat would reveal its pro-trade hand more and more, leading to accusations by African governments and environmentalists alike of collusion with the ivory traders. There were good grounds for suspicion. Over three-quarters of the budget for CITES' Ivory Unit came from the Far East traders, including K. T. Wang, a dealer said to operate undercover operations in South Africa. Joe Yvino, head of the Ivory Unit, resigned over the scandal.

Ian Parker and his close colleague Rowan Martin, who represented Zimbabwe, leapt to the floor after the opening address and called on African delegates to reject any collaboration with the Ivory Trade Review Group. I fought back, saying the delegates should be open to any information. Martin was back on his feet immediately. "We don't need outsiders telling us what to do," he exploded, determined to work his own xeno-phobia into the debate.

When the debate was put to the vote, Africa spoke. With one dissension, the delegates voted in favor of supporting the independent trade study. The sole dissenter, Rowan Martin, got up in a cold fury and left the room. What followed is one of the most bizarre and scurrilous episodes in the entire debate over elephants.

Unknown to most delegates, the CITES secretariat had secured funds from the Kowloon and Hong Kong Ivory Manufacturers Association to commission its own study on the impact of the ivory trade on elephants. The man selected for the study was Graeme Caughley, a close friend of Parker's. No doubt the secretariat thought that Parker's hired hand would vindicate the ivory trade, hence the funding from the Hong Kong associations.

If that had been the expectation, the cabal behind the study was in for a big shock. Caughley, a lean, sandy-haired Australian with a reserved manner and dry wit, ranked among the world's top population ecologists. A man of unusual dedication to scientific truth, Caughley was no one's hired hand. Flicking through transparency after transparency on the overhead projector, his droll presentation lent him an air of utter indifference and impartiality regarding the fate of the elephant.

"The graphs show a steep incline in ivory yields up until the mid-1980s," he stated in his flat drawl, "then show a precipitous slump. Ivory exports are declining sharply and display all the signs of classic overharvesting—in this case as a result of the ivory trade. If the present trends continue, the ivory trade will collapse within five years in East Africa and over the continent as a whole by 2008. The elephant will be extinct by then, except for a few safe pockets. If the results prove robust, the elephant should be placed on Appendix 1." By that he meant the ivory trade should be banned.

Rather than face the embarrassment of adopting the report, the secretariat equivocated, stalled, and finally buried it.

After winning African backing, the independent ITRG study moved ahead at breakneck speed under Steve Cobb's supervision. On February 15, 1989, barely six months after its inception, the group held its first full meeting to assess the mass of economic and biological data. The results looked discouraging, so discouraging in fact that nothing short of a miracle would change the earlier conclusions Pilgram and I had reached. Two months later, at a second meeting, the results shook even the most ardent advocates of a sustainable ivory trade. "The results are a matter of biology, not economics," David Pearce, the head of the economics team from the Environmental Economics Center at the London School of Economics, muttered when population biologists from the Renewable Resources Assessment Group presented their findings.

The graph of ivory exports confirmed much of what Caughley had already established—a slow, steady rise from 200 tons a year in 1950 to around 500 tons in 1970, followed by a steep increase to 1,000 tons a year by 1983. From then on, there was a free-fall to under 400 tons in 1987 as younger and younger animals were poached.

The economists differed with Parker's earlier conclusions about what drove the trade. The demand for ivory, they explained, running through their tabulations, could be fully accounted for by the direct consumption of ivory in the East and West, coupled with steadily rising incomes. All the ivory exports ended up as trinkets, bangles, carvings, name seals, and other knickknacks, rather than in bank vaults, as Parker insisted in equating ivory with gold and currency trading. "Elephants will continue to decline as incomes in the industrial world grow. In fact from our statistical analysis we can roughly predict that for every 10 percent increase in Japanese GNP, the 'demand' for ivory will increase by 15 percent," the economists concluded.

That was hardly a recipe for the sustainable-use maxim Rowan Martin was arguing for. Substitute the impersonal market term "demand" for "fashion" and the Achilles' heel of the ivory industry was exposed. People who could afford it would no more buy substitute ivory than they would fake Gucci shoes.

The economists made another important finding that undermined Parker's effort to equate trade with conservation. Contrary to his statement that ivory sales sank $50 million into conservation, barely a fifth that figure made it to Africa, and less than half that into conservation. Presidents, ministers, and corrupt wildlife officials stashed away the money in Swiss bank accounts. Worse, over three-quarters of all tusks entering the CITES-sanctioned trade came from poached elephants.

With corruption so rampant and the legal loopholes wide open, CITES was essentially legitimizing poaching.

The final meeting of the ivory study group took place in London on May 22, 1989, with temperatures in the eighties and the press giving daily coverage to the elephant crisis. Throughout the closed-door session, a small contingent of reporters was already gathered outside the meeting room to badger the twenty-five delegates for information.

The first morning brought only one surprise. According to the population models produced by the population group, the African elephant could not recover if annual ivory offtakes exceeded 35 tons, a figure one-tenth of the current exports from Africa. The figure was so tiny that a sustainable trade could all but be ruled out for now. "In the afternoon," I wrote, "we discuss all policy options. None of the pricing policies offer much hope of restraining trade to the point of population recovery. All members vote in turn. Result: twenty for the ban, two abstentions (both of them CITES staff who feel it impolitic to vote). All voters recognize danger of a ban and we spend the rest of the meeting working out a set of recommendations to bolster it."

The problem with a moratorium, as Pearce put it, was no longer the risk of the trade going underground, provided the publicity barrage was kept up, but the danger of a public announcement by the prestigious ivory study group in support of a global ban months before it came into effect under CITES. The way to prevent a poaching holocaust in the interim was to solicit media support in calling for immediate ivory bans in the importing nations. Science was poised to add grist to the mill of the media campaign already well under way.

The media were the second thread in the ivory wars. The publicity campaigns began in 1988 when the extent of the elephant slaughter in Africa made headlines around the world. Until the media barrage over the poaching began, ivory evoked the enchanting music of a Steinway piano, the fine art of a Japanese name seal, and the chic jewelry of Parisian haute couture. Our infatuation with ivory dates back to the dawn of civilization. The hauntingly powerful face of the Ice Age hunter unearthed in Dolni Vestonice in Czechoslovakia, the voluptuous fertility figures with pendulous breasts and curvaceous hips, and the graceful pendants carved of mammoth tusks 30,000 years ago attest to of the timeless allure of ivory. Smooth, hard, exciting. Warm to the touch, inviting to the eye. With its delicate translucent lattice beneath a burnished white surface, ivory exudes luxuriance and sensuality. With such a history, ivory spelled opulence and status, not slaughter and environmental destruction.

Within a few months, the media blitz launched by conservation groups and lobbyists changed the imagery and did for the elephant what it had done earlier for the Vietnam war: it brought the carnage and trauma of a bloody bush war into American and European living rooms. The film clips of elephant carcasses with hacked-off faces were gruesome enough, but these paled beside scenes of entire herds crumpling like discarded sacks as tiny orphaned babies raced around their fallen mothers trumpeting in abject fear. Worse still, the victims as often as not included game guards lying face down, riddled with AK 47 bullets sprayed by poachers scouring the continent for ivory.

The link between ivory and elephant finally clicked in the western world's collective consciousness. Press coverage of the bloodshed succeeded where the hullabaloo over DDT and the ozone hole failed. It made it all but impossible for the consumer to buy an ivory bangle without thinking about bloated carcasses and orphaned babies. Overnight ivory jewelry in Tiffany's New York store became as untouchable as radioactive waste from Three Mile Island and the elephant became a newfound symbol of a greening world, the environmental touchstone of presidents, humane groups, schoolchildren, rock stars, and fashion moguls.

That the elephant slaughter touched a raw nerve is not surprising. It spoke of a heinous crime to nature, stirring up American guilt over the bison massacre of the nineteenth century. The killings evoked the horrors of drug wars, criminal overlords, and laundered money. The implication was unavoidable: buying an object of art and beauty can be ecologically as ruinous as torching Africa's rain forest.

Cynthia Moss's book *Elephant Memories*, which became an instant best-seller in 1988, added a touching, almost human side to elephants, much as Dian Fossey had done for the mountain gorilla. "I am not afraid to say that ethics and morality should be essential considerations in our decisions for their future," she concluded after painstakingly documenting the lives of Teresia, Slit Ear, and Echo for thirteen years. Her funding organization, the African Wildlife Foundation, used the book to launch its Year of the Elephant and hired Sachi and Sachi to buy space on prime-time TV to show elephants falling to the rat-tat-tat of automatic gunfire and being hacked up by poaching gangs. The message was unavoidable. This is you doing the buying which does the killing: don't buy ivory.

Moss's message in 1988 generally voiced the consensus reached at Nyeri a year earlier. "What I feel is needed now is a worldwide campaign to reduce the demand for ivory. I would ask people not to buy ivory until the time comes when one can be sure that the tusk is either from an elephant killed legally or from one who died of natural causes."

The animal rights groups entered the fray with a simpler cogent message: killing elephants is wrong. Period. In contrast, Moss's appeal to common sense and conscience buying seemed anemic. In an astute move, the African Wildlife Foundation demanded an outright ban on ivory. Overnight the obscure organization enlisted droves of new members, convinced that they could save the elephant by killing the ivory trade.

The list of organizations and individuals who campaigned in favor of a ban on trade during 1988 and 1989 reads like a *Who's Who* of conservation. The most prominent were the World Wildlife Fund, the New York

Zoological Society, and the African Wildlife Foundation, most of them long concerned about elephants and rhinos and engaged in a methodological search for a solution. To the newer, more radical entrants, the old guard's methodological search seemed more like foot-dragging. Broadly labeled as the animal welfare and animal rights groups, the coalition included the International Foundation for Animal Welfare, the Environmental Investigation Agency, the Humane Society of the United States, Friends of Animals, and the Animal Welfare Institute. Their message was as cut-and-dried as it was pungent: the issue is the right and wrong of killing, not the ivory trade, sustainable or otherwise.

The conservation groups and media eagerly awaited the results of the ITRG study, proceeding concurrently. Would the team of technical experts support the opponents of trade or the advocates of sustainable use, creating a fault line in the West paralleling the divide within Africa?

After the May 1989 meeting of the study group in London the pressure from the media and conservation organizations was relentless. Charles de Haes, director-general of the World Wildlife Fund in Switzerland, joined his adviser John Hanks and the southern Africans in an implacable opposition to a moratorium and did everything he could to embargo the study's results. His position put the U.S. WWF, which had been working with the trade study from the outset, in a predicament. Should it break ranks with its international, parent organization or fall in line and face the fury of the radical animal rights groups? At the urging of Buff Bohlen, attending the meeting on behalf of the U.S. WWF, I telephoned de Haes and told him that the results would be released publicly with New York Zoological Society backing, whether he supported the recommendations on a ban or not. De Haes said he needed to consult with Hanks. A few minutes later he was back on the phone and on board. For a man known for his hardball tactics and given to calling on WWF's President, Prince Philip, when things didn't go his way, he had zero leverage and knew it. He wasn't about to miss out on the biggest media story on elephants about to break. So we agreed—a joint press release in the United States and Switzerland.

The moment the scale of the media event dawned on the public-relations machines in the conservation organizations backing the trade study, collegiality broke down in a sordid battle over credits. By hook or by crook, the image-makers in WWF were going to play a lead role at the press conference in Washington and erase the stigma of foot-dragging suffered at the hands of the press and animal rights groups. By then I was out of it all, riding with the Ortenbergs on their wooded ranch and absorbing the grandeur of Montana's snowclad peaks. Enjoyable though the field aspects of international conservation were, the angst, pettiness, and internecine struggles during the ivory wars brought out the worst in the conservation fraternity. How I longed to be done with it and back in Amboseli, where the daily contact with animals made it all seem worthwhile.

In Washington on May 31, barely a week after the London meeting of the ITRC study group, the publicity battles between the image-makers had subsided, and all that remained was to go over the final details of the press release. Buff Bohlen, who had been busy since the London meeting alerting his political contacts in the State Department and White House to the study's recommendations, pressed the Bush administration to act promptly after the announcement. After six months in office, George Bush, who had run as the "environmental president," still had nothing to show and was under pressure from conservationists to establish a contrast with the Reagan administration, when Secretary of the Interior James Watt gave free rein to developers on public land. With World Environment Day on June 5, the release of our findings was carefully timed to give President Bush a golden opportunity for a magnanimous, risk-free gesture. Not only would a unilateral ban on ivory imports show his green color with a dramatic flair, it would also pip Margaret Thatcher at the post. Rumor had it that she was anxious to take the lead in putting an ivory ban proposal before the European Community on June 8.

The packed meeting at the Press Club in Washington began promptly at 10:00 A.M. I felt distinctly uncomfortable that a decision about the fate of the African elephant and Amboseli was to be announced in a high-rise building in downtown Washington packed with reporters rather than at a Maasai meeting under a tortilis tree with the animals roaming all around. Like it or not, this was the reality. No ecosystem operates as an island in today's world, and its fate is decided as much by the international press as by the local herder. How the barriers between science, conservation, and politics had tumbled in a decade.

Russell Train, president of U.S. WWF, announced the study's recommendation of a global ivory ban in the interests of averting a poaching holocaust. I followed, elaborating the findings and recommendations of the study, stressing the credentials of the group which had produced it. An hour and a half later the press rushed for the doors to announce the news. The next day the call for a ban hit front pages worldwide, with the *New York Times* warning of a poaching holocaust unless the main consumer nations imposed domestic bans immediately.

On World Environment Day five days later, President Bush slapped a domestic ban on ivory imports; within a week Margaret Thatcher declared a unilateral ban on ivory imports into Britain. Within two weeks the European Community, Dubai, Hong Kong, and Japan followed suit.

The door had been slammed on the ivory trade.

By August 1989, ivory that had sold for sixty dollars a kilo in Somalia was being dumped for five. Across the border in Kenya, elephant poaching dropped from 3,000 a year to under 50, a stunning turnaround. No poachers, not even the shifta, were willing to risk their lives for a pittance.

The stage was set for the entry of the third and decisive voice on the ivory trade. Media coverage, public indignation, and the powerful lobby groups counted for everything in the West, but the West itself accounted for a paltry fifth of the 100 votes in the crucial CITES decision in October 1989. The one-country/one-vote procedure put the fate of the elephant overwhelmingly in the hands of the developing world, and, if past experience was any indicator, Africa's voice would be decisive. The Africans alone could block the two-thirds vote needed to invoke a ban. At the time, the elephant was listed as a threatened species under CITES' Appendix 2; its products, including ivory, could be legitimately traded between signatory countries under CITES certification. Appendix 1 species, in contrast, are classified as endangered and all trade in their products is strictly banned. If the CITES meeting failed to upgrade the African elephant to Appendix 1, the status quo would prevail, and trade would continue unabated.

If anything, the wave of reaction in Europe and America convinced most Africans that the West still cared more about wildlife than about Africans. The gap between Africa and the West seemed unbridgeable at the start of the elephant campaign, and the media blitz widened it. The emotional outpouring over elephants had more coverage than the drought in Sudan and the antiapartheid struggle in South Africa, giving the impression of western indifference to the human suffering in Africa.

The chasm dividing Africa and the West surfaced at the very start of the media campaign, at a congressional hearing of the House Subcommittee on Fisheries and Wildlife Conservation and the Environment held on June 22, 1988. Should the United States unilaterally ban ivory, import only from countries with effective elephant conservation programs, or impose a tax on ivory imports to plow back into conservation in Africa? That was the question Gerry Studds, chairman of the subcommittee, asked the crowded hearing room.

Russell Train claimed the backing of 450,000 members in the United States in proposing a campaign to reduce ivory demand, ban imports from renegade countries, and pump funds into African conservation. WWF's proposal was carefully formulated to bring Africa into the picture and reduce the demand for ivory.

Susan Lieberman, the representative of the Humane Society of the United States, was not impressed by WWF's membership or by its weak-kneed response to the elephant crisis, and dismissed its claim to represent American feelings about ivory. "I represent twelve animal welfare groups with a combined membership of at least two million Americans," she announced in a show of one-upmanship and moral outrage. "The American people overwhelmingly support the maximum protection for the elephants. They want to bequeath a world where elephants remain free in Africa."

Sitting next to me, Willie Nduku, director of Zimbabwe's Parks and Wildlife Department, stiffened at the hyperbole. Like many Africans, he was too polite to let his feelings show. What exactly did America's bequeathing elephants to posterity mean? Where did Africans come into the picture?

"We should be realistic here," Nduku told the packed attentive room in his written submission. "You are asking a man who has a gold mine at the corner of his vegetable patch to ignore that natural wealth and to carry on planting cabbages. It will not happen." A U.S. ban would not work, he added. It would drive the trade underground, deprive wildlife departments of money for conservation, and commercial farmers of any economic incentive to conserve wildlife. "I represent the views of the nine southern African countries," he concluded.

In my own submission I pointed out that the United States accounted for such a small fraction of the world market that a unilateral ban would be totally ineffective. A unilateral domestic ban at this point would merely sweep the problem under the carpet and weaken American ability to curb the global trade. The most sensible approach would be to support the World Wildlife Fund position and await the results of the ivory study, due out in a few months. If the next meeting of CITES failed to act on the recommendations of the ivory study, then the United States should push for unilateral bans by all consumer countries.

This approach, along with a fund for elephant conservation in Africa, was the one that Congress adopted. The decision pleased neither the advocates nor the southern Africans bent on sustainable utilization of elephants. Elephants engendered deep passions in Africa and America, but for different reasons. The question of ownership, who gained and who suffered from conservation, racism, free-market principles, the morality of killing animals and the immorality of human poverty and suffering, sentimentality, emotionalism, ignorance, symbolism, and ecological disruption were some of the issues running through the debate. The stage was set for an epic battle in the five months remaining before the CITES meeting.

The first change in Africa's position came not from the media coverage, but from scientific data and the futility of the poaching. By early 1989 Caughley's projections of an imminent extinction of East Africa's elephants and the first alarming findings of the ivory trade study had reached government officials in Africa. Tanzania tacitly admitted defeat in its war against poaching after losing 200,000 elephants in ten years. Even the Selous elephants which Ionides had fought so tenaciously to preserve slumped from more than 100,000 to fewer than 30,000. The new director of the Tanzania Wildlife Division, Costa Mlay, made it clear that he didn't have the resources to stop the slaughter. He was open to other options.

Jorgen Thomsen, a trade specialist with WWF engaged in the ivory trade study, and his colleague Joyce Poole hurriedly slapped together a Tanzanian proposal for an Appendix 1 listing. The proposal "had the authority of a scientific paper and the persuasiveness of a Supreme Court brief," Bonner wrote in *At the Hand of Man.* By this he implied that African governments were so weak and compliant that they fell prey to the connivance of the humaniacs, as the animal welfare groups were disparagingly called by the international conservation organizations. Bonner was right in his characterization of white dominance of wildlife conservation in Africa, but he missed a vital shift in African perceptions: East Africa was unable to cope with poaching and was ready for draconian measures. Thomsen's proposal was not imposed against African wishes. On the contrary, the facts and figures provided the evidence that Costa Mlay needed to make an impassioned plea to stem the elephant slaughter. Tanzania was ready to use scientific data to that end, no less than the United States did in imposing its own domestic ban a few months later.

Within three months, Kenya unexpectedly entered the fray and soon became the most persuasive African voice lobbying for an ivory ban. A new figure in the form of Richard Leakey emerged on the international conservation stage, deepening the divide within Africa by siding with Tanzania. In retrospect it is not hard to see why elephants came to occupy center stage in Kenya's struggle to save its wildlife from poachers in and outside the Wildlife Department. With the population having collapsed from 160,000 to 20,000 in twenty years, the elephant became a symbol of Kenya's conservation failure and hopes of a revival.

Kenya's abysmal poaching statistics hit the headlines first in August 1988 and again a few months later when Somali poachers turned their guns on tourists. With tourists under attack, the government could no longer ignore the poachers. Saving the elephants became a litmus test of Kenya's resolve to stop corruption, save wildlife, and rescue its faltering tourist industry. Its only hope of that happening lay in cleaning up the Wildlife Department.

I had purposely stayed away from the department after my futile meeting with Sindiyo, hoping against hope that it would miraculously improve. Instead, things went from bad to worse, and the government did nothing. Given the ministerial connivance in poaching, the inaction surprised no one.

"How are things going in the wildlife world?" an influential business person and friend of the president's asked me late in 1986 when we both attended a lecture at the National Museums.

"Disastrously," I said in desperation. "In fact things have never been worse, and there's not a hope in hell until something's done about the Wildlife Department."

The president's friend looked surprised. "But, Jonah, you're always so optimistic. If it's really that bad, why not tell the president in person? He's the only one who'll do anything about it. I can introduce you if you like."

A month later I sat in President Moi's spacious office with a precious few minutes to spell out the problems facing Kenya's wildlife. He grew visibly alarmed at the skein of poaching, corruption, and incompetence that was killing off the animals and destroying the national parks. With tourism having recently overhauled coffee as Kenya's largest source of foreign exchange and the country's economy in trouble, the point hit home. He jumped up angrily, grabbed a pen and paper from his desk, and asked for suggestions so that he could act immediately, scrap the Wildlife Department, and start a new organization.

This brief talk cut through the labyrinthine bureaucracy and political interests blocking progress in Amboseli and destroying Kenya's wildlife. Presidential directives were not uncommon in African single-party states in the 1980s. Though often vehicles of corruption, directives could also cut through the tangled web of vested interests, and in this case did. Wildlife had never been high on any African country's agenda, but with the president's attention focused on conservation, the situation soon changed in Kenya.

On February 13, 1987, Daniel Sindiyo was sacked, and Perez Olindo took over as director of the Wildlife Department. His instructions were to clean up the mess and to submit plans for an entirely new wildlife organization.

Conservationists and the tourist operators were full of high hopes and Olindo made a promising start. I worked closely with him, pushing for a new wildlife agency, one that resembled the former Kenya National Parks he had run so successfully under an autonomous board of trustees. Six months later, in August 1987, Moi approved the new agency, the Kenya Wildlife Service. By December we were negotiating with the World Bank on a $50 million loan for the new institution, and other donors were showing keen interest. Then, inexplicably, the momentum slowed as the poaching syndicate Sindiyo had run up against fought to retain its grip on the lucrative ivory trade.

Olindo's problems began when he fired forty linchpins in the Wildlife Department's poaching ring. Days later, they were reinstated. Olindo could no more withstand the tribalism, nepotism, and corruption than Sindiyo without the backing of a political godfather. Having lost the decisive battle for control of the department, Olindo was henceworth marked for failure. It was a bitter second blow for the man who had once run Kenya's national parks so ably.

Far from stopping the poaching, Olindo was saddled with the blame. Late in 1988, ninety-two elephants were poached in a few weeks in the center of Tsavo National Park. Tour operators and hoteliers panicked and appealed to Moi to save the elephant and the tourist industry. Riveted by the carnage, CBS broke the footage on its world news, forcing the minister of Tourism and Wildlife, George Muhoho, to go public. The next day Kenya's largest daily, the *Nation*, ran a giant headline, "Elephants' Graveyard," with Muhoho promising to get tough on poachers.

Within a half-hour of Muhoho's announcement, anthropologist Richard Leakey, then the director of the Kenya National Museums, entered the fray. Come clean on elephant statistics and the people behind the poaching, he told the minister through the international press.

Muhoho had estimated Kenya's total elephant figure at 22,000, less than one-seventh the number estimated in 1973. Leakey, with a network of press contacts, accused the minister of fudging the figures and shielding the culprits. There are only 12,000 elephants, he insisted, and the ministers behind the poaching were named in a secret report submitted to Muhoho himself. Muhoho furiously hit back through the press, denouncing Leakey as a cheeky white, rejecting his elephant figures, and telling him to shut up or to name names himself, if he had the report.

Leakey was indeed wrong about the elephant figures, and the big names he had alluded to were no longer ministers. But what difference did a paltry few thousand make among the 150,000 or more lost in the last twenty years? Nothing would change until the Wildlife Department was scrapped and serious money pumped into conservation, I wrote to the local press during the height of the debate.

Leakey was clearly grandstanding. Why, as chairman of the influential and formerly outspoken East African Wildlife Society, did he wait a decade before saying anything about elephant poaching? And why wait until Muhoho was forced to speak out, then muscle in on his press conference only to quibble about numbers?

Olindo's weakened position, elephant poaching, shortage of funds, and Leakey's undisguised aspirations for his job sucked the new director into the same quagmire that had overborne Sindiyo. With Olindo floundering and conservation grinding to a halt, everything hinged on scrapping the Wildlife Department and starting a new organization.

Under pressure from the constant threats on his life and political intimidation, Olindo withdrew into a cocoon of denial and eventually ended up defending the very institution he promised to bury. He was a brave lonely man fighting gargantuan political battles, some real, some imagined, with failing ability to distinguish between the two. On one occasion he opposed a street march by thousands of school kids rallying under the Wildlife Clubs of Kenya banner to protest the elephant slaughter. He even denied reports emanating from his own field officers of elephant poaching in Tsavo. In the ultimate act of denial, he claimed in a *Time* magazine advertisement profiling Kenya's twenty-five years of independence that elephants had disappeared gradually since the turn of the century. His denials and defensiveness eroded the last of his credibility, leaving him isolated and impotent.

With Olindo's days numbered, I pushed hard for the Kenya Wildlife Service and began to lobby the minister of Tourism and Wildlife, George Muhoho. Knowing the president was still waiting for recommendations, Muhoho asked me to draw up a framework for the new organization. On December 20, 1988, the minister finally announced the government's plan for the Kenya Wildlife Service.

Sadly, the one man who had done so much to launch it, Perez Olindo, would not be part of the new organization. His day was over. Fifty elephants fell to poachers in Tsavo National Park during February 1989. In Meru National Park the remaining 200 of its 2,500 elephants huddled around the headquarters for safety, and that's where the inevitable happened. The poachers, having run out of ivory, turned their guns on the next most lucrative target and gunned down two tourists and a driver. The incident made headlines worldwide and rocked Kenya's tourist industry. With three bullets, the survival of the elephants had become synonymous with the fate of Kenya's tourist industry. From then on, Kenya's entire conservation effort—the rehabilitation of parks, tourism, donor support, and community programs depended upon the success of the Kenya Wildlife Service and curbing the elephant poaching.

On April 20, 1989, Kenya Broadcasting Service announced that Richard Leakey would replace Olindo. The news took everyone by surprise. In many ways, Moi's appointment of Leakey was an astute move, sure to win widespread national and international acclaim. As a Mr. Clean—the man who had challenged Muhoho over corruption and poaching—Leakey stood a good chance of being able to rid the new wildlife agency of corruption where Olindo had failed. Not only was he free of tribal affiliation; he also had strong presidential support and international stature. Leakey also brought to the job fund-raising skills learned during his twenty years as director of the National Museums.

These strengths aside, there were two strikes against Leakey. First, he was out of touch with the deeper conservation challenges in Kenya and subscribed to Ionides' fortress approach to cordoning off parks, and writing off the wildlife outside them. This outlook did not augur well for either wildlife outside parks or local participation. Second, he had an enormous ego and had run the Museums as a one man show. All the same, I was pleased rather than disturbed by the news. I had seen the job grind down Sindiyo and Olindo, and it would take someone with Leakey's ambition, backing, and gall to root out the corruption in the department and start afresh.

Leakey's entry into the ivory wars boosted the support for ban in Africa and the West and turned the war of words between eastern and southern Africa into a political standoff. President Moi, at Leakey's urging, turned up the heat by torching twelve tons of ivory in a dramatic display of his commitment to keep the trade closed. "I appeal to people all over the world to stop buying ivory," he told a jostling crowd of two hundred reporters.

The ivory burning was a bold and dramatic gesture which went down well in the West. Victoria Chitepo, Zimbabwe's fiery minister of Natural Resources, was furious. Egged on by Rowan Martin, she excoriated East Africa for its hypocrisy and abysmal wildlife record. Her message was carefully designed to blame Africa's newfound zealotry on the West and play on third world sensitivities about meddling rich nations. "We don't like the way the West dictates terms to us. Do not take your lead from the countries in Africa that have failed, the Kenyas and Tanzanias. Listen to us, copy our success, spread it through Africa," the Zimbabwe Department of National Parks wrote in *Swara* magazine alongside an article I wrote favoring a ban.

The stage was set for a showdown between African states at the decisive CITES meeting in Lausanne.

‹ ‹ ‹

JULY 4, 1989. The doors of the conference room slammed shut on the cloudless Botswana sky and the international press corps milling around in the lobby. Inside the cavernous hall African delegates from more than thirty countries sat tensely as dozens of conservationist observers sat in the back row whispering expectantly.

"I know there are very strong feelings about the ivory trade on either side," Richard Leakey began in a masterly understatement. "But I want the debate to be technical, apolitical, and open. The African Elephant Working Group is, after all, a technical body. We must recommend to CITES what position to take at Lausanne. The future of the African elephant is at stake."

Leakey, chairman of the working group, looked distinctly uneasy. Anthropological fame and his media battles with Don Johanson over the ancestry of man had not prepared him for the ivory wars, and the southern African states had already come close to unseating him as chairman.

A hefty two-volume report by the Ivory Trade Review Group sat solidly in front of the delegates. Graeme Caughley's slim and damning indictment of the ivory trade prepared at the request of the CITES secretariat at Parker's urging had been conveniently buried. Jacques Bernais, the graying secretary to the CITES secretariat, would have loved to bury the ITRG report too. "The study should present the facts and not its recommendations," he was saying in French as I walked to the lectern to summarize the trade study:

"As chairman of AERSG [African Elephant and Rhino Specialist Group] I initiated the study because we needed an impartial review of the ivory trade," I began. "The report is the work of more than thirty-five biologists, economists, and trade specialists working in Africa, Asia, Europe, and America." Rowan Martin, the most articulate and vociferous opponent of ivory trade sanctions in southern Africa, sat stonyfaced at the Zimbabwe desk. This was the report he and Parker had done everything they could to block at the first African Elephant Working Group in Nairobi a year earlier.

"The report looks at all aspects of the trade, from biology to economics." I continued, carefully avoiding any show of emotion. "It bears out Caughley's conclusion that the elephant faces extinction in the next twenty years. Which brings us to the recommendations."

Jacques Bernais jerked upright and frantically signaled Leakey to cut me off. Leakey leaned across to Bernais, listened politely, and crossed his arms, leaving me to continue. I drew to a close, grateful to Leakey for the opportunity to state the recommendations. "In summary, while we support the policy of sustainable use, the elephant and the trade are doomed as things stand. We recommend that elephants be transferred to Appendix I to ban the ivory trade."

Rowan Martin waved the Zimbabwe nameplate wildly. "The trade report is technically flawed," he said in his precise clipped accent when Leakey gave him the floor. "The elephant is not endangered. To the contrary, it is increasing and becoming a nuisance in southern Africa. We have to cull elephants to save farmers' crops and the habitat of our national parks."

The central African delegates were nodding in agreement. "Sensationalism has got the better of scientists with all this talk of bloody massacres, orphaned babies, and leaderless herds," Martin continued, trying to undermine the technical impartiality of the report. "The study team held press conferences around the world calling for an ivory ban without ever consulting southern Africa. We sell ivory to support rural communities and plow money back into antipoaching. That is why we have succeeded where East Africa has failed. We will continue to sell ivory."

The Congolese delegate waded in to support Martin with a long, rambling monologue on his country's exemplary conduct in the ivory trade.

"Lies! Lies!" a voice erupted from the back. "Who's the name behind Congo's ivory exports?" Pierre Pfeffer, a small wiry animal rights advocate from France, didn't mince his words: he had the president's wife, Marie Antoinette, in mind.

The meeting became raucous and personal as the scientific evidence bolstering the media campaign increased the southern Africans' desperation. To East Africa, the issue was not so much a repudiation of the south's conservation policies as that its continued trading would inevitably leave a loophole in a ban. The loophole, according to Craig van Note, a tall, gaunt conservationist with a bloodhound's nose for wildlife crime and a journalist's flair for exposé, amounted to a politically powered suction pump. He had unearthed an ivory-for-arms deal between Savimbi, leader of the rebel UNITA movement in Angola, and Magnus Malan, South Africa's reviled minister of Defense. Other connections were also surfacing.

João Soares, son of Portugal's president, had been badly injured when a plane overloaded with ivory destined for South Africa crashed on takeoff in Angola. Soares had been whisked to a Johannesburg hospital and secluded from the press. Zimbabwe was also allegedly covering up its own poaching crisis. Although it continued to insist that its much-vaunted antipoaching operations were holding firm, rumors of rampant rhino slaughter and a cover-up operation were beginning to leak out. If all was well, why was Zimbabwe talking about relocating rhinos to safer localities as Kenya had done?

Despite the wrangles, the ivory wars had finally switched the burden of proof from conservationists to traders. With the inner workings of the ivory trade revealed and in disrepute, a ban in place, ivory out of fashion, prices slumping, and the Hong Kong traders screaming because they had been caught with more than 400 tons of immovable stockpiles, the tide had finally turned for the elephant. The anger and fear were palpable when I visited Japan and Hong Kong with Perez Olindo, Joyce Poole, and Ruth Mace to present the study group findings and lobby for support of Appendix 1 listing in October. At meeting after meeting the ivory traders and government spokesmen talked of having been taken by surprise, of being unaware of the pending extinction of the elephant and the collapse of the ivory trade. Why had the CITES secretariat not informed them, they asked. And why had their friend, Mr. Parker, misled them about the elephant?

In the end the Japanese conceded our case, not in response to any emotional appeal, which they firmly rejected whenever Joyce Poole voiced it, but because the way things were going the trade was doomed. "What about the 10,000 employees in the Japanese ivory trade?" they lamented as they edged toward capitulation. "What about the hundreds of Africans killed by the ivory trade every year?" Olindo responded.

In Hong Kong we received a decidedly more hostile reception. Caught with huge stockpiles of ivory and facing a Chinese takeover in 1997, they had reason to be jittery. Dominic Ng, the head of the Ivory Manufacturers' Union, took us out to supper to show us he was human, he insisted, not to talk ivory.

Within minutes he launched into a diatribe—against the West for conspiring to cheat Hong Kong traders, leaving them with immovable stocks; against conservationists for emotionalism; and against Africans for greed and corruption.

"What can I give you that will shock you, to show you how we feel?" he asked angrily. "Shrimp! Yes, shrimp." When they arrived live and squirming in a huge cauldron placed in the center of the table, he poured boiling water over them in a defiant gesture. "Here is what we Chinese think of animals."

Olindo looked sick. Joyce's face tightened. "Elephants, too?"

For another hour, Ng threatened to trade offshore and do whatever else it took to keep the supply of ivory flowing. He was a frightened and confused man, caught in the spotlight, not knowing where to turn. By the time we left Hong Kong, the discussion was no longer about resuming the trade, but about how to offload 400 tons of ivory before the CITES deadline in January. Given the domestic bans in place around the world, the trade study findings, the media coverage, and the changing mood in Africa, a moratorium on ivory was all but inevitable.

◀ ◀ ◀

THE AFRICAN ELEPHANTS dominated CITES' Seventh Conference of Parties in Lausanne that October. Outside, hundreds of school kids filed through the concourse, waving placards and singing songs calling for an ivory ban. Inside, the southern African states made a last-ditch effort to keep the ivory trade open against a united stand by the rest of Africa. Rowan Martin made a fine showing, arguing to the last that a vote against the trade was a vote against sustainable utilization policies. He and the pro-traders in support of sustainable utilization did in fact defeat a straight Appendix 1 listing, forcing a search for a watered-down ivory ban.

On Tuesday, October 17, at 2:54 P.M., an amended Appendix 1 vote, easing the burden of downlisting for countries with safe elephant populations, carried 76 to 11. The auditorium erupted into a prolonged round of clapping, and the press corps charged for the exits to announce the ivory ban to a waiting world.

‹ 14 ›

Back to Roots

O CTOBER 1989. I AM ON
the final leg of the long journey
home, burned out and starved for the wilds after logging 100,000 miles on
the elephant campaign over the last year. Twenty thousand feet below, the
eastern wall of the Rift Valley rises dark and rugged above the arid lava
flats, its cedar-clad peaks shrouded in mist. Shadowy fingers stretch across
the valley still suffused with the vivid red and brown hues of early morning. Soon the harsh equatorial sun will turn the eroded, fractured surface
of the Suguta Valley into a bleached-out landscape of barren earth, bush,
and baking rock.

Pastoral homesteads scattered in the bush miles from any road come
into view as the plane descends. Herds of livestock are moving off to distant water points and grazing grounds. How reassuringly ageless Africa is
from high overhead.

It takes an experienced eye to read the past in the pastoral lands of
Africa. The trained eye of an ecologist—or the African herder—can infer
historical perturbations from the composition of plant species and the age
structure of long-lived trees. In the Suguta Valley the informed eye is startled by the backwash of a tidal event—the extermination of the elephant.
Uniform stands of *Acacia* and *Commiphora* choke the valley floor, where
too many livestock have grazed for too long without the relief of elephants.
The tapestry of habitats is disappearing as the ecological minuet of people
and elephants slows to the repetitive stomp of a new refrain—sedentari-
zation.

Suguta is a microcosm of ecological loss taking place across the continent. The valley's flat monotony of tangled thorn is spreading across the

vastness of Tsavo and other parks, wherever elephants have fallen prey to the poacher's bullet. Remoteness is no longer assurance of ecological diversity when the consumer in New York or Tokyo can have such a profound impact all across Africa.

How small and interconnected our world has become as the homogenization and impoverishment of ecology and culture invade the remotest Sugutas around the world. Is uniformity the fate of the world? Cannot awareness and action change the course of events?

Five years ago, no one imagined elephants to be vital to the maintenance of Africa's biological diversity. Nor did anyone anticipate that within another few years whirring computers in London and crowded press conferences in Washington and Tokyo would snip the fashion link, allowing the first few elephants to tentatively return to the Suguta Valley.

The Athi Kapiti Plain flickers through a low bank of cloud as we begin our final descent into Jomo Kenyatta Airport. Peering out of the port window, I glimpse a solitary house perched above a deep gorge winding through the plain. To the south lies Maasailand, stretching eighty miles to Kilimanjaro; to the north, Nairobi National Park. Soon I will be home sitting on the veranda of that solitary house with my family, catching up, taking in the wooded valley below. With any luck, a rhino will wander down to drink in the river thirty feet below. If not, there is bound to be a bushbuck shyly picking its way through the thickets, alert to leopards, or perhaps a buffalo or eland, nibbling the riparian shrubs.

I lean back happy at the thought, letting my mind wander back over my long search for an answer to coexistence. Now that I am on the homeward path, do all the paths and diversions make sense?

I think back to the trailhead where it all began—Mbwamaji. From the coastal thickets where Mohamed Mbwana taught me to track, the trail leads to shamba-raiding hippos, then to Mikumi and the promise of big tuskers. The trail breaks up, meandering confusingly as farmers moving in from Tanganyika's growing agrarian centers and elephants from Selous Game Reserve's expanding herds meet and clash. The anguished voice of the Momba farmer overrun by elephants and the proud dignity of the old Swahili hunter doomed by hunting laws and poaching gangs are still fresh in my mind. Rushby, Rufiji, Ionides, and my father's transformation from hunter to preservationist made no sense to me then. Their concern to save rather than kill animals made sense only once the gunshots, snare lines, meat racks, wheeling vultures, and vanishing herds spoke out more loudly and more eloquently than they ever could.

With the approach of independence, the killing proliferated as Africans flouted the colonial laws that had robbed them of their land and animals. As a youngster confused by it all, I nevertheless saw no hope in yet more parks, harsher laws, and stronger ranger forces if the outcome meant greater poverty and deeper hostility among Africans.

After my father's unexpected death the trail led to England, where, oddly, the clashes between farmers and elephants finally made sense. The inevitability and desirability of African development became obvious. The dangers of carving up ecosystems into one place for animals and another for people now set me off on a deliberate, active search for an alternative rooted in coexistence rather than in segregation. One step led to another, and years of research, planning, and lobbying in Amboseli, all in the hopes of getting the new integrated approach to conservation approved, funded, and implemented.

Setbacks to the new approach arose from the Wildlife Department's ineptitude and corruption, compounded by the depredations of poachers in Amboseli. The new threats set me on an erratic new trail in Kenya and around the world in an effort to restore integrity and balance in the ecosystem.

How many trails had there been, how many guises had I worn on the path from Mbwamaji to Lausanne? Thousands of conservationists around the world have similar stories to tell, of beginning in some distant trailhead and finding their paths crossing and recrossing around the world. What a fascinating, daunting, frustrating, and finally rewarding challenge modern conservation has become.

We are about to land. I stretch and let out a heavy sigh as tires screech on the tarmac. My own trail had been a long one, but worth every moment. And the payoff? "We can all breathe a little easier knowing we have bought time for the elephant," I wrote Bill Conway and the New York Zoological Society after the Lausanne meeting. I am free to return to my roots.

The black rhino snuffling in the valley below our house on the Athi Kapiti Plain, eight miles from downtown Nairobi, is, like the elephant, better off after years of effort to find the right solution. Like other rhino sanctuaries in Kenya, Nairobi National Park has succeeded where trade sanctions failed. Poaching has tailed off to a handful a year as a result of close protection, and numbers are on the way back up after hitting a perilously low 350. And with Richard Leakey getting strong backing from the president and donors for the Kenya Wildlife Service, the future looks bright. The time has come for me to step down as director of Wildlife Conservation International and chairman of the elephant and rhino specialist group to resume my research and conservation in the field. Finally, I am free to enjoy the wild animals, the bush, and my family. For me, this is what conservation is all about.

Our children, five-year-old Carissa and three-year-old Guy, love the regular trips to Amboseli and to Chololo on the northern Laikipia Plateau, where Shirley still studies the baboons. Shirley and I have a lot of catching up to do, exploring our special worlds with Carissa and Guy, seeing them afresh through their eyes.

Iain Douglas-Hamilton was shocked when I told him of my plans after Lausanne. "You can't drop out, Jonah," he said in disbelief. "There's still so much to be done for elephants."

He is right. The ban has bought some time, but very little, given the threat of more people, continuing poverty, and diminishing wildlands in Africa. Douglas-Hamilton's ambivalence over the ban and his outburst after the final vote at Lausanne, when he castigated conservationists for ignoring the splendid job the southern Africans had done conserving elephants, spoke for most of us involved. Despite all the back-room promises at CITES, only a fraction of the support for Africa has materialized. Donors and conservation groups alike walked away on a cloud of euphoria, blind or indifferent to the fragility of the ban and the outcome for Africa.

The ban has salved the conscience of the West and feel-good conservationists, but it will exacerbate the anger, poverty, and despair at the root of the wildlife crisis once elephants lose their fear of people and begin raiding shambas. It will be Mikumi all over again—unless the roots of the conflict are tackled with the same care and zeal devoted to the ivory ban.

Of all the personalities involved, Douglas-Hamilton did most for the African elephant. All the same, his comment to me about dropping out shows a common misperception about where the ultimate fate of wildlife lies. In the course of all the moral grandstanding and rhetoric over the elephant, a conservation consensus has begun to emerge in Africa: the future of wildlife lies not in ivory bans and antipoaching, however vital as safeguards. The ultimate solution rests on local custodianship—on people like the Maasai, who saved Amboseli's elephants and in whose hands the fate of an entire ecosystem resides.

In a heartening development, the concept of integrated conservation and development is catching on in Africa and spreading around the world. Zambia, Zimbabwe, Botswana, South Africa, and Namibia have adopted local participation as a general policy and are making greater headway than Kenya. Other examples are springing up in Tanzania, the Central African Republic, and Zaire. In the process, conservation has shifted from protectionism to sustainable use. It might not be box-office stuff compared to saving the elephant, rhino, and whale, but local participation will save countless species and conserve entire ecosystems even if comparatively few programs work. Without such success, there is no hope beyond national parks, and no escape from impoverishment within them.

Far from dropping out, a return to Amboseli is a return to the root of the problem—wildlife, people, space. I step off the plane raring to start all over again.

< < <

THE TREES around my house in Amboseli have grown over thirty feet tall in the nine years since the elephant ditch went in. But this is not what grips my attention on getting back. Outside the ditch, where elephants regularly plucked every acacia seedling as if it were the first gray hair, thickets missing for fifteen years have miraculously reappeared. *Solanum, Pluchea, Withania, Abutilon, Achyranthes,* and even *Sesbania*—a bush so common that it merited a distinctive habitat on my 1967 vegetation map—have recolonized the cynodon swards behind my house. In defiance of elephants, patches of regenerating acacia five feet tall are making headway. And, to my delight, a scuffed dung pile in the middle of a thicket shows that an old friend visited last night.

For a moment I feel giddy with déja vu, catching a fleeting image of a fading yellow tent tucked away amid a grove of fever trees, imagining a rhino's heavy hide scraping through the prickly undergrowth. It has been ten years since the last rhino visited my house.

I excitedly fondle each plant like a long-lost friend, crushing and sniffing its leaves to recall forgotten smells. Each species has a distinctive pattern of regeneration in the competition for space, water, and light. *Abutilon* and *Withania*, small and fast-growing, recover first, only to be out stripped by *Pluchea* in drier patches and *Solanum* in the drainage lines. Under the shade of the *Solanum* the acacias grow spindly and tall like beanstalks, eventually dying back exhausted for lack of light. Closer to the edge of the drainage line, where herbivores have more room to evade predators and so punish the vegetation more heavily, the acacia seedlings make their break. Once above shrub height, the saplings overshadow the understory bush, shading out the *Solanum*.

I size up fresh clues to future habitats and conjure up new experiments to untangle the complicated ecological web. The roles of determinism and chance in shaping plant and animal communities take on new meaning. At the scale of an ecosystem, rainfall plays a decisive role in determining the relative shares of large, medium, and small ungulates. At a finer scale within an ecosystem, the plant community changes composition regularly—from woodland to grassland, for example—driven by rainfall flux, elephants, human activity, and a host of secondary forces, affecting its animal occupants in turn.

Walking to the edge of the habitat recovery plot, I duck my head and pass underneath a single electric wire, the reason for the lush vegetation round my house. The high-voltage wire is all that keeps out elephants, allowing other herbivores to pass underneath, graze the cynodon sward, and accelerate the recovery of Amboseli's diversity. The electric wire is the ecological equivalent of Maasai cattle, as far as the elephant is concerned. Both deter elephants and encourage the trees to grow. My mind is racing ahead, thinking through the options for restoring the diversity over the whole ecosystem.

Without space, the options come down to culling elephants to maintain biodiversity or, as Cynthia Moss insists, declaring Amboseli an elephant park and forgetting about ecological diversity. The trouble with a save-elephants-and-forget-the-rest policy is that in the long run it doesn't do the elephant any good, either. In the long run, the park could support fewer than a third of its present numbers; hundreds of elephants would die of starvation.

The better alternative, surely, is to win back the nine-tenths of the ecosystem the elephants abandoned, now that poachers no longer pose a threat. First, the Maasai need good reasons to accept elephants back on their land. One reason is that elephants open up the bushland thickets and improve livestock grazing, another that the tourist dollars earned from elephant watching would bring good income.

My thoughts are cut short by a white Land Rover pulling up to the house.

"Jonah, you are back." Kerenkol clambers out with the Ogulului committee—Marinka, Leboo, the whole crowd. They greet me with a traditional handshake: hand to thumb, followed by hand to hand, then thumb to hand again. "You've been gone a long time. We thought you had left us. Welcome back."

As David Maitumo boils up tea in my kitchen, the committee fills me in on Amboseli news. Marinka begins. "The Namelok fence is up and working. You must come and see it. The first day the elephants touched it they screamed in fright and haven't been back since. And the warriors, well, you know what they're like. They dare each other to see who is brave enough to touch the fence and laugh at their donkeys when they get a shock. We are also putting up an electric fence around the campsite to protect the trees from elephants and give the tourists shade."

When Marinka has finished Kerenkol looks around the room and grins conspiratorially.

"Jonah, the elections are coming up soon. We want someone who will bring us development to stand as our member of parliament. You have done a lot already. We want you to stand."

I laugh, amused and pleased by the invitation. Conservation and development are finally allied in their minds. The gulf no longer exists. Then, looking round the room, I point at Marinka. "He's your person. Not me. I'll help, but I'm no politician."

Everyone laughs, including Marinka. He is short as Maasai go, with an easygoing disposition. He lacks Kerenkol's regal bearing but makes up for it with a ready smile and infectious humor. His leadership qualities have emerged during his handling of wildlife matters on behalf of the group ranch, and his education gives him a definite edge when it comes to national politics. Soon he will in fact declare his candidacy in the upcoming elections.

"What news of KWS?" the chairman of the committee asks. "Is it any better than the Wildlife Department? We see improvements in the park, but will Leakey restore the revenue-sharing? If he doesn't, we will fight for it. We are ready to do our part. We want to keep the area open for wildlife and cattle, to employ our own scouts to patrol the areas outside the park, even to set up a wildlife association."

The chairman's assertiveness typifies the change among the Maasai, a change brought about by the tide of democracy flooding through Africa and by the emergence of a younger, politically savvy generation. As in the days leading to independence, political and economic reforms are rapidly penetrating the rural areas. Unless the Maasai gain economically from Amboseli as part of these reforms, wildlife will again become a focus of discontent. Even with benefits flowing, not all is well. Leaders have become greedy for money and are denying the poorer families any of the fruits of development. The next challenge will be to get the benefits to the families who have made the biggest sacrifices. For the moment, though, the Maasai are united and the chairman speaks for them all.

◀ ◀ ◀

BY HIS OWN ADMISSION, Leakey's first priorities for the Kenya Wildlife Service lay in eliminating corruption and poaching and reviving the parks. He made a flying start and quickly imposed a semblance of law and order. With the ivory ban putting an end to poaching, Leakey's mercurial style changed the entire institution, setting it back on its feet. He even began to concede the need for local participation in conservation and set up a community wildlife service within KWS. He earned high marks and considerable respect, including my own. But when I kept after him to visit Amboseli to get a flavor of the problems facing the park, he seemed less inclined than ever to see the human threats beyond the boundary. "I can't afford to be compassionate about the Maasai," he told me over lunch in Nairobi when I tried to brief him on a string of Maasai grievances and the dangers of ignoring them.

When Leakey did finally get down to Amboseli, he came with an ever-present retinue of reporters. Our scheduled meeting with the Maasai was

conducted in a brisk manner, with Leakey talking in English for the benefit of the press and a translator talking in Swahili for the Maasai. Despite
the brevity of the meeting, the Maasai made their points clearly and
forcibly, offering to help conserve wildlife in exchange for a share of the
park revenues. Leakey listened thoughtfully and responded that he was a
man of action, not words. The Maasai were cheered and hopeful.

Weeks passed. Nothing happened. The mood in Amboseli grew worse.
Angered at the lack of response, Leboo wrote to Leakey saying that unless
KWS began putting something back in the hands of the Maasai, they
would fence off the park. Days later the reply came: money from the park
would be given to the Maasai.

Leakey's pledge was a turning point. The Maasai were finally learning
the power of their own voice. The park would be left open, the ecosystem
intact, and wildlife free to migrate.

The changing times were even more evident at a *harambee*, self-help
meeting, at Namelok. Hundreds of Maasai gathered to raise money to
expand their first primary school. I sat under a marquee waiting for the
guest of honor to arrive, fascinated by the bewildering diversity of dress.
Old men in shukas and young men in business suits stood around talking
animatedly. The women stood apart, some in traditional shawls, others in
bright printed dresses. A funnel of ululating girls festooned with necklaces
and bracelets greeted the parliamentary representative, Ole Singaru, when
he arrived. Many of those accompanying him were young Maasai who had
made it in the larger world as farmers, ranchers, bankers, accountants,
salesmen, university lecturers, and professionals and intended to help others do the same. They were all proud of their roots and what they had
accomplished. Nothing rallied them more than the education of Maasai
children.

An elderly man in a crumpled suit and dark sunglasses walked up and
pumped my hand vigorously. "Yonah, I'm back." His face was strong and
heavily lined, his eyes intense and unwavering. Then he snorted gently.

"Parashino!" I couldn't believe it. He had aged. His face was thin and
lined, his skin sallow. I grabbed his hand and pumped hard. "You're back?
You mean living in Amboseli?"

"Yes. I've taken a shamba at Namelok and am settling down here for
good. But look, the meeting's starting. I will see you later."

As the meeting got under way I looked around, staggered by the changes since the drought ended fifteen years ago. The Maasai had been a dying people then, clinging to a lifestyle collapsing as cattle fell and rotted in the thousands. They survived only as wards of state, as famine relief victims with no education and no future in the modern world. Land shortage and drought had pushed them to the brink of cultural disintegration, but somehow they had drawn on their awesome pride and resourcefulness and survived.

Parashino, looking on happily as the contributions for the new school rolled in, exemplified both the modern and the traditional Maasai. He was comfortable, even successful by Kenya standards, and still had a good herd and two shambas. Now that the electric fence was up at Namelok, he could move back and grow commercial crops in the irrigated fields. The elephants, though close by, were safer than in decades—and so were the Maasai shambas.

Kerenkol looked on proudly, with good reason. He represented the ruling class of elders, savvy if largely illiterate. No longer wards of the state, they had become farmers, ranchers, and businessmen, making their own way in the world and proud of it.

The huge stone house rising behind the croton fence was Kerenkol's latest venture. Within a year he would move his three wives into a fifteen-room mansion and educate all eight kids at a boarding school in Gilgil. He hadn't stuck to his vow to marry just one wife, but three was a step down from Oloitiptip's thirteen and sixty-odd children. By any standards, Kerenkol was a wealthy man. He had recently bought a new Isuzu seven-ton truck for $40,000 cash, acquired two shops, and would soon invite a tour operator to build a lodge on his land at Kitirua.

Marinka, master of ceremonies, was dressed in a black two-piece suit with a huge bandanna round his shoulders and a party badge on his lapel. He was the aspiring politician, taking charge and canvassing support for his upcoming election. After the money had been pledged, he pointed out to the crowd that wildlife had largely footed the bill for the school. He reiterated the same point Oloitiptip had made fifteen years earlier: wild animals were the Maasai's second cattle—and more important than ever before.

I was getting ready to leave when Marinka ushered me back and announced that the Maasai wanted to make a rare award. At this point his father, a tall, regal man dressed in traditional robes, stepped forward and began to speak. "We are today awarding daktari something special. Let me tell you why. He has told us for years how important wildlife is to us and that we should look after it and benefit from it. He fought for us in Nairobi when we could not speak for ourselves. He worked with us, lived with us as warriors, joined our meat feasts, and learned our ways.

"Today we see the wisdom of using wildlife all around us, in the flourishing shambas over there, in the new school classrooms, in the campsites we operate and the lodges we are building. We also have our revenue-sharing back, and it is helping us with development. We have our own scouts to protect wild animals. We have pledged to keep our land open to wild animals and make them our second cattle as our forefathers did.

"Today we want to acknowledge daktari as a leader among the Maasai. We want to award him the *orinka*, the black stick carried by our spokesman. Whenever he attends a meeting, he will have the authority to carry this orinka and speak on our behalf."

Despite my ease in an international forum these days, my old self-consciousness welled up as I walked forward to receive the ornately beaded orinka and ceremonial beads Marinka placed over my shoulders. Then he presented me with a goat, a bag of onions, and a sack of tomatoes.

"These gifts are symbols of our lives and culture, the old and the new, and we want to give them to you to acknowledge what you've done. You have been with us through the bad times and the good, and we want you to be a part of our future too."

The meeting over, Parashino rushed forward to be photographed with me holding the goat and the orinka. "Jonah, I am proud of what we did together. I saw what you didn't, and you saw what I didn't. I have decided to write a book about the Maasai and wildlife. Unless our children know how it was, how can they understand and value wildlife? I want to tell them these things."

It was like old times again. Here we were, talking about wildlife and the Maasai as we had done a hundred times, but now with pride rather than anger and bitterness. Everything had changed—the Maasai, their lifestyle, the habitat, and even the wildlife. Everything except Kilimanjaro. Fittingly, the mountain was clear, rising high above Amboseli, presenting the same face it had for thousands of years.

A few days later I headed for Lake Amboseli, starved for its solitude and austere beauty. I needed to think, to be alone, to feel Amboseli's pulse again and renew my sense of wonder.

A new lake had sprung up on the plains in the last year. Thousands of pink flamingos shimmered in the haze, filtering the fresh algal bloom from the water with the slow sideways sweep of their upturned bills. A small shift in Longinye Spring had changed the alignment of the stream, circumventing the swamp. A minor twitch, combined with seasonal rainfall gushing into Longinye across the elephant-denuded flats, disgorged enough water onto the plains to create the new lake and attract the flamingos, pelicans, ducks, and flocks of waders.

I drove on across the *Suaeda* flats, caught up in the vortex of change. In 1968 the woodlands had been so dense that I could barely locate the heavily shaded grove where a pride of lions had killed two giraffe. The image of young cubs frolicking around the carcass among the *Lycium* and *Salvadora* bushes and rolling on their backs in the dense sward of cynodon was still vivid. Could the open grassland dotted with *Suaeda* bush really be the same spot? Only the rotting tree trunks, choked by bush like an unattended graveyard, alluded to some tumultuous transformation. It took a long memory—or old photos—to tell the story of cardinal woodpeckers, African eagle owls, vervet monkeys, giraffe, lesser kudu, bushbuck, and dozens of other woodland species supplanted by two-banded coursers, fisher's sparrow larks, zebra, wildebeest, and Thomson's gazelle.

Passing through the Olengaiya grove where Parashino had first introduced himself, I stopped briefly, recalling our surreal encounter over the stolen fence wire. We had both been young and impetuous then and full of dreams—he of herds of cattle large enough "to crush the stones of streambeds," of lion hunts, meat feasts, cattle raids, and young girls, I of exploring Amboseli and new ways to conserve it. It took a stolen roll of wire to bring our two cultures together in the quest for common ground.

I thought back on how apprehensively I had once viewed the inevitability of Africa's development. Over the course of forty years, remote villages scattered in the endless bush have become linked by road, radio, and trade. Mbwamaji is a residential suburb of Dar es Salaam, Mikumi a staging post on Tanganyika's southern tourist circuit. Parashino and Kerenkol have survived drought and cultural disintegration and adapted to the New Africa, and in their own way are molding it.

Undeniably, their New Africa has less place for wildlife. Two decades ago the question was whether it would survive at all—and the answer was an emphatic no, according to Peter Beard in his *End of the Game*. Today, as Africa enters a new century, Beard's skepticism offends most Kenyans. Wildlife has already passed into African hands, and over 90 percent of all Kenyans regard it as important to the nation. With such a large and expanding constituency, the tide has turned for national parks, and for elephants and rhinos too. County councils across the country are voting to turn land into wildlife reserves, rhinos are increasing by 6 percent a year, and elephants by nearly 1,000 animals a year.

I REACH THE EDGE of Lake Amboseli. Getting out, I take a long, solitary walk onto the dusty flats, past herds of zebra staring head up and ears forward in curiosity. Returning to fringing vegetation, I listen to the crunch of salty grass beneath my feet and the cackle of crowned plovers protesting my intrusion. My father would be an old man by now, his adventures over, the killing done. I imagine how he would love to join me here amid the grandeur, the bleakness, and the tame animals. This is the serenity he saw in Manyara and dreamed of in Mikumi but never lived to see. He would take satisfaction in watching Carissa and Guy, racing around throwing elephant dung at each other as Martin and I did as kids. He would enjoy seeing his love of wildlife passing on. Guy cries for four hours when his cat kills a cliffchat, less when a leopard mauls his dog. "This is their home," Carissa tells Guy sagely—referring to both the leopard and the cliffchat. When I ask Guy what he wants to do when he grows up, he tells me in all seriousness, "Save the world." They understand the fragility of nature and the importance of protecting and nurturing it; they see no contradiction in the Maasai and wildlife living side by side in Amboseli. Someday, I promise them, we will visit Mikumi, where their concern and caring began.

Appendix

In recent years, the conservation approach I advocate in the book has acquired two names: community-based conservation and locally based conservation. In both cases, the focus is the same. Community-based conservation is personal, rooted in societies and groups living side by side with wildlife, as opposed to conservation emanating from national legislation and enforcement or international treaties. Each has its place. I stress the local approach because it has a place in most traditional societies and also has enormous potential to improve the lives of rural communities and the status of wildlife on a global scale. In the last fifteen years, community-based conservation has been growing apace. Farmers in eastern India have worked with one another to conserve and manage their dwindling forests; Indonesian fisherman in the Maluku Islands have resurrected traditional harvesting practices, with a modern twist, to prevent the overexploitation of valuable trochus shells; Aborigines in Australia have entered a novel agreement for the joint management of Kakadu National Park; and sheep farmers in the United Kingdom have struck an innovative deal with government to protect the rural landscape in return for subsidies which pay manifold benefits in visitor returns. Even the venerable Yellowstone National Park has its local support group, the Greater Yellowstone Coalition, dedicated to finding a balance between people and wildlife in the interests of keeping the entire ecosystem open to the endangered grizzly and migrating elk. The exciting reintroduction program now under way for the gray wolf would have been inconceivable without cooperation from the owners of surrounding lands.

Sitting in on a meeting of the Yellowstone Coalition is like listening to a meeting of conservationists and Maassai in Amboseli. The issues—space and coexistence—are the same worldwide. Despite such initiatives, ecologists and conservationists have only recently turned their attention to rural areas and examined seriously the options for coexistence. At stake is nothing less than the fate of the natural world and our natural resources. In the rural areas, either we value the land, live within it sustainably, and find an extensive place for nature, or we face a biologically and physically degraded world. Overuse of the land will reduce its ability to provide our most basic needs and overwhelm the self-replicating and self-cleansing capacity of our soils, waters, and the atmosphere. The warning signs are already there in greenhouse warming and ozone thinning.

If present trends of population growth and destructive economic practices continue, nature, will be reduced and confined to hypermanaged ecological islands and megazoos. Even if the 8,000 or so protected areas, which cover a mere 4 percent of the earth's surface, were doubled in size, they would be insufficient to preserve animal and plant life if confined and cut off from the space beyond them. Locally based conservation in the rural landscape can help buffer such protected areas and reduce the scale of extinction. A bigger opportunity by far lies in the conservation and sustainable use of rural lands for their inhabitants, thus forestalling the loss of species which necessitated the protected areas in the first place.

For those who are interested in the larger conservation issues, a number of recent publications will be helpful. One volume in particular, *Natural Connections: Perspectives in Community-based Conservation,* * published by Island Press, draws together case studies from all over the world, including Amboseli, and takes a hard look at the future challenges facing community-based conservation. My concluding chapter in that volume, reprinted here, and the list of books which follows give a flavor of what is entailed.

Vision of the Future: The New Focus of Conservation

The global changes of the last half-century have been disastrous for the environment. Human numbers have tripled; energy consumption has quadrupled; pollution has fouled our atmosphere, oceans, and soils. Natural habitat is being reduced to vestigial fragments, and thousands of plant and animal species are being driven over the precipice of extinction.

Push the trends another fifty years into the future, and the outlook is calamitous. The exponential curves of consumption and degradation show a world running out of agricultural land and essential resources. Global cli-

---

* *Natural Connections: Perspectives in Community-based Conservation,* edited by David Western and R. Michael Wright, Shirley C. Strum, associate editor (Washington, D.C.: Island Press, 1994), pp. 548–556.

mate will be several degrees hotter and the ozone layer dangerously thin. City skies will be acrid with pollution, rivers and lakes heavily acidified, and groundwater contaminated with toxic waste. Perhaps half of all species will have disappeared in a mass extinction spasm.

These apocalyptic scenarios are based on computer predictions made during the last twenty years. Any conservationist brave enough to look ahead is sure to be demoralized. There is no glimmer of hope in a future viewed through the prism of past human excesses. Conservationists might as well pack up and enjoy nature as long as it lasts—or should they?

Fortunately, there is scope for change and room for hope—if we take our cues from the positive trends. Several recent projections take a more sanguine view of the future. I share this optimism, not so much because of any giant strides yet taken, but because of the changes now fermenting in the human mind and because of examples, here and there, where the distillation process has manifested itself in the first small steps in a new direction. My optimism is based on a quarter-century of improvements in and around Kenya's Amboseli National Park, an area that was regarded as a conservation disaster in the 1960s. The improved outlook for the ecosystem convinces me that conservation, when alert and responsive to local needs, can find an enduring place in our future.

From Despair to Hope

In addition to changes in the human mind that portend changes in our behavior toward the environment, a number of more visible trends run counter to the apocalyptic scenario. These trends suggest that awareness and action can slow and ultimately reverse the precipitous slide toward environmental catastrophe.

In 1798, when Thomas Malthus made his abysmal forecast of a Europe plunging into overpopulated misery, Britain had fewer than 10 million people, most of them living in poverty. Today, Britain's population is six times as large, and its people are wealthier and healthier. In other words, the link between population size and poverty is weak at best. This is not to dismiss the Malthusian theory of limits to growth; the ceiling is simply higher than Malthus and many ecologists allow. This in itself is important, since we have more time than anticipated before the crunch—time in which to do something about the warning signs showing up in the environment.

The significance of time becomes all the more apparent when we consider the momentous changes of the past century. World population growth began to climb steeply only in the mid-1800s. The growth rate peaked in the 1950s and has steadily declined ever since. As a result, present projections predict world population will level off between 10 and 14 billion people, one-third of the number forecast in the 1960s. Today, demographers are concerned less about running out of food and space than they are about a powder-keg world divided into rich and poor.

Even more significant for environmental pressure points is urban drift. At current rates, withdrawal to urban areas will cause populations in rural areas to peak in 2050, at numbers about one-third greater than at present. Thereafter the figures will fall rapidly, repeating the transition in the West from an agrarian to an urban society in less than a century. Rural depopulation, among other factors, saw the recovery of wildlife populations in much of the eastern and southern United States.

If changes in sensibilities in the West are anything to go by, the urban population of the developing world will become more sympathetic toward nature, as well as a financial force in keeping it intact. Environmental awareness is already on the rise, alongside education and urbanization. In Kenya, the Wildlife Clubs movement has enrolled well over a million schoolchildren eager to see the lion and cheetah they have heard about only in fables. Similar youth movements have sprung up throughout Africa and the rest of the Third World.

Countertrends are present in other indices of environmental quality, too. Many airborne pollutants are declining in major industrial nations. An increasing number of lakes and rivers, including Britain's once-foul Thames, are being cleaned up at public insistence. Habitat-restoration and species-recovery plans constitute something of a growth industry in the conservation world.

Offering yet more reason for hope is the welter of new policies, laws, and enforcement measures aimed at cleaning up the environment. Environmental impact assessments have become mandatory in many countries. Endangered-species legislation and national conservation strategies are commonplace. The Wetlands Convention, the Convention on International Trade in Endangered Species (CITES), the Mediterranean Treaty, the Convention on Climate Change, and the Biodiversity Treaty are just a few of the dozens of international conservation agreements that have come into force during the past two decades. The growth in numbers of conservation organizations has been nothing short of phenomenal. Peru alone has more than 500 nongovernmental conservation organizations—up from a handful in the 1970s. As of 1990, virtually every major bilateral and multilateral donor agency had adopted environmental policies.

The rise of the environmental movement and its influence on national and global politics culminated in the Rio Declaration of 1992. Although the declaration fell short of expectations in several respects, the fact that the Earth Summit took place reflects the new global environmental agenda adopted by many heads of state.

These countertrends show that environmental degradation can be slowed and reversed. Societies freed from poverty are choosing cleaner and more diverse environments in which to live, and they are willing to pay for that privilege. The encouraging trends anticipate future directions in conservation. If promoted energetically, the future need not be some nightmarish rendition of the past. In the most paradoxical twist of all, development is no longer seen as the archenemy of conservation. According to the new paradigm, conservation and development are complementary. Development eliminates poverty and paves the way for conservation. In a reciprocal link, conservation preserves the resources essential for sustaining development.

Changing Our Minds

Although the trends are encouraging, the positive signs don't yet signify a sea change in our relationship to the environment. To catch the winds heralding such a change, we have to look for subtle cues—the first small eddies and ripples. Step back, and the signs are there, in changing behavior patterns, in the attitudes that mold behavior, and, most of all, in the awareness that precedes both.

The rise of environmental awareness in the last two decades is captured in the new words entering popular speech: *ecology, ecosystem, biosphere, green labeling, greenhouse warming, ozone hole, ecotourism, biodiversity,* and dozens of others. Several events helped to raise public consciousness, among them the 1970s oil crisis; the Torrey Canyon and *Exxon Valdez* oil spills; the destruction of the Amazon; the slaughter of whales, elephants, and tigers; and the fragile appearance of our blue planet seen from outer space. The regular press coverage of population growth and environmental destruction is almost impossible to ignore. The message of earthly bounds and limits finally has been driven home to the general populace.

The recognition of bounds and limits is hardly new to ecologists. They justifiably claim that governments are finally coming around to their position. Margaret Mead's admonition—"Never forget that a small group of thoughtful committed citizens can change the world; indeed this is the only thing that ever has"—is germane to their cause.

Evidence suggests that coercive governments can bring about improvements. Fertility control in China and the establishment of protected areas around the world are two examples that come to mind. Coercion has limits, though, and is as futile as trying to row up a waterfall when it runs against the perceptions and wishes of a population. The litter of parks around the world that exist on paper but are otherwise unsupported and unregulated is a reminder of how fruitless token conservation can be. Conservation cannot spread as long as its roots are confined to the high ground of the wealthy or academic few. Coercive programs are everywhere bending to the strong winds of liberty and ensuing proprietary claims eddying around the world since the collapse of the Cold War.

The new environmental awareness is no longer constrained by class and race. Environmentalism has entered the collective public consciousness on a monumental scale. Forty-eight top commercial companies led by Swiss industrialist Stephan Schmidheiny, for example, came together as the Business Council for Sustainable Development to prepare their own contribution to the Earth Summit. Their message? Markets must reflect environmental as well as economic truths.

Environmental awareness is not confined to urban areas, either; encouraging signs are cropping up in rural areas. Local communities are taking a fresh interest in the conservation of renewable resources, natural habitats, and wildlife. These are admittedly small steps, but they are steps taken in the face of enormous obstacles, and often without outside help.

From Awareness to Action

Only by looking back at the distance already covered is it possible to get a glimpse of the way ahead. The schism between nature and humanity caused by industrialization, commercialism, urbanization, and population growth over the last half-century reflects a profound loss of contact with the land. The centralization of authority, particularly in totalitarian and authoritarian states, made matters worse by dishonoring traditional property rights and encouraging open-access resource abuse. Knowledge, respect, and caring for the land died for lack of contact.

The small, localized efforts taken here and there around the world amount to a renewal of sorts. They reflect grass-roots changes and a profound shift in the center of gravity among developmentalists and conservationists. Conceding that local people can become the chief beneficiaries and custodians of natural resources and biodiversity is a truly momentous stride; this one leap opens the door to a rural conservation long thwarted by misguided policies.

Perhaps the most encouraging aspect of community-based conservation is that it is happening spontaneously. Many communities close to the land that have suffered the costs of mismanagement are taking the initiative. Conservationists and developmentalists who take the time to look, learn, and think about natural justice—and what works and fails in conservation—are buoyed by these grass-roots initiatives. As a result, conservation policies are nudging the locus of action from the center to the periphery.

One last link in the chain connecting awareness, attitudes, and behavior is necessary in order for community-based conservation to work. That link is responsibility. Behavior well may mirror concern, but whether that behavior helps or hinders conservation is another question altogether. Tens of thousands of campers feeding grizzly bears in Yellowstone National Park have turned the animals dangerous, causing their destruction. Nature lovers en masse have destroyed high Himalayan pastures. When it comes to nature, destruction is destruction, whether the cause is poverty, greed, or the crush of admirers.

Few governments are willing to empower communities without some assurance of their capacity and sense of responsibility. A community's future security, no less than society's, is jeopardized by environmental abuse. Environmental responsibility, then, is the flip side of freedom. Without responsibility, individual freedom tramples the rights of other individuals, communities, nations, humanity, and future generations. The

NIMBY (not in my backyard) mentality, for example, ensures that pollutants are not dumped in our own backyard but fails to ensure that they are disposed of in an environmentally harmless way.

On the positive side, localizing conservation action is likely to foster the responsibility that goes with rights. Thinking globally and acting locally closes the circle of action and consequences in three essential ways: environmentally, economically, and socially. Localization rebuilds the connections lost in today's amorphous and transient society. If the responsibility that comes of living within a community and on the land cannot be established locally, can it ever be established in the less personal and less intimate global setting? If caring and responsibility do start locally, will it not be easier to expand the sensibilities they engender from individuals to communities, nations, humankind, and even future generations?

Changing Roles

If the gulf between conservation and development has closed, however slightly, what does this augur for the future? What will it take to fulfill the promise of conservation in the rural landscape? And what are the challenges for conservationists?

In practical terms, community-based conservation calls for sweeping policy reforms on a grand scale. If the community is to be the locus of action, conservation policies and practices must be turned on their heads. The approach must be bottom-up rather than top-down, and local rather than national. Diverse (rather than uniform) environmental values and conservation practices also must be encouraged.

Here is where community-based conservation becomes more revolutionary than evolutionary: Such changes call for nothing less than a turnaround in entrenched political norms.

Every aspect of conservation, from user rights to donor roles, must be rethought. Local initiatives and skills must become the driving force of conservation. The role of government must move from center stage to the periphery and change from coercive to supportive. Governments must think in terms of integrating the activities of many conservation-oriented groups and individuals and arbitrating their disputes.

The future, for conservationists, lies not in trench warfare fought by ecowarriors, but in building local awareness and local capacity. The role of national nongovernmental organizations lies in linking up interest groups and encouraging reciprocal exchanges between them. Local communities will become the real conservation practitioners who experiment with new techniques and disseminate them by example. National and regional conservation organizations will become the partners of local communities. International conservation bodies will become the antennae, technical innovators, and watchdogs of conservation. They will look ahead for the pressure points and devise new and better tools and skills for conservation. They will become global monitors who advocate compliance and change. Conservation organizations, together with bilateral and multilateral donors, will become resource brokers looking for innovative conservation enterprises to support and foster.

Community-based conservation should draw strength from connections between the many groups and individuals with a stake in conservation. Yet, however many connections may be built, the obstacles to environmental sustainability still must be removed. Populations cannot continue to grow and poverty to deepen without threatening the future. Rapid cultural change, with its attendant problems of community breakdown and loss of traditional values, is an equally big if overlooked threat. At the opposite extreme lies the tyranny of factionalism: equating freedom with political separation. Solving every cultural difference by division traps human beings in an infinite regression and removes an important incentive for accommodation. Learning to live with our own differences is the first step on the road to learning to live with other species.

The problems of free trade are no less a threat to self-determination and community conservation. The General Agreement on Tariffs and Trade (GATT) and the North American Free Trade Agreement (NAFTA), among many other global and regional free-trade agreements, risk scuttling local conservation efforts and progress made at the Earth Summit—unless, that is, trade agreements are sensitive to environmental and local concerns. The ecological truths acknowledged by the Business Council for Sustainable Development, in other words, must quickly assume the stature of economic truths.

The list of problems goes on. In some cases, breaking with the past is as difficult as embracing the future. Institutions in the developed world have become so atomized and bureaucratized that reintegrating their activities will be no less formidable than building up skills and institutions from scratch.

A New Vision

Locally based conservation calls for a brave new vision rooted in interconnections. If conservation is to become embedded in our daily activities, nature and society must be intimately linked in our minds. This is a radical departure from the western view of the separateness of Man and Nature—one that rekindles a holistic, ancestral way of thinking about our species in relation to the rest of the natural world. Research, knowledge, and education all will have a central role to play in the conceptual shift if we work on the premise that rural communities have as much to teach others as they have to learn about how to live in a more integrated world.

Holism has an important contribution to make in balancing the widespread reductionist and purist view of science. Ecologists will need to come to grips with biodiversity and biological processes within human-modified landscapes. They will also need to develop new theories to accommodate the complex and shifting mosaic of habitats occurring over millions of square kilometers and many centuries. Discrete ecosystems in steady state and coevolved species will almost certainly be the exception rather than the rule, whether or not this was true in the past. Economists will also need to deal with the externalities in conservation, with the enormous social inequities, with the long-term sustainability of renewable resources, and with the maintenance of genetic adaptability.

The possibility exists that sustainability in a single location is an illusion, a romantic ideal made wholly unattainable by the tremendous flux in cultures, populations, economies, and land-use practices. If this turns out to be true, there will be all the more reason to view sustainability in global and generational terms. Humans will need to think big to exploit the niches opened up by the continually changing modes and shifting centers of production. In this event, conservationists will have to learn how to deal with moving targets of opportunity and threat.

Conservation will cease to be a singular activity based on biology and resource use. Instead, it will be the sum of many interrelated and integrated activities that contribute to the sustainability and maintenance of biological diversity. How well we succeed in embedding conservation in daily practices will depend on the extent to which its precepts become basic rights and freedoms we value and insist upon. Sensibilities and rights have expanded continually in modern times. There is reason to believe our environment and the natural world will be drawn deeper into that expanding circle.

Conservation arose as a singular, distinctive human activity based on scarcity, threat, and aesthetics. It follows that if humans embed conservation in their psyches and behavior, and if they tackle scarcity and poverty with the same zeal given to space exploration, conservation will cease to be a discrete human activity.

If this vision is ever realized, conservationists will become redundant. It will be time to hang up our consciences and our indignation and retire on the pension fund of nature we have so regularly paid into for decades. Until then, there is much to be done. The best hope for sustaining life's diversity lies in embedding conservation values in the lives of rural people.

If conservationists can take up the challenge of this new and unfamiliar terrain, they will help move the impetus from North to South and from center to periphery. They will, in the process, help conservation become multiethnic and multiethical, thus healing its deep schisms with an array of approaches no less diverse than biodiversity itself.

Recommended Reading

Constanza, R., B. G. Norton, and B. D. Haskell, eds. 1992. *Ecosystem Health: New Goals for Environmental Management.* Washington, D.C.: Island Press.

Engel, J. R., and J. G. Engel, eds. 1990. *Ethics of Environment and Development: Global Challenge, International Response.* Tucson: University of Arizona Press.

Herman, E. D., and K. N. Townsend, eds. 1993. *Valuing the Earth: Economics, Ecology, Ethics.* Cambridge, Mass.: MIT Press.

Kemf, E., ed. 1993. *The Law of the Mother.* San Francisco: Sierra Club Books.

McCormick, J. 1989. *The Global Environmental Movement: Reclaiming Paradise.* London: Belhaven.

Meadows, D., D. L. Meadows, and J. Randers, eds. 1992. *Beyond the Limits: Confronting Global Collapse, Envisioning a Sustainable Future.* Post Mills, Vt.: Chelsea Green.

Nash, R. F. 1989. *The Rights of Nature: A History of Environmental Ethics.* Madison: University of Wisconsin Press.

Piel, G. 1992. *Only One World: Our Own to Make and Keep.* New York: Freeman.

Repetto, R., ed. 1985. *The Global Possible: Resources, Development, and the New Century.* New Haven: Yale University Press.

Shabecoff, P. 1993. *A Fierce Green Fire: The American Environmental Movement.* New York: Hill and Wang.

Southwick, C. H., ed. 1985. *Global Ecology.* Sunderland, Mass.: Sinauer.

Thomas, K. 1983. *Man and the Natural World: A History of the Modern Sensibility.* New York: Pantheon.

Weiner, J. 1990. *The Next One Hundred Years: Shaping the Fate of Our Living Earth.* New York: Bantam.

Western, D., and M. Pearl, eds. 1989. *Conservation for the Twenty-first Century.* New York: Oxford University Press.

World Commission on Environment and Development. 1987. *Our Common Future.* New York: Oxford University Press.

World Development Report. 1992. *Development and the Environment.* New York: Oxford University Press.

Editor's Note

In March 1994, Richard Leakey abruptly resigned as director of the Kenya Wildlife Service. In announcing his decision to step down, Leakey claimed that he could no longer freely direct the organization in the face of government interference and burdensome operating procedures. His resignation followed a government review of the Kenya Wildlife Service which called on the organization to address the mounting conflict between people and wildlife and to halt the rising toll of human deaths from wildlife, especially elephants.

Five days after Leakey resigned, President Daniel arap Moi named David Western director of the Kenya Wildlife Service. In the eyes of many, Western was a logical choice. Not only did he have a lifelong commitment to conservation, but he had proved that the needs of people and wildlife can be balanced to the benefit of both.

Since Western's appointment, support for wildlife has grown steadily in Kenya. In 1996, under his guidance, the Kenya Wildlife Service launched the fiftieth anniversary celebration of Kenya's national parks. The theme of the anniversary, Parks beyond Parks, celebrates the success of the national parks today while promoting local participation in conservation throughout the country. In December 1996, Kenyans for the first time outnumbered foreign visitors to Kenya's national parks. The same year saw the first community-based wildlife sanctuary established at Kimana, adjacent to Amboseli National Park.

Stimulated by the success in Kenya, community-based conservation programs are being adopted elsewhere in Africa and throughout the world.

Index